CHILD ABUSE

CHILD ABUSE

A GLOBAL VIEW

Edited by Beth M. Schwartz-Kenney,
Michelle McCauley, and
Michelle A. Epstein

Foreword by David Finkelhor

A World View of Social Issues
Andrew L. Cherry, Series Adviser

Greenwood Press
Westport, Connecticut • London

Library of Congress Cataloging-in-Publication Data

Child abuse : a global view / edited by Beth M. Schwartz-Kenney, Michelle McCauley, and Michelle A. Epstein ; foreword by David Finkelhor.
    p. cm.—(A world view of social issues, ISSN 1526–9442)
    Includes bibliographical references and index.
    ISBN 0–313–30745–8 (alk. paper)
    1. Child abuse. I. Schwartz-Kenney, Beth M., 1964– II. McCauley, Michelle, 1962–
III. Epstein, Michelle A., 1969– IV. Series.
    HV6626.5.C472   2001
    362.76—dc21   00–035364

British Library Cataloguing in Publication Data is available.

Library of Congress Catalog Card Number: 00–035364
ISBN: 0–313–30745–8
ISSN: 1526–9442

First published in 2001

Greenwood Press, 88 Post Road West, Westport, CT 06881
An imprint of Greenwood Publishing Group, Inc.
www.greenwood.com

Printed in the United States of America

The paper used in this book complies with the
Permanent Paper Standard issued by the National
Information Standards Organization (Z39.48–1984).

10 9 8 7 6 5 4 3 2 1

CONTENTS

SERIES FOREWORD

Why are child abuse in the family and homelessness social conditions to be endured or at least tolerated in some countries while in other countries they are viewed as social problems that must be reduced or eliminated? What social institutions and other factors affect these behaviors? What historical, political, and social forces influence a society's response to a social condition? In many cases, individuals around the world have the same or similar hopes and problems. However, in most cases we deal with the same social conditions in very dissimilar ways.

The volumes in the Greenwood series A World View of Social Issues examine different social issues and problems that are being faced by individuals and societies around the world. These volumes examine problems of poverty and homelessness, drugs and alcohol addiction, HIV/AIDS, teen pregnancy, crime, women's rights, and a myriad of other issues that affect all of us in one way or another.

Each volume is devoted to one social issue or problem. All volumes follow the same general format. Each volume has up to fifteen chapters that describe how people in different countries perceive and try to cope with a given problem or social issue. The countries chosen represent as many world regions as possible, making it possible to explore how each issue has been recognized and what actions have been taken to alleviate it in a variety of settings.

Each chapter begins with a profile of the country being highlighted and an overview of the impact of the social issue or problem there. Basic policies, legislation, and demographic information related to the social issue are covered. A brief history of the problem helps the reader better understand the political and social responses. Political initiatives and policies are also discussed, as well as social views, customs, and practices related to the problem or social issue. Discussions about how the countries plan to deal with these social problems are also included.

These volumes present a comprehensive and engaging approach for the study of international social conditions and problems. The goal is to provide a convenient framework for readers to examine specific social problems, how they are viewed, and what actions are being taken by different countries around the world.

For example, how is a problem like crime and crime control handled in third world countries? How is substance abuse controlled in industrialized countries? How are poverty and homelessness handled in the poorest countries? How does culture influence the definition and response to domestic violence in different countries? What part does economics play in shaping both the issue of and the response to women's rights? How does a national philosophy impact the definition and response to child abuse? These questions and more will be answered by the volumes in this series.

As we learn more about our counterparts in other countries, they become real to us, and our worldview cannot help but change. We will think of others as we think of those we know. They will be people who get up in the morning and go to work. We will see people who are struggling with relationships, attending religious services, being born, and growing old, and dying.

This series will cover issues that will add to your knowledge about contemporary social society. These volumes will help you to better understand social conditions and social issues in a broader sense, giving you a view of what various problems mean to different people and how these perspectives impact a society's response. You will be able to see how specific social problems are managed by governments and individuals confronting the consequences of these social dilemmas. By studying one problem from various angles, you will be better able to grasp the totality of the situation, while at the same time speculating as to how solutions used in one country could be incorporated in another. Finally, this series will allow you to compare and contrast how these social issues impact individuals in different countries and how the effect is dissimilar or similar to your own experiences.

As series adviser, it is my hope that these volumes, which are unique in the history of publishing, will increase your understanding and appreciation of your counterparts around the world.

Andrew L. Cherry
Series Adviser

FOREWORD

This book is to be greatly welcomed because it adds considerably to what we know about child maltreatment and child maltreatment advocacy in an international perspective. Up until now, disappointingly little organized and published information has been available that takes a consciously comparative perspective on the issue, even though a great deal of informal international exchange and reflection have occurred at such forums as the biennial international meetings sponsored by the International Society for the Prevention of Child Abuse and Neglect (ISPCAN), which extend back to 1976. Several world data books on child abuse and neglect have been organized in conjunction with recent ISPCAN conferences which do provide some crude categorical comparisons among countries, but they nonetheless leave much to be desired in regard to qualitatively comparing the nature of the problem and the responses to it in different environments. Thus, the present volume fills an important gap.

This book confirms the two clear, if perhaps simpleminded, conclusions one can draw from international comparison. First, evidence of child maltreatment exists in all locales where it has been sought. Second, advocacy on behalf of maltreated children continues to expand within and across national boundaries.

But the chapters of this book highlight many more questions to which we have no answers, to which, in fact, we have hardly even begun to address ourselves. The questions that have probably been asked most frequently concern comparative epidemiology: Where are different forms of child maltreatment more common, and why? On these epidemiologic questions, we have at least formulated some ideas about how to get an answer, and some initiatives have been undertaken and more are under way to collect comparative data with methodologies and definitions that have some uniformity. One frequently articulated hope for such research of this sort is that it will point out social structures or cultural influences that contribute to or protect from child maltreatment. Thus, we might find hypothetically that in contexts where women are more educated, child neglect tends to decline. But attractive as the dream of such conclusions is from a theoretical perspective, I believe the likelihood is remote that it will yield practical hard scientific results in the near term that will be applicable to the prevention of child maltreatment. This is because teasing out the relevant components of large social and cultural systems is a very difficult challenge, and so, to continue the example, societies that have more educated women may differ on a host of other variables that may be extremely difficult to measure. It is probably easier to test the hypothesis by experimentally educating groups of women and following them to find out whether child neglect declines. The challenges of large multinational theoretical inquiries are very daunting for a topic like child abuse.

Other questions that are posed about the response to the child maltreatment problem in a comparative perspective are at an even more primitive stage of development, and the appropriate methodology for answering them is even less clear. As the chapters in this book show, there is no simple inventory or yardstick that can be applied to comparing where countries are in their social response. Part of the problem is that different countries have very different historical and institutional frameworks into which concern about child maltreatment gets assimilated. Another part of the problem is that child maltreatment advocacy is not as discrete a concept as it is often considered by child maltreatment advocates themselves. It seems very possible that systems of universal medical care, child care, family planning and contraceptive services, as well as economic supports for families, may be as influential in reducing child abuse as any specific child maltreatment intervention such as home visitation. Many countries have adopted and continue to adopt such social welfare concepts for reasons that have little to do with advocacy from those concerned specifically about child maltreatment. One hypothesis worthy of consideration is that there is very little association between the level of advocacy about child maltreatment, in the narrower sense that most of the contributors to this volume discuss it, and the actual occurrence of child maltreatment or its reduction. But though this is an interesting question to consider, the obstacles to answering it in any formal way are so great that it seems almost academic to ask it in the first place.

So we are a long way from being able to make many useful grand international comparative generalities about child maltreatment. I believe that the best place to start in comparative studies, and the approach most likely to produce immediate scientific and policy payoffs, is with much more modest comparative efforts at a micro level. There is a lot to be gained in comparing the operation of specific institutions in a couple of countries and looking at their strengths and weaknesses. How do child protection investigators go about their business in country X and country Y? Similarly, one can compare the entire systems of different countries in terms of how well they accomplish different specific goals. For example, how do country X and country Y protect children from the negative impact of involvement in the criminal justice system when crimes have been committed against them? I think these comparative studies might be the most useful exercises for people in one national context who are trying to think creatively about how they might approach their tasks in a new way. The current volume may give inspiration to such undertakings.

We live in a world where the sharing of technological and cultural inventions has become very widespread and fast-paced. The rate of diffusion and exchange of social welfare practices has also increased, but at nowhere near the same pace. Clearly, however, the tempo at which such exchanges are taking place is increasing. It is incumbent on us to become knowledgeable about the international context in which such exchanges will occur, and to be ready to take a thoughtful and critical approach to them. This book is a good first step on that path.

David Finkelhor

ACKNOWLEDGMENTS

A project such as this is not possible without the support of a great number of individuals. First, we thank all the contributors for their patience and willingness in responding to our many requests concerning their chapters and for the strength of their contributions. Special thanks and acknowledgment go to David Finkelhor for providing an insightful foreword for this volume. Many people behind the scenes deserve recognition for their contributions. We would like to thank the following students for their invaluable research assistance: Taisha Nurse, Carla McDaniel, and Kimberly Cuevas at Randolph-Macon Woman's College, and Jean Burr, Juli Krulewitz, and Michelle Young at Middlebury College. We also thank Bette Bottoms at the University of Illinois at Chicago for her ongoing guidance during the editing process of this book. We are indebted to Kimberly Svevo at the International Society for the Prevention of Child Abuse and Neglect (ISP-CAN) for her assistance in helping us identify potential contributors. The book also benefited from the helpful advice from our editors, Emily Birch at Greenwood and Andrew Cherry at Barry University. Finally, our greatest thanks go to our families and colleagues for their ongoing encouragement and support.

INTRODUCTION

Children are our future, yet we still resist knowing historically what we have done to create the future. We deny knowing about childhood, because then we might have to face how we have treated our future.
　　　—H. Lawton, 1988, *The Psychohistorian's Handbook*, p. 124

In this volume, we asked experts from sixteen different countries to discuss the issues of child abuse and neglect in their countries, including the following: the history of child abuse and neglect, legal definitions of abuse, the prevalence of abuse, children's role in the legal system, and penalties for abusing a child. In addition, authors have touched on the resources available for investigating allegations of abuse, for treating victims and (occasionally) perpetrators, and for gathering statistics about abuse and neglect. Chapters are arranged alphabetically by country, and similar topic headings are used in each chapter to help readers compare issues across countries. In addition, we have provided a brief description of each country at the beginning of each chapter.

Reading the chapters in this volume reveals that there is amazing overlap in the problems faced by each country regardless of its economic resources, political structure, or whether the majority of the people live in urban or rural regions. For instance, many authors note that their societies have only recently acknowledged the existence and prevalence of child abuse and neglect. Many chapters reveal the ongoing struggle to find adequate definitions of child abuse and the need to draw distinctions between acceptable traditional child rearing practices and inappropriate child maltreatment. Many authors expressed frustration with the lack of monetary, organizational, and informational resources for dealing with newly recognized child abuse and maltreatment problems. However, lack of adequate resources is not a problem only for those countries that have recently begun to recognize and address child abuse and maltreatment. Even countries with a long history of addressing these problems appear to have difficulty funding the governmental and social agencies needed to prevent and treat the problem and getting adequate information on the prevalence of child abuse and maltreatment.

Although there are tremendous similarities among these countries' problems, many face unique concerns as well. For example, D. G. Harendra de Silva discusses the negative effects that conscription has had on children during Sri Lanka's recent civil war and argues persuasively that child conscription should be recognized as a form of child abuse in its own right. Akihisa Kouno and Charles Felzen Johnson, writing about Japan, suggest that economic stresses brought on by the influence of Western values since World War II have led, among other problems, to increases in infanticide (e.g., coin-operated locker babies) and violence perpetrated by juveniles.

Furthermore, while many countries (e.g., the United States, England, and Canada) have accumulated an extensive body of research on the causes, effects, prevention, and treatment of child abuse, other countries (e.g., Russia and Romania) have little published work on the subject. Similarly, some countries have well-established databases assessing the prevalence of various types of abuse, while others lack the informational resources to accurately estimate prevalence.

The authors are all experts involved within their own country in some aspect of the problems of child abuse and neglect. Many hold office in international organizations, others head (or have headed) governmental agencies within their country, while others are primarily academic researchers (and some have held all of these positions). Although it was not possible to include all of the countries we would have liked to, we believe that this volume will provide the reader with a survey of how child abuse is dealt with across different cultures, regions, and political systems. We are confident that readers will find this volume helpful in understanding the challenges faced worldwide in our attempts to prevent child abuse.

1

AUSTRALIA

Suzanne E. Hatty and James Hatty

PROFILE OF AUSTRALIA

The Commonwealth of Australia, an island in the Pacific Ocean, has an area of 7.7 million square kilometers. The capital is Canberra, and the country's population of 18.7 million is comprised of various ethnic groups, including Europeans, Asians, and Aboriginals. The people speak English and are mostly Anglican, Roman Catholic, and other Christian denominations. The infant mortality rate is 6 per 1,000. Life expectancy is seventy-five years for males and eighty-one years for females. Children are required to attend school until the age of fifteen, except in Tasmania, where the age is sixteen. The overall literacy rate is 99 percent. The age of universal suffrage is eighteen, and the gross national product per capita in 1998 was $20,300 (U.S.). The government is a democratic, federal-state system, but the British monarch is recognized as sovereign.

A CASE STUDY

Jeffrey was five months old when a hospital notified the Child Protection Agency that he had a broken limb and bruising on his forehead, upper arm, and buttocks. Jeffrey's parents could offer no explanation for his injuries. The hospital doctors, however, were of the opinion that the injuries were non-accidental. A full skeletal survey revealed several additional fractures that were up to two months old.

Despite this evidence, Jeffrey was released back into his parents' custody with only minimal intervention provided by the Child Protection Agency.

Further, it was later determined that the agency offered inadequate supervision, because only two weeks later Jeffrey was found dead, face down in his cot. Unfortunately, there was insufficient evidence to establish the cause of Jeffrey's sudden and unexpected death. Thus, it was never determined if it was accidental or not, and his parents could not be held accountable.

PREVENTION AND CHILD PROTECTION

Long concealed by a conspiracy of silence, child abuse is now an issue that commands the attention of mainstream Australian society. Many groups and organizations work to maintain community awareness of the problem and to press for measures to eliminate all abusive treatment of children. They also provide support networks for victims of abuse and informative material designed to help parents and children recognize abusive behaviors.

Among the more prominent groups that focus on child protection are the National Child Protection Council, the National Association for the Prevention of Child Abuse and Neglect, Australians Against Child Abuse, the Australian Institute of Family Studies, Survivors on the Net-Australia, and the Child Safety Network. Most of these organizations have a presence on the Internet, providing parents and children with direct access to information and support. There is also another service that caters specifically to children, called the Kids Helpline. This is a free phone service that is available throughout Australia for children who need advice, wish to report incidents of abuse, or want to discuss fears that they are at risk of abuse.

Australia was the birthplace of the Safety House program which, since its introduction in 1979, has been adopted by several other countries. This is a nationally organized, but local community–based, child protection program that has networks of clearly identified houses and schools where children can gain refuge if they encounter threatening behavior on the streets. Schools and police also cooperate in these programs, which rely on the voluntary help of local householders. In the earlier phases of this program, the accent was largely on "stranger danger." However, later evidence that indicated that a child is more likely to be abused by someone known and trusted has caused programs in schools to cover a wider range of situations, with particular emphasis being placed on sexual abuse. This increasing emphasis on ensuring that all children can recognize situations in which they are at risk of sexual abuse stems from the realization that such abuse is much more widespread than had been previously acknowledged (Calvert, 1993).

PREVALENCE

No reliable statistics are available in Australia regarding the overall extent of child abuse. In this respect, Australia does not differ from most other countries. Several factors contribute to the lack of data. First, it is generally conceded that child abuse frequently goes unreported. Second, there are significant definitional differences as to what constitutes sexual abuse, there is disagreement as to what age groups should be classified as "children," and there are differences in methodology used to obtain such rates. As a result, annual reports compiled by aggregating figures from each jurisdiction in Australia must be interpreted with caution, particularly for figures which purport to show the total number of cases of abuse in Australia.

Nevertheless, much valuable information is contained in the latest annual report on child abuse and neglect in Australia (Broadbent & Bentley, 1997). The following comparisons are based on substantiated abuse cases originally reported to various child protection agencies in each state. It is reasonable to assume, however, that these rates also generally reflect patterns of abuse for unreported cases in Australia. In the 1995–96 year, physical abuse represented 28 percent, emotional abuse 31 percent, sexual abuse 16 percent and neglect 24 percent of the substantiated cases recorded. Since sexual abuse is arguably the behavior least reported, the incidence of such abuse might well be understated in these comparisons (Family Law Council, 1988, p. 3).

Further analysis of the patterns of abuse contained in this report shows that boys were more likely to be victims of physical abuse than girls until the age of thirteen, with physical abuse of girls being markedly higher than boys from age thirteen to sixteen. The incidence of emotional abuse was very much the same for boys and girls, again until around thirteen years of age, after which notifications involving girls rose, while those for boys fell. Sexual abuse of girls was reported more often than for boys. The patterns of sexual abuse for boys peaked at around five or six years of age and then declined, while the patterns for girls had a small peak at about age three or four, and then a large peak between twelve and sixteen years of age. Substantiated cases of neglect primarily involved young boys and girls, at similar rates of involvement.

Researchers and other professionals in the field of child protection, as well as groups representing survivors of child abuse, provide their own estimates of the overall incidence of child abuse in Australia to supplement the acknowledged deficiencies in official statistics. In particular, they address the hidden extent of sexual abuse. These estimates vary marginally, but all suggest that some 28 percent of girls and 9 percent of boys will have been sexually exploited by an older person before they reach the age of eighteen. These rates differ to some extent from estimates of sexual abuse in North America. After allowing for definitional and methodological differences, however, there is no reason to assume that child sexual abuse is more or less likely to occur in Australia than in other Western industrialized countries (Youth and Family Services, 1997).

LEGAL ISSUES

Local Organizations and Child Protection

There are three levels of government in Australia: the Commonwealth of Australia, the states and territories, and local government. The last has no role in framing legislation on child welfare. In broad terms, local government involvement with children is limited to the operation of community child care centers. In this context, local authorities have a direct interest in ensuring compliance with the requirements of Commonwealth and state laws on child welfare.

The role of the Commonwealth government in children's affairs is mainly limited to issues of custody and child support that arise in divorce proceedings before the Family Court of Australia. The Commonwealth government also deals with issues related to the nation's international obligations. Thus, primary responsibility for protecting the interests of children in Australia rests with the governments of the six states and two territories that constitute the Commonwealth of Australia.

At this stage, all states and territories have broadly similar legislation dealing with protecting the interests of children. The titles of the various acts differ, but all address the same issues: prevention of child abuse, and intervention when abuse occurs or when it is considered likely to occur. There are, however, small differences in the way in which the various state and territory acts were drafted and the manner in which their provisions are implemented. Despite these differences, which are relatively minor, Australian legislation on child protection is generally based on the principle that the best protection for children is usually to be found within the family. Nevertheless, it recognizes that intervention is necessary in instances where a child is considered to be at risk of abuse or where abuse has already occurred.

DEFINITIONS

Current legislation on child abuse in Australia establishes definitions of child abuse and provides procedures to be followed in reporting and investigating such reports. Actions to be taken on substantiated cases are also defined within child protection legislation. Abusive treatment is now defined under all Australian legislation within the following categories: neglect or abandonment, physical abuse, emotional abuse, and sexual abuse. It is also now required by law that any actual or suspected cases of child abuse, or perceptions that a child is at risk of abuse, must be reported to the relevant state child protection agency. Established instances of abuse may then be addressed in one or more of the following ways: by provision of family support and counseling, by separation of the child from the abuser, or by retributive punishment or diversionary programs for the perpetrator of the abuse. We return to these issues below.

All Australian jurisdictions have legislation in place to combat child pornography. Most provide for this by creating separate sections within the Criminal Code, others by introducing legislation specific to this type of offense. For example, in South Australia, child pornography is now covered specifically within Section 33 of the Summary Offenses Act 1953, while in New South Wales such offenses are covered by a separate act, the Crimes Amendment (Child Pornography) Act 1995. Some jurisdictions have also found it necessary to enact legislation to ban particular practices that have been traditional in some other countries, but are viewed in Australia as acts of gross child abuse. In these states, any form of female genital mutilation is prohibited unless it is part of a surgical procedure necessary for the health of the child.

INVESTIGATION

Recently, two new independent bodies have been established under state legislation to review child deaths: the New South Wales Child Death Review Team in 1995 and the Victorian Child Death Review Committee in 1996. These review committees are required to establish whether the deaths arose from natural causes, were of an accidental nature, or whether abusive treatment contributed to the child's death. Where child abuse was a factor, the case is transferred to the justice system. All findings and recommendations of these committees are included in annual reports submitted to the state legislatures and are available to the public. Recommendations generally focus on the elimination of system failures within child welfare and related agencies.

The gradual convergence of state and territory legislation on issues of child welfare has been facilitated by regular meetings of the responsible ministers from each state and territory and a senior representative of the Commonwealth government. In the early 1990s, the National Child Protection Council was established to develop a national approach to the prevention of child abuse. When Australia began to establish its National Strategy in 1992, it broke new ground. At that point, no other country had an overall plan to target all forms of child abuse (Spall, 1995). The National Strategy is still being vigorously pursued, focusing on protection of the child rather than traditional approaches based on intervention and treatment. Implementation of the strategy involves the use of educational and preventative measures and the provision of support for affected families.

HISTORY

There is ample evidence available to show that many children have been maltreated or abused by adults for many centuries (Hatty & Hatty, in press).

Until relatively recently, however, many of the behaviors now considered abusive were acceptable, or at least condoned, within patriarchal societies of the West with their entrenched views of the inherent rights of the father.

Over the intervening centuries, some of the more extreme forms of child maltreatment gradually became unacceptable, but not until the late nineteenth and the early twentieth centuries have we witnessed a growing recognition of the child as an individual with his or her own rights. This has led to more rapid changes in community attitudes toward child welfare. These shifts were due, in large measure, to the efforts of social reform groups championing the rights of children. The causes espoused by these advocacy groups became politicized as the general public became convinced of the need for change. Finally, with growing demands for legislative action to remedy perceived injustices or abuses suffered by children, governments felt compelled to respond by enacting laws which would address these issues.

The politicization of the child gathered momentum in the second half of the twentieth century. This process has been hastened, in part, by the globalization of channels of communication. Accordingly, the issue of children's rights has become an important topic debated throughout the Western world and in many other countries. The international nature of children's rights is evident in the United Nations Declaration of the Rights of the Child of 1959, and the subsequent United Nations Convention on the Rights of the Child of 1989. Within the debate on children's rights, the discourse of the "abused child" featured prominently in Australia, as it did throughout the West. The essence of late twentieth century attitudes toward child abuse was captured in the European Charter on the Rights of the Child, which expressed the view that the physical and psychological maltreatment of children was one of the most abhorrent abuses that could occur in any nation.

Such pro-child attitudes did not crystallize rapidly. Early reports of physical abuse of children in the 1960s were initially received in Australia, as they were in other Western countries, with a mixture of disbelief, anger, and denial. For many, these accounts were the overreactions of well-meaning but misguided individuals or groups who misunderstood the dynamics of family relationships. A similar response was evident in the next decade, when social reform groups drew attention to the fact that some adults, including parents and other caregivers, were sexually abusing children. This was seen by some as an exaggerated claim, but evidence from medical practitioners and social workers as well as reports from adults abused as children soon revealed the widespread nature of the problem (Family Law Council, 1988).

Although it became clear that existing child protection legislation was completely inadequate, state governments did not act swiftly to correct the situation. Those with a more conservative approach to social policy adopted a wait and see attitude. Others, mostly the more populous states, established task forces to investigate effective ways of framing legislation to protect children from abuse. The establishment of the New South Wales Government Child Sexual Assault Task Force in 1984 is an example of the typical way that governments set up public inquiries that invited input from anyone with an interest in protecting children. The aim of the NSW Task Force was to investigate the extent of child abuse in the community and recommend strategies to prevent or minimize its incidence in the future. Submissions were sought from all professionals working in the area of child abuse, and from the general community. The findings of this and similar task forces were used as the basis for either amending existing legislation on child welfare or introducing entirely new legislation to address current child protection issues. Most state jurisdictions have opted for the latter and maintain a continuing process of review to ensure that the laws on child protection are kept up-to-date. This process is aided by recommendations made on a regular basis by various groups, such as semi-government bodies and other child rights' advocacy groups. Recommendations may also come from other sources, such as from inquiries where the principal objectives are not the investigation of child welfare. For example, a recent Judicial Inquiry in New South Wales found persuasive evidence that some members of the police service and judicial officers were protecting small groups or individuals engaged in pedophile activities (Wood Royal Commission, 1997). At the request of the government, this inquiry also made recommendations for the improvement of child protection legislation in New South Wales.

The image of the abused child is now firmly entrenched at every level of community discourse in Australia. The print and electronic media give extensive coverage to reports of child abuse, apparent failures of agencies responsible for child protection, and challenges to the way child protection law is administered. Similarly, protecting children from abuse is a prominent focus of research and publications emanating from local professionals associated with child welfare.

The states and the territories have long accepted a limited responsibility for child welfare, and have enacted legislation to cover such matters as adoption, neglect, or abandonment of children. Until the last twenty years, maltreatment of children, except for the most blatant offenses, has received only passing attention from state governments. The way that children were treated within the family was considered to be a matter best left to parents. This stance reflected traditional perceptions of the parental role. It also tapped into the complacent view of many in the community that, while the existence of neglect and maltreatment of children is most reprehensible, it is not their problem. To these people, such situations only occurred in other families. In general, it was left to charitable organizations such as the Society for the Prevention of Cruelty to Children, established in the nineteenth century, to discover and report cases of child maltreatment. Beyond that, the police were charged with the responsibility of investigating any such reports, and, if deemed appropriate, taking action under the Criminal Code.

From the 1970s onwards, public opinion in Australia began to change markedly. With this gradual shift in community discourse, demands for changes to social policy increased. First, there was increasing media coverage of the previously unknown, or at least unacknowledged, extent of physical abuse of children within the community (e.g., Krugman, 1996). The battered child syndrome, which refers to a group of symptoms and behaviors exhibited by a child who has been repeatedly physically abused, sprang into prominence (Kempe & Helfer, 1980). As a result, previously condoned behaviors were questioned. For example, the use of corporal punishment was banned in most school systems. Public opinion remained divided, however, on the extent to which it was acceptable to use physical punishment to correct a child within the family. Hence, there have been no legislative changes to cover such actions within the family environment, such as has happened in some European jurisdictions.

At much the same time, the public protests of the feminist movement against the physical and sexual maltreatment of women inevitably brought to light the extent to which girls had been, and were still being, sexually exploited (Family Law Council, 1988). Women and girls were encouraged by this publicity to come forward and report their experiences. In many cases, they also identified their abusers. Revelations about the sexual abuse of young males followed. It became clear that many cases of physical and sexual abuse of girls and boys had occurred within government institutions and that the practice had continued over a very long time. Official investigations also led to the conclusion that some responsible individuals, and in fact organizations, had either ignored the problem or concealed these abusive practices. In this regard, the Australian experience simply replicated the institutionalized abuse of children that has been revealed in many other parts of the world.

The growing sense of community revulsion about any type of abuse directed against children created great pressure for changes to social policy and legislation in all Australian jurisdictions. As a result, all states and territories reviewed existing legislation on child welfare and modernized or completely replaced statutes that were no longer appropriate to the times. The way in which this process was handled in the state of Victoria is typical of the outcome in other states.

During the 1970s, the Victorian government began subsidizing the investigative work of the Children's Protection Society (originally the Society for the Prevention of Cruelty to Children), a charitable organization. Then, following a major review of child welfare practices in 1984, the state took over the work of this society. The review also prompted a complete overhaul of all existing legislation concerned with child protection, resulting in the introduction of a new measure, the Children's and Young Person's Act 1989. At the same time, the earlier Children's Court Act of 1973 was repealed, as were almost all of the provisions of the Community Services Act

1970. The sole responsibility for implementing the provisions of the new act and investigating all reports of suspected child abuse was given to a state government agency, the Department of Human Services. From that point, the role of the police was limited to investigating criminal matters arising from reports received by the Department of Human Services. In all states and territories, review of child protection legislation is now a continuing process that frequently incorporates representations made by many groups within the community championing the rights of the child.

While the incidence of physical abuse appears to be higher than that of sexual abuse, the latter tends to attract stronger condemnation within the community (Broadbent & Bentley, 1997). This has led to pressure on the Commonwealth government to address the sexual exploitation of young girls and boys by Australian nationals visiting Asian countries. Many men, not only Australian citizens, join "sex tours" to the Philippines, Thailand, and neighboring countries to seek sexual encounters with children as young as four to eight years of age (Sex tourism, 1996). However, the Australian government, in collaboration with the governments of Asian countries, has developed protocols for the exchange of evidence on such sexual exploita-tion of children and has legislated for offenders to be tried in Australia for offenses of this type committed in other countries. The relevant legislation, the Crimes (Child Sex Tourism) Amendment Act 1994, may not have elim-inated all offenses, but it appears to have substantially reduced the number of offenders.

Coming to Terms with the Past

Australia is currently confronting large-scale maltreatment of children from the past. This abusive treatment stemmed from earlier governmental social policies and the way they were implemented in a variety of institutions.

From the late 1940s, Australia, along with other countries that then had links with Britain, joined in programs to bring children from institutions in Britain to Australia. In theory, the aim was to give disadvantaged children an opportunity to resettle in a new land where they could help boost the population and provide the countries with cheap, young, and healthy mi-grants. In reality, however, children in Britain were deceived, often being told that they were orphans or that their families did not want them. Not only were they separated from their families, but on arrival in Australia, siblings were separated and sent to different institutions, mostly run by church organizations. The truth about what happened to many of these children has only recently emerged. Specifically, many of these boys and girls were physically, sexually, and emotionally abused, and treated as slave labor (MPs arrive, 1998). Recent campaigns to gain recognition of their plight and provide some assistance for victims have gained some ground. Church organizations have belatedly, and often grudgingly, offered some support and an apology for the abuses suffered at the hands of members of their orders. In addition, the government of Britain has set up a committee to determine what can be done, at this stage, for victims of these past policies.

Previous Australian governments, Commonwealth and state, were also responsible for much misery experienced by Aboriginal children and their families. Based on now-discarded policies of forced assimilation, Aboriginal children, particularly those of mixed-race parentage, were forcibly separated from their families and communities and placed in institutions run by church organizations or government instrumentalities. These children have now become known as the "Stolen Generation" (Freedman & Donaczy, 1991). Boys and girls were subjected to physical and sexual abuse, as well as being emotionally deprived of their cultural heritage. Vigorous campaigns seeking acknowledgment of the distress caused by this, a formal apology, and some form of compensation for victims who were alienated from their families and traditional culture have been only partly successful to date.

Past abuses of children at the hands of governmental instrumentalities also took other forms. Again, these abuses have only recently become public knowledge. For example, orphaned babies and children in various Victorian institutions were used to test a range of vaccines and antigens, some of which were toxic. This continued without challenge for several decades, being justified both by medical researchers and by those who supervised the orphans as being for a good cause. The second example of authorized abusive treatment occurred in New South Wales institutions and involved the forced sterilization of teenage girls deemed to be sexually irresponsible. Parental permission was not obtained in such cases.

Social policy in Australia, and in other Western countries where similar situations have been uncovered, has shifted a great deal since these abusive practices were considered acceptable. Public anger, which has been aroused by revelations of institutional abuse, has ensured that such abuse can no longer be countenanced.

LEGAL INNOVATIONS

There are still differences of opinion as to the effectiveness of some of the recently introduced legislation and policy initiatives for the protection of children. The most significant of these involve mandatory reporting of cases of actual or suspected child abuse, the issue of court testimony in cases involving children, and the ways in which to deal with child abusers.

All states except Western Australia now have legislation requiring compulsory reporting of child abuse and neglect (Broadbent & Bentley, 1997, p. 5). A similar outcome is achieved in Western Australia through interagency protocols that have been adopted. In general, legislation designates a range of professionals working with children who must report all signs of actual or suspected abuse. As a result, there has been a considerable increase in the number of cases of abuse reported in every jurisdiction. To many, this demonstrates the effectiveness of the program. Others are not so convinced, claiming that mandatory reporting increases the risk of unnecessary intervention and involves child protection agencies in trivial or vexatious claims at the expense of more serious cases of abuse. There is also some concern that mandatory reporting may discourage people in crisis from discussing their problems with professionals. Despite these doubts, mandatory reporting remains in force.

Considerable attention has been given recently to the way in which evidence of abuse is presented to courts. The Australian judicial system leans toward an adversarial rather than an investigative approach, a pattern recognized as highly unsuitable in cases involving children. Further, traditional methods of gathering evidence from children, and the requirement that an abused child appear in court to face the alleged abuser, are now seen as totally unacceptable practices (Cashmore, 1995). A fairly recent case in New South Wales has highlighted these deficiencies. Specifically, charges of sexual abuse were made against a husband and wife who operated a child care center. This became known as the so-called Mr. Bubbles case, taking its name for the clown persona adopted by the husband for the amusement of the children (Hatty, 1991). Both husband and wife were accused of sexually molesting the children by some, but not all, parents. Considerable doubt as to the veracity of the claims arose from suspicions that the children's statements had been colored by parental questioning and the ineptitude and inexperience of social workers and police who later interviewed the children. Subsequently, the case collapsed and was dismissed when the court found that the children's evidence had become contaminated by poor interviewing techniques.

In other cases of child abuse to come before the court, it has become apparent that children can become confused and intimidated by the presence of the alleged abuser in court and by the frequently adversarial nature of the defense case. Two major changes have resulted from these and similar experiences. To avoid adverse effects for children, specialists are now trained in child protection agencies and in police services to conduct investigations of child abuse and to gather evidence from children in an appropriate manner. In addition, to eliminate the confrontational aspects of court cases involving children, some Australian jurisdictions have introduced closed-circuit TV or videotaped evidence for child witnesses in abuse cases.

There are also marked differences of opinion concerning how to deal with abusers, particularly those involved in sexual abuse. Community views tend to support programs of intervention that are used as alternatives to court proceedings to support victims, abusers, and the families in cases involving neglect, emotional abuse, and lower levels of physical abuse (Tomison, 1996). These interventions are aimed at helping abusers to recognize the causes of their behavior and to modify their attitude toward children. For more violent cases of physical abuse, and certainly for cases of sexual abuse, community attitudes show little sympathy for abusers. Fired by media coverage of such cases, the general community expects an offender to be subjected to retributive and harsh punishment. The alternative model of diversionary programs for offenses involving sexual abuse is not advanced by its proponents as the solution in all cases. It is only considered to have application where the safety of the victim can be guaranteed and where the offender has acknowledged guilt and consents to undergo a rehabilitation program. Repeat offenders are not eligible for diversionary programs. Overall, the Australian community remains skeptical concerning the efficacy of rehabilitation programs. As a result, the retributive punishment model, with no "soft options," is thought to be more appropriate for individuals who sexually abuse children, and is likely to prevail for some time.

LEGAL ISSUES

Systemic Failures

Although a great deal of attention has been focused on protecting children from harm over the past decade or so, the systems set in place to deal with the issue have failed on many occasions. This has been evident in the various jurisdictions throughout Australia. The most serious evidence of systemic failure is the death of a child while ostensibly being monitored by a child welfare agency called the New South Wales Child Death Review Team (NSWCDRT, 1997). Such deaths have occurred on a number of occasions in the last few years and have drawn strong media criticism of the agency held responsible for child protection. Although child protection agencies carry primary responsibility for minimizing the risk of harm to children, ineffective interagency liaison must frequently share the blame (Cashmore, Dolby, & Brennan, 1994). On many occasions, other groups such as the police service, medical practitioners, hospital workers, teachers, and staff in child care centers must take some responsibility. This is frequently overlooked in community responses to the death of a child who had been known to be at risk.

The problems facing all child protection agencies can be seen in recent reviews of operations conducted in New South Wales. The most recent *Annual Report* of the New South Wales Child Death Review Team (NSWCDRT, 1997) reveals that, although significant efforts have been made to eliminate them, systemic failures are still leading to child deaths. For example, in the eighteen-month period from January 1996 to June 1997, the report notes that of the twenty-six children who died from "non-accidental" injuries, half of them had been known to the Department of Community Services. In many cases, the deaths appear to be due to failure to follow up in situations of known risk, not treating the case seriously enough, and not informing other agencies that could have helped. Taking a broader view of the total of 1,201 child deaths investigated in the same eighteen-month period, those known to the department prior to the deaths represented a significantly higher percentage (7 percent) than the 2 percent of children known to the department in the general population (NSWCDRT, 1997).

Causes of systemic failures resulting in child deaths and instances where harm was of a nonlethal nature have been identified by the Child Death Review Team and form the basis for recommendations for corrective action. The team found that allegations of abuse were, at times, not taken as a formal "notification" and not recorded or cross-referenced. Inadequate risk assessment was also a factor, together with inadequate monitoring of children apparently at risk. A significant increase in the number of cases of abuse reported has only served to exacerbate the situation. Recommendations from the Wood Royal Commission (WRC) confirmed these inadequacies but underscored the fact that inadequate funding, lack of adequate training, and understaffing mean that the workload of field officers is "beyond human capacity" (WRC, 1997, p. 862). Taken together with the inadequacies of interagency liaison, this produces a "dysfunctional environment, whilst trying to treat dysfunctional families in which child abuse is occurring" (WRC, 1997, p. 890). The recommendations of the Child Death Review Team and the Wood Royal Commission are currently the basis of legislative, administrative, and funding changes aimed at eliminating systemic failures in New South Wales. Other jurisdictions have taken note of these findings and have their own situations under review.

CONCLUSIONS: OVERVIEW AND FUTURE DIRECTIONS

Mainstream Australian society now recognizes that child abuse and neglect are more common than previously acknowledged. There has also been a growing realization that such abusive treatment endangers the physical, social, intellectual, and emotional development of affected children, and that corrective action is urgently required to minimize the long-term effects of abuse. It is also accepted that there are no short-term solutions to the problem, which stems from a diverse series of complex social and cultural factors. Nevertheless, the issue has become highly politicized, and all programs for the protection of children have been overhauled. In particular, sexual abuse of the young has had a major impact on public debate, and many of the new protection programs have this as the main focus.

A National Child Abuse Prevention Strategy was introduced in 1993 by the National Child Protection Council, a body sponsored by the Commonwealth government and composed of representatives of the Commonwealth, state, and territory governments. The main objectives of the National Strategy are to (a) identify and change attitudes and behaviors which are harmful to children, (b) identify and change factors contributing to harmful parenting practices, and (c) teach children to form nonexploitative relationships and to develop their emotional care and personal safety skills (Spall, 1995). The implementation of this strategy requires public awareness campaigns, support for families in crisis, and programs of education for children and parents on the dangers to be encountered. In addition, it relies on the strengthening of legislation for child protection and better resourcing of services involved in the provision of child welfare services.

All state and territory governments have now reinforced or replaced their previously existing child protection legislation. They have also moved to improve the effectiveness of agencies directly responsible for child welfare and interagency responses to reports of child abuse. Improving parenting skills and providing effective support for families in which children are at risk is a longer-term project. Much remains to be done in these areas, particularly with regard to adequately staffing agencies and in providing ample funding for their work.

Programs aimed at heightening the awareness of children to the dangers of abuse have been completely overhauled and greatly strengthened. From the beginning of 1999, for example, New South Wales will introduce a new child protection curriculum. Children will be introduced to this program at their point of entry into the school system and remain involved with it until the completion of their secondary school education. All circumlocutions and euphemisms have been abandoned in favor of frank discussions of the facts. The course aims to have all children understand that they have the right to feel safe and that they also have the right to say no to any person who touches them inappropriately, makes them feel uncomfortable, or threatens their safety. Further, they are encouraged to tell trusted adults of threatening situations. Through the use of situational examples, children will learn to recognize behaviors, in addition to direct touching, that are considered to be sexually abusive.

While there is still much work ahead to eliminate all forms of child abuse, Australia is committed to implementing the United Nations Declaration of the Rights of the Child. Inevitably this requires changes in social attitudes and practices and the abandonment of some inherited cultural values. Those committed to the National Strategy aim to have child abuse prevention a reality in Australia by the year 2010.

REFERENCES

Broadbent, A., & Bentley, R. (1997). *Child abuse and neglect Australia 1995–96.* Canberra: Australian Institute of Health and Welfare.

Calvert, G. (1993). *Preventing child abuse: A national strategy.* Canberra:National Child Protection Council.

Cashmore, J. (1995). *The evidence of children*. Sydney: Judicial Commission of New South Wales.

Cashmore, J., Dolby, R., & Brennan, D. (1994). *Systems abuse:Problems and solutions*. Sydney: New South Wales Child Protection Council.

Family Law Council. (1988). *Child sexual abuse: A discussion paper*. Canberra: Family Law Court of Australia.

Freedman, L., & Donaczy, T. (1991). The stolen children: A personal account. *Children Australia, 16*, 19–22.

Hatty, S. E. (1991). Of nightmares and sexual monsters: Struggles around child abuse in Australia. *International Journal of Law and Psychiatry, 14*, 195–199.

Hatty, S. E., & Hatty, J. (in press). *Boys, crime, and justice*. New York: State University of New York Press.

Kempe, C. H., & Helfer, R. E. (1980). *The battered child*. Chicago: University of Chicago Press.

Krugman, R. D. (1996). The media and public awareness of child abuse and neglect: It's time for a change. *Child Abuse and Neglect, 20*, 259–260.

MPs arrive to help UK war "orphans." (1998, June 14). *Sydney Sun-Herald*.

New South Wales Child Death Review Team [NSWCDRT]. (1997). *Annual Report 1996–1997*. Sydney: Author.

Sex tourism. (1996, August 3). *Philippines Reporter*.

Spall, P. (1995). *The development of a national strategy for preventing child abuse*. Sydney: New South Wales Child Protection Council.

Tomison, A. (1996). *Child maltreatment and family structures*. Melbourne: Australian Institute of Family Studies.

Wood Royal Commission [WRC]. (1997). *Wood Royal Commission: Final report*. Sydney: NSW Government Printer.

Youth and Family Services Division. (1997). *Child sexual abuse: Understanding and responding*. Melbourne: Youth and Family Services Division, Victorian Government Department of Human Services.

2

CANADA

Marcellina Mian, Nicholas Bala, and Harriet MacMillan

PROFILE OF CANADA

Canada, located in northern North America, has an area of 9.9 million square kilometers and a population of 30.2 million people. Ottawa is the capital. The diverse ethnic background of Canada includes British, French, other European, Asian, Arab, African, indigenous Indian, and Eskimo. Canadians speak French and/or English and are mostly Roman Catholic or Protestant. The infant mortality rate is 7 per 1,000, and the life expectancy is seventy-five years for males and eighty-two years for females. Ninety-nine percent of Canadians fifteen years of age and older have at least a ninth grade education. In 1998 the gross national product per capita was $20,020 (U.S.). The government is a confederation with a parliamentary democracy, which includes a constitutional monarchy and a federal system.

A CASE STUDY

In 1986, at nine months of age, Crystal was admitted to the Hospital for Sick Children with the diagnosis of "near-miss" sudden infant death syndrome (SIDS). Her twin brother had died of SIDS at four months of age. She was failing to thrive and had one small bruise on her forehead and extensive retinal hemorrhages. Diagnostic imaging revealed a skull fracture, numerous rib fractures, and acute subdural hemorrhages on both sides of her head. The family doctor knew that both she and her twin brother had rib fractures at four months of age, but he attributed the fractures to neonatal interventions that were performed due to the twins' prematurity and mild respiratory distress. Despite intensive intervention, Crystal died. Her autopsy confirmed that she had suffered numerous unexplained injuries, and the diagnosis of shaken baby syndrome was made. Crystal's mother later told police that Crystal's father would often "thump" Crystal on the chest to quiet her when he was watching television. Fortunately, Crystal's father was charged and convicted of aggravated assault.

HISTORY

Until the latter part of the nineteenth century, there was little social or legal recognition in Canada of the special needs and vulnerabilities of children. Child abuse and neglect were common, and children often worked in factories, mines, and farms starting at a young age. Religious orders established orphanages for infants, but it was common for children whose parents and relatives were dead or unable to care for them to be "apprenticed out" to work on farms and in shops, often under exploitative conditions (Neff, 1994).

Toward the end of the nineteenth century, reformers began to advocate for compulsory school attendance, the abolition of child labor, and the establishment of juvenile courts and training schools to deal with older children who were neglected, orphaned, or delinquent. In 1893, the first Canadian legislation was enacted for the establishment of Children's Aid Societies, and judges were given broad authority to commit to Society guardianship young children who were "dependent and neglected," as well as older youths who were "immoral or depraved" (Protection of Children Act, 1893). By early in the twentieth century, child welfare agencies were established in each Canadian jurisdiction.

Mandatory child abuse reporting legislation was enacted in Canada in the mid-1960s. This intrusion of the state into family life contrasted with the growing recognition of civil rights and the right to restrictions on state interference in the lives of individuals. During the 1970s and 1980s, a number of related social work and judicial developments led to significant changes in the child welfare system, supporting the concept of "family preservation" (Heneghan, Horwitz, & Leventhal, 1996) and placing greater emphasis on the legal rights of parents and children. As a result, child protection agencies devoted greater attention and resources to justifying involuntary interventions, leading to a decrease in the number of children in state care.

In the early 1980s, adults who had experienced sexual abuse in childhood, feminists, and professionals raised public awareness about child sexual abuse, including that it was dramatically underreported and that child welfare, legal, and medical professionals were not dealing adequately with cases. A federal commission, chaired by sociologist Robin Badgley, was appointed to determine the extent of child sexual abuse in Canada and to formulate recommendations to respond to the problem. Data were collected from surveys of hospitals, police records, child protection files, and the general population. "The Badgley Report" (Badgley et al., 1984) concluded that in Canada, one in four girls and one in seven boys are subjected to some form of unwanted sexual contact before the age of eighteen. In 1985, a Special Advisor to the Minister of Health and Welfare was appointed to report on long-range federal child sexual abuse initiatives that were based on nationwide consultation with professionals as well as with survivor groups. The resulting document, "Reaching for Solutions" (Rogers, 1990), made wide-ranging recommendations about child protection, government funding, and legal reform. These two reports resulted in heightened public awareness, increased political pressure on the government to deal more effectively with child sexual abuse, and significant changes to legislation governing criminal prosecutions for sexual offenses and child witnesses (Bala, 1990).

Examination of child abuse in Canada revealed patterns of extensive abuse in child welfare and educational institutions that were under church or government control. Government policies aimed at the forced acculturation of Native people into the mainstream white society gave rise to institutional abuse of children of Aboriginal ancestry (Monture, 1989).[1] Use of residential schools for Aboriginal people occurred from the late 1800s through the 1950s (Postl, Irvine, MacDonald, & Moffatt, 1994). Aboriginal children were sent from their families and communities to live primarily in these institutions, which were usually operated by religious orders, under the direction of the federal government. Besides being wrenched from their homes, these children were forbidden to speak their language, their culture was denigrated, and they were frequently subjected to abuse by teachers, nuns, and priests in the residential schools. Only recently has this widespread, systemic abuse and its profound effect on Aboriginal communities become apparent (Canada Royal Commission on Aboriginal Peoples, 1996). The federal government and churches are now faced with the prospect of substantial civil liability to victims. In fact, official apologies have been made and plans are being developed to offer compensation and support to adults abused as children (Scrivener, 1988).

One of the most publicized institutional abuse cases in Canada was at Mount Cashel Orphanage in Newfoundland, where boys suffered chronic physical and sexual abuse at the hands of the Catholic Christian Brothers who operated the institution. Reports made by the boys to the police, child welfare authorities, and church officials at the time of their maltreatment in the 1960s and 1970s were ignored (Bessner, 1998). Following disclosures of the abuse, the Newfoundland government and the Catholic Church established commissions of inquiry that made a number of recommendations for the clergy, the larger religious community, police, and child welfare authorities to prevent similar occurrences in the future (Archdiocese of St. John's, 1990).

There have also been recent disclosures of abuse, particularly of males, that occurred during involvement in recreational activities. Circumstances range from a small city Anglican cathedral where boys were molested by their choir master (Steed, 1994) to hockey leagues where boys were preyed on by coaches and staff at arenas (Robinson, 1998). Again, in almost all of the cases, some responsible adults had information from youth at the time that the abuse was occurring but failed to take protective action.

In the last century, Canada has moved from a dearth of services for children, through a period of broad state powers and instances of institutional abuse, to a time of greater family rights. Now there exists a heightened awareness of child abuse and the need for judicious proactive societal intervention.

Aboriginal Children and Families

A Canadian perspective on the response to child maltreatment must include specific reference to the child welfare system's approach to Aboriginal children and their families. Before the mid-1970s services to this population were extremely underresourced (Timpson, 1995). Community-based services were rarely provided on reserves (i.e., land that was often located in quite remote places and specifically set aside for Native populations with Native local government), and the typical response to "extreme" cases (e.g., abandonment) was removal from the home and community. Aboriginal children were typically sent far from their communities with minimal preparation and follow-up and placed with white families who had a culture and language that often differed significantly from their own (Monture, 1989). Native children were (and still are) vastly overrepresented among children in agency care. This high number of Aboriginal children in foster care can be attributed, at least in part, to "cultural colonialism." Non-Aboriginal child welfare professionals tended to devalue traditional native family structures and child care arrangements, considering children neglected if their families failed to meet the standards and expectations of middle-class, white families. This displacement and the special risks created by residential schools were among the many factors which contributed to the breakdown of Native families, the loss of good role models for young Native parents, and, consequently, the intergenerational problems of abuse and neglect (Bala et al., 1991).

By the 1970s, Aboriginal communities began to assert claims for control over child welfare decision making and service provision, as well as for a range of other social, judicial, and educational services (Monture, 1989). In several jurisdictions, child welfare legislation was amended to create a preference for Aboriginal children who were removed from parental care to be placed in Aboriginal homes. By the mid-1980s, control over child welfare services for Aboriginal communities began to be transferred to their own organizations, although provincial and territorial governments continue to maintain administrative and financial control (Davies, 1992). Aboriginal organizations are increasingly involved in the design and delivery of child and family services to their communities, both on reserves and in large urban centers, where Aboriginal people are only a relatively small but greatly disadvantaged segment of the population. Models are now being developed for the treatment of maltreated children and their families by community healing, and services are increasingly being provided by Aboriginal paraprofessionals and lay persons, with the assistance of non-Aboriginal professionals (Musto, 1990). Canada has an increasingly racially and culturally heterogeneous population, and there are growing efforts to include representatives from each culture in child protection services, in an attempt to meet the needs of particular religious or language groups (Timpson, 1995).

DEFINITION

Children's services, including education, health, adoption, child protection, and child abuse reporting requirements, are primarily a provincial responsibility. A key legal definition of "child in need of protection," which is used by child welfare agencies to determine whether there is a basis for involuntary intervention, is similar across Canada. In practice, the initial assessment of whether a child is "in need of protection" (i.e., has suffered or is at risk of suffering harm through the caregiver's abandonment, neglect, or inflicted injury) is based on the judgment of child protection workers.

In the majority of cases, child protection agencies become involved on a "voluntary" basis. Most of these voluntary cases involve supervision of the children in their homes or temporary removal from the home. Court proceedings take place if the parents and agency cannot agree on the nature of the intervention, and are most likely to occur if there is the prospect of long-term removal of a child from the home (Bala, Hornick, & Vogl, 1991). The onus is then on the state agency to justify involuntary intervention.

PREVALENCE

There are at present no national statistics on abuse and neglect in Canada. However, the first survey to collect information on official reports of child maltreatment from provinces and territories across the country is now under way. By the end of 2000, data providing estimates about the incidence of reported child maltreatment in Canada should be available (Phaneuf & Tonmyr, 1998). Studies that have examined the incidence of one or more types of child maltreatment in certain provinces of Canada include work by

Trocmé and colleagues (1994) and Wright and coworkers (1997). The Trocmé study evaluated the incidence of reported and substantiated child maltreatment in Ontario in 1993, revealing an estimated annual incidence of child maltreatment investigations of 21 per 1,000 children in Ontario. In close to 60 percent of these cases, maltreatment was suspected or substantiated by child welfare authorities upon completion of the investigation. Wright examined the incidence of reported child sexual abuse in Quebec using data from child welfare services. The number of confirmed cases of sexual abuse by a parent or guardian of children below the age of eighteen was 0.87 per 1,000 in 1995/1996.

Data were also obtained from the Mental Health Supplement to the Ontario Health Survey (1990/1991), hereafter referred to as the Supplement, an epidemiologic study of psychiatric disorders which included a self-administered questionnaire used to collect retrospective information about physical and sexual abuse in childhood (Offord et al., 1996). Childhood physical abuse based on acts of violence (spanking and slapping were excluded from the definition) was reported by about one in three males and one in five females (MacMillan et al., 1997). Sexual abuse was reported by one in eight females and one in twenty-five males. The dramatic differences between child welfare data and retrospective survey data suggest that many cases of abuse are not coming to the attention of child welfare authorities.

Data from the Supplement indicate that one of the major risk indicators for psychiatric disorders in the general population is a history of child physical or sexual abuse. This suggests that a history of child maltreatment is as important as a family history of psychiatric disorders in determining risk of developing a subsequent psychiatric disorder (Offord et al., 1994). Reducing child abuse could potentially have major implications in decreasing the portion of the population with serious emotional problems.

Additionally, while children from all socioeconomic and cultural backgrounds may be maltreated, the incidence of some forms of abuse, and especially neglect, is inversely correlated with family income (Steinberg, Catalano, & Dooley, 1981). Progress in establishing programs to reduce child poverty has been slow, and Canada continues to have high levels of child poverty (National Council of Welfare, 1998).

Unfortunately, the state continues to have difficulty caring adequately for children. A 1998 Ontario report based on interviews with adolescents in state care contained accounts of staff and foster parents being physically and verbally abusive to children in their care (Ontario Office of Child and Family Service Advocacy, 1998). Many of the youth experienced frequent moves and placement changes. Such placement breakdowns increase the risk for aggressive and self-abusive behaviors among these youth. Disturbingly, over half of the youth in young offender facilities were previously in the care of the children's service system (Ontario Office of Child and Family Service Advocacy, 1998).

INVESTIGATION

Child Protection Services

Each province or territory has a government department responsible for child welfare and protection services that develops policies and procedures for their delivery, either through government agencies alone or in combination with mandated nongovernmental agencies (Federal-Provincial Working Group on Child and Family Services Information, 1994). Provinces vary in their levels of funding for child welfare services and in the implementation of child protection programs and services. In recent times, budgetary constraints have necessitated significant restructuring in most child protection agencies in Canada as well as the development of liaisons with other service providers in the health, education, and social service systems. Child protection workers often carry heavy caseloads and report that they must make critical decisions without sufficient resources to assist families adequately (Gove, 1995).

The multidisciplinary approach, which was ill-defined in responding to physical abuse, became critical in addressing sexual abuse. Most jurisdictions now have joint police-child protection protocols to provide a coordinated response to all types of abuse. The police are responsible for any criminal prosecution that may arise, while child protection workers are responsible for protection of the child and the provision of services to the family. Most protocols provide specific guidelines on the investigation of child abuse reports, including time lines for response and criteria for intervention.

Medical practitioners play an important role in this field because of the importance of physical findings in confirming abuse. Thus, most hospitals have specific policies for involving child protection agencies if child abuse or neglect is suspected. There continue to be concerns, however, that some professionals in the community, including physicians, are failing to identify and report child abuse adequately (Loo, Bala, Clarke, & Hornick, 1998).

TREATMENT

Canadian communities provide a spectrum of support services. These can be arranged by voluntary agreement of the family, at the request of the child protection agency, or by court order. Services include day care, respite care, homemakers' and public health home visitation, and programs for substance abuse, parenting skills, and anger management. The level of services available is dependent on many factors including geographical location, community size, degree of neighborhood involvement, and how high the risk is of a family being neglectful or abusive to its children. Unfortunately, these support services are often difficult to access and in some cases unavailable.

Health personnel are key service providers, both in the assessment and treatment of at-risk and maltreated children and their parents. Crisis support group programs, which may include an assessment component, are available in some communities for immediate help to children and their parents. Referrals may then be made for ongoing treatment as appropriate. In some locales, group or individual counseling is available for offenders. The availability of these services varies widely. Since Canada has universal health care coverage, there should be reasonable access to psychiatrists and other physicians. In reality, however, there is a significant shortage of these and other mental health services for children and families, especially in rural and remote communities. Access to other mental health professionals, such as psychologists or social workers, may also be limited by cost.

CHILD PROTECTION

In Canada the trend toward giving individuals greater rights in their relationship with the state was both reinforced by, and reflected in, the introduction of the Canadian Charter of Rights in 1982. At the same time, there was a growing challenge to the practice of removing children from parental care, based on arguments that the process of separation of children from parents was emotionally damaging to children who were "attached" to their parents, even if the parents were far from ideal (Goldstein, Freud, & Solnit, 1973).

The move toward a "family autonomy" model was most apparent in the Ontario and Alberta legislative reforms of 1984. These acts included statements that favored "support for the autonomy and integrity of the family" and the "least disruptive alternative" for agency intervention. The definition of "child in need of protection" was narrowed, so that it was no longer sufficient for a social worker and a judge to conclude that a child was living in an "unfit" place, but rather it became necessary to establish a "substantial risk" of serious harm. As a result of these legislative and policy changes, the number of children in care in Ontario was cut by almost half from 1971 to 1988. However, there was a 160 percent increase in the number of families receiving child welfare services, reflecting population growth, more stress on families, and identification of more child welfare problems in the community (Trocmé, 1991).

In the 1990s, research on child development has emphasized the importance of the first years of life in terms of social, psychological, and neurological development. This has raised questions about "family preservation" policies that leave children, especially very young children, in homes with clearly inadequate parental care (Steinhauer, 1996). Also at issue is inadequate planning on the part of child protection workers for young victims of maltreatment (Steinhauer, 1984), resulting in emergency placements, unstable environments, and multiple moves.

More recently, concern that agencies were not doing enough to protect children has resulted in investigations and inquiries in British Columbia, Quebec, Ontario, Manitoba, and New Brunswick. The British Columbia public inquiry by family court judge Tom Gove was sparked by the death of a five-year-old boy, whose case was known to child protection agencies, following physical abuse and neglect by his mother. This led to the most comprehensive assessment of the child welfare system to date. The "Gove Report" (1995) resulted in new legislation, as well as substantial changes in the administration of child welfare services in British Columbia, including the creation of a new Ministry of Children and Families. In Ontario, following a series of coroner inquests, the Ministry of Community and Social Services developed an agenda for action with respect to child maltreatment. A committee, chaired by family court judge Mary Jane Hatton, was appointed to review Ontario's child welfare laws. The committee completed its report in June 1998 (Hatton et al., 1998), and the government has responded by enacting significant amendments to the 1984 law, although they did not adopt all of the committee's proposals (Child and Family Services Amendment Act, 1999).

The Gove (1995) and Hatton et al. (1998) reports indicate that some social workers and judges applied child welfare legislation in a way that placed too much emphasis on family preservation and left children exposed to parental abuse or neglect. The statutory changes emphasize that the paramount consideration is "to promote the best interests, protection and well being of children," rather than the rights of the parents. Further, changes placed greater statutory recognition on the problems of child neglect and emotional abuse. For example, in emotional abuse cases it will no longer be necessary to find that "severe" harm has occurred, and it will suffice if there is a "risk" that a child is likely to suffer "serious emotional harm" from parental neglect or abuse (Child and Family Services Amendment Act, 1999). There is an emphasis on making permanent decisions for young children sooner, thereby reducing the time these children spend in temporary care arrangements. This is especially true for children under the age of six years, for whom the maximum period in temporary care has been reduced from twenty-four to twelve months.

In the 1970s, the first legal aid programs were established to represent low-income parents facing intrusive state action in their families. While there was significant variation across Canadian jurisdictions, the trend was toward the establishment of programs for legal representation of children involved in protection proceedings. The precise role of these lawyers in court was, however, controversial. By the 1990s a more conservative approach prevailed in Canada, with greater emphasis on individual responsibility and accountability and less focus on societal support and responsibility. "Family values" remain important, but society appears more prepared to intervene in the lives of children when their parents are seen to be inadequate. The notion of "children's rights" is still emphasized, but these rights are now more likely to be defined as the right to protection and safety, as opposed to strict legal rights. While there continue to be significant programs of legal representation for children involved in child protection proceedings (particularly in Ontario and Quebec), resource cuts have led to reduced use of lawyers for children in protection cases.

There are concerns that any child welfare law reforms should continue to recognize the risks of excessive intervention. In addition, politicians may focus on the relatively inexpensive task of legislative reform and fail to provide the resources and administrative supports required for a more effective child protection system. More comprehensive data about the number and circumstances of children taken into care and the outcomes of their involvement with the child welfare system are essential in exploring these controversial issues (Bala, 1998).

Criminal Law Reforms

Until recently, the criminal justice system in Canada regarded child witnesses as inherently unreliable, and very little effort was made to accommodate them. Beginning in the late 1980s, there have been significant changes in criminal law, resulting in substantial improvements in how the Canadian justice system deals with child victims of maltreatment (Bala, 1990). New offenses have been created to address sexual exploitation of children, and testimony by children has been facilitated.

LEGAL INNOVATIONS

Programs are available to support children who have to testify in court. These programs prepare children for the court experience by explaining the procedure and the role of each participant in the process, including the child witness. Such programs also provide advocacy for children in court. One of the first such child victim witness support programs was established in London, Ontario (London Family Court Clinic, 1999), and is operated by mental health professionals and social workers who work in liaison with police and Crown prosecutors. This program conducted research on the experience of children who have to testify about their victimization (Sas et al., 1993) and determined that while children have negative perceptions of their court experience, there are no long-term consequences of testifying per se. Significantly, they identified children who require more intensive support services, particularly children who do not have a parent who can provide effective support.

It is now accepted that a child does not have to demonstrate an understanding of the religious significance of an oath to give sworn testimony. A child who has the capacity to communicate in court and can "promise to tell the truth" is allowed to testify in criminal proceedings without the need for corroboration (Bala, 1990). Canadian judges are becoming more sensitive to the needs and capacities of child witnesses, but there is still considerable variation in judicial attitudes toward child witnesses, and the process of testifying can still be a traumatic and confusing experience for young children (Bala, 2000).

In an effort to accommodate child victims, they can now testify from behind a screen or from another room via closed circuit television. The legislation allows videotapes of an investigative interview with a child made by police or child protection workers to be admitted into evidence, provided that the child is a witness and that the child testifies that the content of the videotape is true. This provision does not eliminate the need for the child to testify, as the videotape is received in addition to the child's testimony, but it allows the court to receive a fuller account of the alleged abuse (Bala, in press).

The Supreme Court of Canada decision in R. v. Khan (1990) allows the admission of a child's out-of-court statements (hearsay) that disclose abuse, provided that the statement is considered "reliable" and it is "necessary" to admit this type of hearsay evidence. For example, if the child is too young to be accepted as a witness in court, the judge may admit evidence of a child's disclosure to a parent or doctor, given that there is some assurance of the reliability of the statements (e.g., the statements were given in a relatively spontaneous manner). This approach ensures that the trier of fact (i.e., the judge or jury) has a relatively complete description of the alleged acts, without compromising the rights of the accused to fully cross-examine the person to whom the statement was made (Bala, in press).

In 1993, the Criminal Code was amended to specify that in child abuse prosecutions, if the prosecutor requests an order to exclude the public while the child is testifying, the judge must consider "the interests of the child witness, as well as concerns about the administration of justice." The prosecutor may call an expert witness or others who can testify about the likely effect on the child's emotional well-being of permitting members of the public or supporters of the accused in court. It is also an almost invariable practice for judges to make an order prohibiting the publication of information that would serve to identify the victim in any sexual offense (Bala, in press).

The dominant model for dealing with child abusers (especially sexual offenders) in Canada is prosecution and imprisonment. In some Aboriginal communities, however, programs are being implemented to achieve accountability without imprisonment. Treatment options are limited in prison, although some facilities offer both individual and group therapy.

In some provinces, child perpetrators' names are placed on "Child Abuse Registers." There has been considerable controversy about the usefulness and effectiveness of these registers. In Nova Scotia and Manitoba, these registers can be used for employment checks for individuals seeking positions that involve work with children (Bala, Hornick, & Vogl, 1991). In other provinces, child-serving organizations are starting to screen workers and volunteers for criminal records involving offenses against children.

Increasingly, adults who were victimized as children are seeking legal redress from individual abusers for maltreatment that occurred years earlier. In cases where abuse occurred in an institution, Canadian courts have been increasingly willing to hold the organization or government that was responsible for the institution civilly liable, even if directors of the institution cannot be proven to have been negligent (*Bazley v. Curry*, 1999).

PREVENTION

Efforts to prevent child maltreatment in Canada can be classified into three types of programs: (1) early intervention community-based programs, (2) safety prevention programs, and (3) a miscellaneous group of interventions.

Early intervention community-based programs focus on the prevention of physical abuse and neglect by providing services to high-risk individuals or communities. Such services have two major subcategories: (1) home visitation and (2) parent training programs. Home visitation programs have been promoted in many developed countries as an early intervention strategy for improving the health and well-being of children. There is a wide range of programs which vary in terms of service provider (e.g., nurse, social worker, lay home visitor), duration, visit frequency, and activities of the intervenor during the visit (American Academy of Pediatrics: Council on Child and Adolescent Health, 1998). The majority of programs emphasize parental education, social support, and links with community services. Despite American studies that show the effectiveness of home visitation by nurses in preventing child abuse and neglect (e.g., Olds et al., 1997), budget cutting in the 1980s forced reductions in some of these programs in Canada. More recently, there has been pressure on provincial governments to increase funding available to home visiting programs (Else, Williams, Wilson, Watson, & Bradley, 1998), but debate continues about the most effective and inexpensive methods of providing the service to high-risk families.

The second major group of early intervention programs includes parent training programs. These initiatives generally focus on providing education about child rearing and child development to individuals considered at risk for experiencing problems in parenting (Wekerle & Wolfe, 1993). Most of these programs aim to improve child-parent interactions and emphasize behavioral management strategies in an effort to prevent child physical abuse and neglect. They are generally provided by community agencies. While there is some evidence that such programs improve knowledge and parenting behavior, there is not yet evidence that they actually reduce occurrences of child physical abuse and neglect (MacMillan, MacMillan, & Offord, 1993). There is some suggestion that the parents that typically make use of these programs are not the ones whose children are at greatest risk for experiencing physical abuse and neglect.

Over the past fifteen years, many safety programs have been developed for children that focus generally on the prevention of sexual abuse and abduction (Wurtele, 1987). Most of these interventions are school-based and directed to children from the general population. Some have included parents and/or teachers. Identifying inappropriate touching or advances by an adult and saying no are common elements of the educational curricula. Participants range in age from preschoolers to children who are twelve years of age. Interventions have included a range of approaches including film or videotape with instruction, skits, use of printed material such as coloring books, behavioral rehearsal, and a combination of these methods.

In summary, while there is evidence that these programs significantly increase children's knowledge about sexual abuse and enhance awareness of safety skills, there is as yet no evidence that they actually reduce the occurrence of sexual abuse or abduction (MacMillan, MacMillan, & Offord, 1993). In Canada, as in other countries, these school-based prevention education programs put the onus on children to resist sexual abuse. Thus, they can be falsely reassuring to parents who assume that a child's participation in a prevention program inoculates the child from sexual abuse and abduction. Research by Finkelhor and Dziuba-Leatherman (1994) suggests that adequate supervision is one of the major determinants in increasing the likelihood that children are protected from sexual abuse and abduction, as well as other types of victimization.

Miscellaneous

There are a variety of other initiatives that emphasize the prevention of child abuse as one of their goals. For example, a national toll-free telephone hot line called the Kids Help Phone was developed and provides advice to children and youth about a range of issues. The actual benefits of this program are not known. While the Kids Help Phone does monitor the number of calls, it is difficult to determine the impact of such a program in preventing outcomes such as child maltreatment.

CONCLUSION

One of the most significant developments in the child welfare field in Canada in the mid-1990s has been the public focus on child abuse and neglect deaths, particularly in situations where the children were known to agencies but were not removed from parental care. While there is no clear evidence that the child welfare system is providing less protection than in the past, the public and politicians are now demanding improved measures to reduce child abuse and neglect. There has also been greater media coverage about the need to prevent child abuse than in past years. This has led to child abuse forums that focus public attention on child maltreatment. Despite this, the actual effect of such events in preventing child maltreatment is not known. Fortunately, there have been recent developments at the federal level to increase awareness about child maltreatment that may assist in the development of programs and policies. Health Canada is funding research to better assess outcomes for children taken into care by child welfare agencies.

Significant work has been done in Canada in the recognition of child abuse and neglect and interventions to address these social ills over the past century, but further emphasis on the need for prevention and evidence-based treatment services is necessary.

NOTES

Nicholas Bala was supported by a grant from the Social Sciences and Humanities Research Council of Canada.

Harriet MacMillan was supported by a W. T. Grant Faculty Scholar Award.

1. The term "Aboriginal" in Canadian usage refers to people whose ancestors were native to Canada. The terms "Aboriginal" and "Native" will be used interchangeably. Many Aboriginal people object to the term "Indian," so this term will only be used when required to describe information from the original source accurately.

REFERENCES

American Academy of Pediatrics: Council on Child and Adolescent Health. (1998). The role of home-visitation programs in improving health outcomes for children and families. *Pediatrics, 101*, 486–489.

Archdiocese of St. John's. (1990). *The Report of the Archdiocesan Commission of Enquiry into the sexual abuse of children by members of the clergy.* St. John's, Nfld.: Author.

Badgley, R. F., Allard, H. A., Proudfoot, P. M., Ogilvie, D., Gelinas, P. M., Sutherland, S., McCormick, N., Fortin, D., Rae-Grant, Q., & Pepin, L. (1984). *Sexual offences against children* (catalogue J2–50/1984E). Ottawa: Department of Supply and Services Canada.

Bala, N. (1990). Double victims: Child sexual abuse and the Canadian criminal justice system. *Queen's Law Journal, 15*, 3–32.

Bala, N. (1998). Reforming child welfare policies: Don't throw out the baby with the bathwater. *Policy Options, 19*, 28–32.

Bala, N. (in press). Child witnesses in the Canadian criminal courts: Recognizing their capacities and needs. *Psychology, public policy and the law, 5*, 1–32. Washington, DC: American Psychological Association.

Bala, N., Hornick, J., & Vogl, R. (1991). *Canadian child welfare law: Children, families and the state.* Toronto: Thompson Educational Publishers.

Bazley v. Curry (1999), S.C.J. No. 35 (Q. L. online), 174 D.L.R. (4th) (S.C.C.).

Bessner, R. (1998). *Institutional child abuse in Canada*. Ottawa: Law Commission of Canada.

Canada Royal Commission on Aboriginal Peoples. (1996). *Final report*. Ottawa: Author.

Child and Family Services Amendment Act (Child Welfare Reform) S. O., C. 2. (1999).

Davies, C. (1992). Native children and the child welfare system in Canada. *Alberta Law Review, 30,* 1200–1215.

Else, P., Williams, R. C., Wilson, I., Watson, B., & Bradley, S. (1998). Healthy babies, healthy children: An early intervention/prevention program for Ontario. *Ontario Medical Review, July/August,* 20–21.

Federal-Provincial Working Group on Child and Family Services Information. (1994). *Child and family services statistical report 1994–95 to 1996–97*. Ottawa: Minister of Supply and Services Canada.

Finkelhor, D., & Dziuba-Leatherman, J. (1994). Victimization of children. *American Psychologist, 49,* 173–183.

Goldstein, J., Freud, A., & Solnit, A. (1973). *Beyond the best interests of the child*. New York: The Free Press.

Gove, T. (1995). *Report of the Gove inquiry into child protection in British Columbia*. Vancouver: Attorney General, Province of British Columbia.

Hatton, M. J., Campbell, G., Colantoni, H., Ferron, R., Huyer, D., Ortiz, T. J., MacMillan, H. L., & Trocmé, N. (1998). *Protecting vulnerable children: Report of the panel of experts on child protection*. Toronto: Ontario Ministry of Community and Social Services.

Heneghan, A. M., Horwitz, S. M., & Leventhal, J. M. (1996). Evaluating intensive family preservation programs: A methodological review. *Pediatrics, 97,* 535–542.

London Family Court Clinic. (1999). *Child witness project*. www.lfcc.on.ca/cwp

Loo, S., Bala, N., Clarke, M., & Hornick, J. (1998). *Reporting and classification of child abuse in health care settings*. Ottawa: Health Canada.

MacMillan, H. L., Fleming, J. E., Trocmé, N., Boyle, M. H., Wong, M., Racine, Y. A., Beardslee, W. R., & Offord, D. R. (1997). Prevalence of child physical and sexual abuse in the community: Results from the Ontario Health Supplement. *Journal of the American Medical Association, 278,* 131–135.

MacMillan, H. L., MacMillan, J. H., & Offord, D. R. (with the Canadian Task Force on the Periodic Health Examination). (1993). Periodic health examination, 1993 update: 1. Primary prevention of child maltreatment. *Canadian Medical Association Journal, 148,* 151–163.

Monture, P. A. (1989). A vicious circle: Child welfare and the First Nations. *Canadian Journal of Women and the Law, 3,* 1–17.

Musto, R. J. (1990). Indian reserves: Canada's developing nations. *Canadian Family Physician, 36,* 105–116.

National Council of Welfare. (1998). *Profiles of welfare: Myths and realities*. Ottawa: Author.

Neff, C. (1994). The Ontario Industrial Schools Act of 1874. *Canadian Journal of Family Law, 12,* 171–208.

Offord, D. R., Boyle, M. H., Campbell, D., Cochrane, J., Goering, P., Lin, E., Rhodes, A., & Wong, M. (1994). *Ontario Health Survey 1990: Mental Health*

Supplement: Selected findings from the Mental Health Supplement to the Ontario Health Survey. Toronto: Ontario Ministry of Health.

Offord, D. R., Boyle, M. H., Campbell, D., Goering, P., Lin, E., Wong, M., & Racine, Y. A. (1996). One-year prevalence of psychiatric disorder in Ontarians 15 to 64 years of age. *Canadian Journal of Psychiatry, 41,* 559–563.

Offord, D. R., Kraemer, H. C., Kazdin, A. E., Jensen, P. S., & Harrington, R. (1998). Lowering the burden of suffering from child psychiatric disorder: Trade-offs among clinical, targeted and universal interventions. *American Academy of Child and Adolescent Psychiatry, 37,* 686–694.

Olds, D. L., Eckenrode, J. R., Henderson, C. R., Kitzman, H., Powers, J., Cole, R., Sidora, K., Morris, P., Pettitt, L. M., & Luckey, D. (1997). Long-term effects of home visitation on maternal life-course and child abuse and neglect: Fifteen year follow-up of a randomized trial. *Journal of the American Medical Association, 276,* 637–643.

Ontario Office of Child and Family Service Advocacy. (1998). *Voices from within: Youth in care in Ontario speak out.* Toronto.

Phaneuf, G., & Tonmyr, L. (1998). National incidence study of child abuse and neglect [letter]. *Canadian Medical Association Journal, 159,* 446.

Postl, B., Irvine, J., MacDonald, S., & Moffatt, M. (1994). Background paper on the health of Aboriginal peoples in Canada. In Canadian Medical Association, *Bridging the gap: Promoting health and healing for Aboriginal peoples in Canada* (pp. 19–56). Ottawa: Canadian Medical Association.

Protection of Children Act, 45 S.O., s 14 (1893).

R. v. Khan (1990), 79 C.R.(3d) 1, 59 C.C.C. (3d) 92 (S.C.C).

Robinson, L. (1998). *Crossing the line: Violence and sexual assault in Canada's national sport.* Toronto: McLelland & Stewart.

Rogers, R. (1990). *Reaching for solutions. The report of the special advisor to the Minister of National Health and Welfare Canada.* Ottawa: Supply and Services Canada.

Sas, L., Hurley, P., Hatch, A., Malla, S., & Dick, T. (1993). *Three years after the verdict: A longitudinal study of the social and psychological adjustment of child witnesses referred to the Child Witness Project.* London: London Family Court Clinic.

Scrivener, L. (1998, October 28). Full apology. *Toronto Star,* p. A3.

Steed, J. (1994). *Our little secret: Confronting child sexual abuse in Canada.* Toronto: Random House.

Steinberg, L. D., Catalano, R., & Dooley, D. (1981). Economic antecedents of child abuse and neglect. *Child Development, 52,* 975–985.

Steinhauer, P. D. (1984). The management of children admitted to child welfare services in Ontario: A review and discussion of current problems and practices. *Canadian Journal of Psychiatry, 29,* 473–484.

Steinhauer, P. D. (1996). Toward improved developmental outcomes for Ontario children and youth. *Ontario Medical Review, 63,* 43–50.

Timpson, J. (1995). Four decades of literature on Native Canadian child welfare: Changing themes. *Child Welfare, 74,* 525–546.

Trocmé N. (1991). Child welfare services. In R. Barnhorst & L. C. Johnson (Eds.), *The state of the child in Ontario* (pp. 63–91). Toronto: Oxford University Press.

Trocmé, N., McPhee, D., Kwan Tam, K., & Hay, T. (1994). *Ontario incidence study of reported child abuse and neglect: Executive summary.* Ontario: Institute for the Prevention of Child Abuse.

Wekerle, C., & Wolfe, D. A. (1993). Prevention of child physical abuse and neglect: Promising new directions. *Clinical Psychological Review, 13,* 501–540.

Wright, J., Boucher, J., Frappier, J. Y., Lebeau, T., & Sabourin, S. (1997, June). *The incidence of child sexual abuse in Quebec.* Paper presented at the Fifth Family Violence Research Conference, University of New Hampshire, Durham, NH.

Wurtele, S. K. (1987). School-based sexual abuse prevention programs: A review. *Child Abuse and Neglect, 11,* 483–495.

3

ENGLAND

Wendy Stainton Rogers and Jeremy Roche

PROFILE OF THE UNITED KINGDOM

The United Kingdom of Great Britain and Northern Ireland, islands in northern Europe, has an area of 244,820 square kilometers. The capital is London, and the population of 58.5 million people consists of British, West Indian, and South Asian ethnic backgrounds. The official languages are English, Welsh, Irish Gaelic, and Scottish Gaelic. The religious faiths include Church of England, Roman Catholic, and Church of Scotland. The infant mortality rate is 6.4 per 1,000, and the life expectancy is seventy-four years for males and seventy-nine years for females. Education is mandatory from the ages of five to sixteen, with an attendance rate of nearly 100 percent and a literacy rate of 99 percent. The government is a constitutional monarchy, and the age of suffrage is eighteen. The gross national product per capita in 1998 was $21,400 (U.S.).

This chapter focuses on England rather than Britain as a whole, since Britain has three different legal systems: one for England and Wales, one for Northern Ireland, and one for Scotland. Each of these systems has somewhat different administrative arrangements.

A CASE STUDY

In the United Kingdom, the state has a responsibility to provide housing for families if they are homeless, but often these accommodations can be very inadequate. For example, Dionne is two years old and lives with her mother in a bed and breakfast that essentially consists of a single room in a cheap boardinghouse. The room is cold and damp, the bathroom is shared with three other families, and the cooking equipment meets only their most basic needs. Dionne's mother found a part-time job in the evenings to help supplement her state benefits. Such employment is strictly illegal; however, many poor parents find such work in order to earn enough money to live adequately. Consequently, Dionne's mother is forced to leave Dionne locked up in their makeshift apartment from 11 P.M. until 7 A.M. every night. Dionne is often frightened when she wakes up alone in this cold dark room.

HISTORY

Concern about what we now call child abuse has a relatively long history in England. In 1883, the National Society for the Prevention of Cruelty to Children (NSPCC) was created in Liverpool and was instrumental in creating legal protection for children through the Prevention of Cruelty Act, 1889. Among other provisions, this act gave courts the power to (a) issue a warrant for the police to enter a home if there were suspicions that a child was being mistreated, (b) arrest individuals suspected of abuse, and (c) remove a child from his/her home. This law was an important turning point in English legal history. It reflected a dramatic change in thinking about children, and, in particular, highlighted an emerging concern for children's welfare.

Not long before this time, young children worked long hours in factories and mines and were hung for petty crimes. For example, in February 1814, at the Old Bailey court in London, five boys were condemned to death for stealing. The youngest was eight and the oldest twelve. Both in schools and at home, children were exposed to severe physical punishment. The maxim for child rearing was "Spare the rod and spoil the child." Susannah Wesley, mother of the religious leader John Wesley, gave parents this advice:

Break their will betimes: begin this great work before they can run alone, before they can speak plain, or perhaps speak at all . . . make him do as he is bid, if you whip him ten times running to effect it. . . . Break his will now and his soul will live, and he will probably bless you to all eternity. (Quoted in Jobling, 1978, p. 24)

Parents were seen as having absolute rights over their children, and this was viewed by many as far more important than potential risks to children. In a 1874 debate in the British Parliament about what might be done to tackle the high rate of infant mortality among the poor, one member stated, "I would far rather see even a higher rate of infant mortality prevailing . . . then [*sic*] intrude one iota further on the sanctity of the domestic hearth" (quoted in Inglis, 1978, p. 24). This historical backcloth is important for understanding how child abuse is perceived today in England, since the attitudes and tensions still resonate. In particular, a punitive view of child rearing still persists in the United Kingdom among some sectors of the community. Indeed, it has taken outside intervention from the European Court of Human Rights to force schools in Britain to give up using the cane on pupils and to treat severe caning of a child by a parent as abuse. Nevertheless, there continues to be ambivalence in England about what constitutes the dividing line between "physical abuse" of children and "physical punishment." Regarding sexual abuse, however, there exists much more consensus. In effect, any sexual contact between an adult and a child is treated as child sexual abuse, whereas physical punishment can still be defended in law by the claim that the child was subjected to "reasonable chastisement" used to control the child's misbehavior.

LEGAL ISSUES

The Legal System in England

The legal system for child protection in England encompasses both criminal and civil law, with civil law comprising public law (where there is a dispute between an individual or a group of people and the state) and private law (where the dispute is between individuals). Criminal law involves the prosecution of crimes against children, including sexual assaults and violence. Currently the age of consent in England is sixteen. An act of sexual intercourse (hetero- or homosexual) with a child younger than age sixteen is, by definition, unlawful (although in practice a criminal prosecution is seldom pursued if the child and the adult are both in their teens). Alternatively, as noted previously, parents and other caretakers who are acting with parents' permission may cite "reasonable chastisement" as a defense against prosecution for a physical assault of a child. In practice, this defense tends to be restricted to smacking without the use of an implement, such as a cane.

Civil public law applies when the state (or, in some cases, the NSPCC) seeks to intervene to protect a child, either in the short or the long term.[1] A number of court orders can be obtained to protect a child. These include an Emergency Protection Order (EPO), a Child Assessment Order (CAO), and a Care Order. The EPO allows for a child with a suspected non-accidental injury to be kept in the hospital without parental consent, or for the removal of a child from a home when there are concerns about the child's immediate safety. A CAO can be used to ensure that a child is medically examined and/or assessed. It is used in situations when there is suspected neglect, and when the concerns about the child's safety are less urgent. A Care Order allows the state to restrict parents' ability to exercise their "parental responsibilities"—by, for example, placing the child with a relative or foster care providers.

Civil private law applies when a private citizen (such as a relative) seeks to modify how a child is cared for. For example, under some circumstances, grandparents can apply to a court for a Residence Order that would specify that the child would come to live with them. In addition, children can, with leave of the court, make an application in their own right. For example, a teenager might apply to the court for permission to live with a relative rather than to remain at home. While its use is restricted in practice, some older children have been able to successfully ensure their own protection in this manner.

In general, the English legal system is adversarial. That is, matters are decided by a court in which different sides dispute a case against one another. In serious criminal cases, outcomes (guilty or not guilty) are decided by a jury. In civil law, a judge or magistrate decides. One unusual feature of the legal system in England is that a very high proportion of public and private law cases are decided by lay magistrates who are appointed from the local community and sit as a bench of three people. Magistrates' courts deal with the majority of legal actions, ranging from family proceedings to small-scale theft (such as shoplifting). Magistrates are trained, but they are not lawyers, and therefore are advised in court by a lawyer (about what actions they can and cannot legally take). The idea behind this system is that the judgments they make are primarily "human," and so best made by community members. Magistrates who hear cases concerning children receive special training, including input from childcare practitioners and academics.

The Legal Framework for Child Protection

Arrangements for child protection in England are framed within the Children Act, 1989. This was a "consolidation law" (i.e., it replaced a body of piecemeal legislation) and, as such, it brought about considerable changes. When introducing the act in the House of Lords, the Lord Chancellor heralded it as "the most comprehensive and far-reaching reform of child care law which has come before Parliament in living memory" (Hansard, House of Lords, December 6, 1988). The Children Act is a large, integrated body of legislation, covering a wide range of matters concerned with children's welfare. It includes provisions for how disputes are settled in court, but also defines the obligations of state authorities in protecting children.

A number of principles underpin this legislation, which was intended to transform child welfare law to make it better suited to the needs and concerns of children (see Stainton Rogers & Roche, 1994 for more detail).

The first and overriding principle is that a child's welfare must be the paramount consideration when making decisions about a child's care and upbringing. One manifestation of this principle is that when a child's welfare is being decided by court proceedings, delay must be avoided. Equally, courts are only permitted to make orders that are in the best interest of the child.

In the spirit of this principle, parents are not seen as having rights over their children, but rather responsibilities for them. The law is intended to positively promote parents' ability to fulfill those responsibilities, even when they no longer have day-to-day care for the children. Except when their children are adopted, parents continue to have parental responsibility for them, regardless of where they reside (e.g., with the other parent following divorce, or in foster care provided by the state). This allows for parents' wishes still to be considered regarding all major decisions relating to their child's upbringing. The aim is to foster children's sense that they have parents who care *about* them, even if they cannot care *for* them. This is felt to be important in preventing future child abuse. Specifically, the hope is that this will reduce the number of children who are so damaged in their childhood that they grow up unable to parent effectively themselves.

Although children are entitled to be protected from abuse, it is believed that children should be brought up by their biological families if at all feasible, and that families should be given assistance, if they need it, to make this possible. The state is required to give this help as a service to the child and the family, working in partnership with parents. In other words, the state is not allowed to enforce intervention unless there are serious shortcomings in the care given to children by their parents. When there is enforced intervention, this intervention must be mandated by a court, where parents have a right of challenge.

As mentioned already, unlike federal systems elsewhere, the law in England is centralized. While England's cities and counties have a degree of devolved responsibility, control over child protection comes very much "from the top." The basic framework is supplied by legal statutes. One innovation of the Children Act was that it was written in clear language to encourage practitioners as well as lawyers to consult it directly. The finer-grained detail is set out in a series of documents, *Regulations and Guidance*, that were prepared by the Department of Health, the ministry responsible for child protection and children's services generally. Again, the *Regulations and Guidance* are intended to be followed by all practitioners who undertake work in this field. *Regulations* have the same legal force as statutes. While *Guidance* is advisory, any deviation from the recommendations can form the basis of a legal challenge, and so they are usually followed.

Criminal Prosecution

Running alongside civil law measures to protect children, criminal prosecutions are pursued against alleged abusers. This, as elsewhere in the world where the legal system is adversarial, presents serious problems in situations where children's testimony is crucial for the prosecution of such cases. However, since Britain, unlike the United States, has no constitution, there are (somewhat) fewer difficulties in devising ways for children to testify without being further traumatized.

The government set up an advisory group to explore this issue, and its report was published in 1989 (Home Office, 1989). Some, but not all, of its recommendations were followed. Now, when there is a suspicion that a child may have been sexually abused, the child's interview is usually videotaped. The interview is conducted by one or two members of a joint police and social work investigative team. This videotaped interview then replaces the child's evidence-in-chief (i.e., the main evidence the child gives) in court. However, the child may still be required to be cross-examined by the defense lawyer, although this can be done via a live video link. Measures have also been taken to speed up cases involving child witnesses and to coordinate cases where both civil child protection prosecutions and criminal prosecutions are being pursued. This has been done because it is believed that having to face one's abuser in court and having to testify repeatedly may be traumatizing for children.

In England, criminal prosecution is not usually pursued in cases of neglect or violence, except in cases of extreme violence. In such situations, it is usually considered to be better for the child to offer help to the parents, if at all possible, to tackle the causes of mistreatment, which are seen to lie in family dysfunction. By comparison, perpetrators of sexual abuse are generally prosecuted if sufficient evidence can be obtained to do so. This division reflects different understandings of the causes of physical and sexual abuse. Stainton Rogers and Stainton Rogers (1992) have shown that these disparate causes warrant different strategic responses.

Physical abuse is believed to arise from stress on families caused by poverty, poor housing, and inadequate social support. Such abuse tends to occur when parents are immature and lack good examples of parenting from their own childhood. Consequently, the strategic response which is viewed as most appropriate is to provide support to families, including help in money management, rehousing, and building social support networks. It is better to work with parents to overcome their inadequacies, including helping them with their parenting skills, than to remove the child.

By contrast, sexual abuse tends to be perceived as arising from the misuse of male power, especially by men who have suffered sexual abuse in their own childhood. Clearly this viewpoint is informed by feminism and by psychodynamic theory. Here the strategy of choice is to remove abusers from the family and to seek prosecution and imprisonment. If this proves impossible, then the next best option is to rehouse the mother and child. If the mother is not amenable to this solution, however, then the only solution is to remove the child from the home. Treatment may be offered to abusers (e.g., in prison), although there are some who believe that rehabilitation of sexual abusers is impossible.

This analysis, of course, oversimplifies the situation, but it does help us to understand some of the difficulties involved in responding to child abuse. The family dysfunction understanding is more traditional, reflecting the theory base that informed professional practice (particularly in social work) in the 1960s and 1970s. At that time, child abuse was generally regarded as primarily a problem of physical mistreatment and neglect. In the 1980s, taking a lead from the United States, both feminism and psychoanalytic theory increasingly began to inform professional practice, as sexual abuse became increasingly recognized as a problem that needed to be addressed. This shifted the perspective on the types of responses that are required. In seeking to meet these two disparate agendas, the child protection system has come under increasing strain.

DEFINITIONS OF ABUSE

The Department of Health has produced specific guidance about how agencies should work together in child protection. It defines physical abuse of children as "actual or likely physical injury to a child, or failure to prevent physical injury (or suffering) to a child including deliberate poisoning, suffocation and Munchausen's syndrome by proxy" (Department of Health, 1991).

As Corby (1993) notes, this very broad definition has proved problematic. In practice, action is seldom taken unless the injury is severe, judged to be deliberate, and the child is relatively young. The Department of Health's definition of neglect is similarly unspecific: "The persistent or severe neglect of a child or the failure to protect from exposure to any kind of danger, including cold or starvation, or extreme failure to carry out important aspects of care, resulting in the significant impairment of the child's health or development, including non-organic failure to thrive" (Department of Health, 1991). Perhaps the department's vaguest definition is for sexual abuse: "Actual or likely sexual exploitation of a child or adolescent. The child may be dependent and/or emotionally immature" (Department of Health, 1991). Most practitioners now draw upon more precise definitions. Corby recommends the following:

Any child below the age of consent may be deemed to have been sexually abused when a sexually mature person has, by design or neglect of their usual societal or specific responsibilities in relation to the child, engaged or permitted the engagement of the child in any activity of a sexual nature which is intended to lead to the sexual gratification of the sexually mature person. This definition pertains whether or not it involves genital contact or physical contact, and whether or not there is discernable harmful outcome in the short-term. (Glaser & Frosh, 1988)

THE CHILD PROTECTION SYSTEM

The basic responsibility for child protection is placed with Social Services Departments. These are located in 108 Local Authorities across the country that constitute local government. The Children Act provides Local Authorities with a number of important powers and obligations. We can divide these obligations into three main categories, those (1) relating to all children, (2) intended to help children and families who face particular problems and troubles, and (3) specifically relating to protecting children who may be at risk.

Local Authorities have a general duty to promote and safeguard children's welfare. But they are also required to take reasonable action to enable children's own families to look after them, as long as this does not place the child at risk of serious harm. In England, provision for children and their families is mainly seen as a state responsibility, within the context of the "welfare state," which was set up in Britain in the 1940s. Health care is completely free for (1) children up to the age at which they leave full-time education, (2) pregnant women (up until a year after their child is born), and (3) families on state benefits who have low incomes. Other adults have to pay some costs (for example, a fixed fee for drug prescriptions), but these are fairly modest.

A specially trained nurse (called a "health visitor") visits all families and holds well-baby clinics, monitors preschool children's development, and provides advice and support to parents. Families also register with a "general practice" (to which the health visitor is attached), which provides primary health care services and access to specialized medical care when needed. This primary health care system is a crucial gateway to other services (such as housing and social care). As a universal service, it offers parents a source of advice and support that does not stigmatize them. This primary care is seen as crucial in advancing children's general health and in preventing abuse by monitoring parental care and dealing with problems before they become too serious.

The Children Act defines children as "in need" if they require certain services in order to attain a reasonable standard of health or development and/or their health or development will suffer without these services. Children who are disabled are automatically considered "in need." Local Authorities have a duty to develop Children's Service Plans that monitor the needs of the children in their area and plan the services that need to be provided to meet such needs. Such services may include housing, respite care, guidance, counseling, and help with housework (including laundry).

The aim here is to limit child protection intervention—to avoid taking children away from their families if at all possible.

Local Authorities also have a specific duty to take reasonable steps to prevent children from suffering from ill treatment or neglect. The key concept for child protection in England is that of "significant harm." Children are regarded as in need of protection if they fulfill two main criteria. First, the child must be judged to be at risk of "significant harm" (see Adcock, White, & Hollows, 1991, for definitions) or are likely to be so (for example, if not removed from where they are or not kept in a hospital). Second, that harm must be attributable to action or inaction on the part of their parent(s). The intention here is to restrict child protection intervention to situations of abuse. When harm can be addressed by providing services to support the family, then the child is treated as "in need."

INVESTIGATION

Local Authorities have a general duty to investigate all reports that a child may be, or is at risk of being, significantly harmed. They must also investigate all cases where a child has been taken into police protection, or where an emergency protection order has been made. England does not have mandatory reporting laws—that is, child welfare professionals in general are not legally obliged to report suspected abuse. This duty to investigate, however, does place social services departments (and hence the social workers who work in them) under an obligation to investigate all referrals. They may decide, after initial inquiries, not to take any further action. But they *must* make at least an initial inquiry (e.g., consulting with the child's health visitor). And while other professional groups are not under this legal obligation, almost without exception, most are required by their professional codes of practice and their employing agency to report any suspicions of abuse.

Finally, this law gives the police special powers to protect children. First, they have a general power to take action to "save life and limb." A court can give them a warrant to accompany social workers, to help them gain access to a child—for example, by forcing entry to a home if entry is refused. They can also take children into police protection if they consider them to be in immediate danger. This can involve taking the child to a police station or standing guard over a child who is in the hospital. When a child is taken into police custody, the police must inform the Local Authority and arrange for the child to be moved, if necessary, to a more appropriate location (such as a foster carer's home).

Other professionals (including social workers) can only impose intervention if authorized by a court. This primarily happens when a child's safety has been monitored for some time (the process for this is described later) and serious shortcomings are observed in the standard of parental care such that the child is at risk of significant harm. In such cases, the Local Authority will seek an order to require supervised parental care or, in the most serious cases, a care order, requiring that a child be taken into the state's care (i.e., place the child with a relative, with foster carers, or in a residential establishment).

In situations where there is imminent danger, professionals may need to apply for an emergency protection order (EPO). For an EPO to be given, the court must be satisfied that "there is reasonable cause to believe that the child is likely to suffer significant harm" if he or she is either not removed from an unsafe place, or not kept in a safe one. Local Authority social workers and those who work for the NSPCC can also get an EPO if they are trying to investigate possible abuse and their attempts to get access to the child are being unreasonably refused.

It is worth noting that *any* person can apply for an EPO. In practice, however, it is almost always a childcare professional—and mostly social workers—who do so. In emergencies, an EPO can be provided by contacting a lay magistrate by telephone at home. So, when there is a situation of imminent danger, an EPO can be obtained in a very short amount of time. Once an EPO has been made, the Local Authority must start an investigation. The EPO can be challenged (usually after seventy-two hours) and it can only last a maximum of eight days, so time efficiency is necessary.

At the end of the eight days (or sooner if it is safe to do so), the child must be returned home, or the Local Authority must go back to court to seek an interim care order. There are limits to the length of such orders. When investigators conclude that a child cannot safely return to his/her family, a full care order must be sought. This will only be granted if it is seen to be the best outcome for the child. In these proceedings, the court will appoint a guardian ad litem. The guardian is an officer of the court who acts independently from the Local Authority. He or she consults extensively (including the child wherever possible) and prepares reports setting out various options and recommendations for the child. For example, a guardian may ask the court not to make a care order, but rather to place the child with relatives who will assume parental responsibility for the child.

Effectiveness of Policies

A number of serious shortcomings have been identified with the current system of child protection in England. As stated by Parton, Thorpe, and Wattam (1997), "child welfare agencies have been virtually overwhelmed in recent years by an explosion of child abuse and neglect reports and referrals" (p. 1). Yet, while the number of referrals has dramatically increased, the number of children identified as abused or at risk remains relatively constant. Hence, a disproportionate amount of effort and resources are now being directed to investigation, taking many highly limited resources away from other work, such as prevention and treatment.

Evidence for this is now well established. For example, Giller, Gormley, and Williams (1992) reviewed the work of four Area Child Protection Committees and found that over 75 percent of cases "dropped out" between referral and the child protection conference. Gibbons, Conroy, and Bell (1995) carried out a detailed study of the child protection work of eight English Local Authorities over a sixteen-week period, tracking the progress of cases over an additional twenty-six weeks. Of the 1,888 referrals during this time, 520 cases were filtered out either immediately or after initial investigation (i.e., after inquiries were made to other agencies but not to parents). An additional 925 were dropped following more comprehensive assessment, and 315 after a child protection conference. Only 17 percent of the cases were retained in the system after this point, and of these, only 15 percent were placed on the "at risk" register.

Given these findings, it is not surprising that serious disquiet is being expressed about the workings of the child protection system in England, both by practitioners and by the government. Perhaps what is unusual is that government policy in this field has, for some time now, been informed by research. Following the Children Act, 1989, the Department of Health commissioned a number of major research projects to evaluate the workings of the new law and the effectiveness of the child protection system. In 1995, it published an overview of this research (Department of Health, 1995).

The results from all of these studies are obviously far-ranging and complex, and it is only possible here to outline some of the key features. The first has to do with what constitutes abuse. The overall finding was that, aside from relatively rare cases of extreme violence or sexual assault, children seldom suffer any serious or long-term harm from a single event or incident of mistreatment. What seems to cause the most severe and long-lasting harm to children is being brought up in an environment which is "low on emotional warmth and high in criticism." This is often—but not always—accompanied by a regime of constant physical punishment. Usually this is justified by parents as "discipline" (see Newell, 1989), but such discipline is frequently erratic and may be associated with alcohol or drug abuse. Surprisingly, however, it is the emotional abuse—that is, humiliation, coldness, and psychological cruelty—and emotional neglect (i.e., the child is not loved or cared about) which seem to be the most severely damaging. Unfortunately, it is exactly these kinds of abuses with which the current child protection system in England is least effective in dealing.

The second key finding is that there was little evidence that children were suffering harm without coming to the attention of child protection agencies. Thus, the considerable effort and resources devoted to investigation appear to be effective in that regard. But it appears to be at considerable cost, swallowing up massive amounts of resources. In Local Authorities, the social work teams specializing in work with children and families did very little else other than investigate. They had little, if any, time and few, if any, resources to provide direct help and support to those parents who were struggling. Even worse, being investigated in and of itself often left parents and children feeling alienated and angry, leading them to refuse help that was offered. The studies found that the child protection system failed to develop any longer-term coordinated treatment or counseling services or to undertake basic kinds of preventive work with families.

It was concluded that many investigations were undertaken, many families were visited and case conferences called, but that, in the end, little support was offered to the family. Not only did the parents become alienated, angry and bewildered, but the children were not helped. Perhaps, more crucially, valuable time and resources were wasted, particularly on investigations, with little apparent benefit. (Parton, Thorpe, & Wattam, 1997, p. 14)

In response to these findings it is now being argued by the government that there needs to be a change in direction and that child protection needs to be pursued "with a lighter touch." Their advice to Local Authorities is that they need to get a better balance between fulfilling their duties specifically to *protect* children from abuse, and their responsibility to help and support families, especially those whose children are "in need."

PREVENTION

Social Services are the lead agency in child protection in England. However, all levels of protection—prevention, investigation, and treatment—involve practitioners from different agencies who need to work together, each having their own particular role to play (see Hallett & Osborne, 1992). Specific *Guidance* is provided by the government to specify how this should be done (Department of Health, 1991). It includes the requirement for each locality to operate a liaison committee (called an Area Child Protection Committee [ACPC]), to hold interagency child protection conferences on a case-by-case basis, and to maintain a register of children considered to be at risk of abuse.

The main tasks of ACPCs are to establish, maintain, and review local interagency procedures that are followed in individual cases and to monitor standards of protection work carried out in their area. They also review (a) significant issues arising from the handling of particular cases, (b) arrangements for access to expert advice and liaison between agencies, (c) progress on preventive work, and (d) interagency training. ACPCs are usually constituted of senior officers from each of the agencies involved: social services, the police, hospital and community medical services, education, probation; and where relevant, organizations such as the NSPCC.

The Child Protection Register consists of a centrally kept list of names of and details about children who are believed to be at risk of significant harm. Such children continue to live with their families even though there are unresolved protection issues. This is accomplished by ensuring that the child's safety is monitored, and parents are helped to overcome their problems according to a plan which details what each agency is expected to do, identifies the child's key worker, and specifies dates for review.

The register is maintained in each area on behalf of the ACPC and is usually administered by the Social Services Department. It provides a central point where information is kept that can be checked out whenever a new referral is received. It also collects information about the numbers and categories of children registered and provides a mechanism for ensuring that cases are reviewed regularly. There are also arrangements for Social Services Departments to inform each other, for example, if a registered child has moved from one part of the country to another. The register is kept under strict guidelines of confidentiality, and only named professionals in the different agencies have the right to access the information.

The main system for coordinating interagency work on a case-by-case basis is usually through a child protection conference. This is generally chaired by the Social Services Department and may include the police, medical and nursing staff, teachers, nursery staff, and probation officers, depending on the circumstances of the case. Other than in exceptional circumstances, parents and children (depending on their age and maturity) are also invited, and provided with support to enable their participation.

The conference does not occur in a court of law and has no legal powers. Rather, it is intended to provide a formal setting within which practitioners and the family can share information and concerns, assess the forms and levels of risk to the child, and make recommendations for action. Conference members pool and discuss information about the child and family under investigation. This usually starts with an account of the precipitating factors that led to the investigation, including the outcome of any medical examinations and/or interviews that have been conducted. The child's state of health and development and the family's situation are usually described, and an initial assessment of family functioning and the degree of risk to the child is made.

The only decision that can be made at the child protection conference is whether or not the child's name should be placed on the Child Protection Register. If this is done, then a key worker (usually from the Social Services Department) will be assigned to coordinate the case. The conference also formulates advice for the agencies involved. For example, plans may be made for a detailed assessment of the child and family and for what will be done to protect the child. The desirability or necessity for legal action may also be discussed. While the conference is not empowered to make decisions on such issues (which remain the prerogative of the separate agencies), it is rare for the recommendations of the conference to be overturned.

The core group of professionals most closely involved with the case will usually be designated by the conference to work together and meet on a regular basis. At periodic intervals (usually every six months), the full conference will be reconvened, the child's and family's circumstances reviewed, a decision made as to whether there is continued need for registration of the child, and future plans for interagency work determined by the professionals and the family.

CONCLUSION

Parton, Thorpe, and Wattam (1997) argue that the present situation arose through a number of sociopolitical shifts. One was the growing impact of pressure groups—the women's movement, groups promoting the rights of children, and parental rights organizations—all of which challenged the institutional power wielded by statutory agencies and professionals, as well as challenging each other. One consequence was that child protection became reconceptualized from a medico-social discourse—in which child abuse was seen as analogous to a disease that needed to be diagnosed so that it can be treated—to a legal discourse. That is, "the significance and social function of the law take on added importance in periods of considerable uncertainty where there are particular problems concerned with managing disappointed expectations and conflict" (Parton et al., 1997, p. 33).

At the same time, the concept of child abuse has undergone what Dingwall (1992) terms "diagnostic inflation," now covering a much wider range of concerns than the original "battered baby syndrome." The net result, exacerbated by politico-economic changes which severely limit resources, is a system which is overwhelmed by carrying out investigations, distorted by the pressure to collect evidence for criminal prosecutions, defensive in its practice and resource prioritization, and alienated from the people it is intended to serve.

If we had been writing this chapter a year or so ago, we would have ended here on a very pessimistic note. For all the good intentions of the Children Act—and there is quite amazing consensus in England that it is good law— the child welfare system seemed to be going severely off-course, with those who worked in it becoming increasingly despairing about their inability to make a real difference. But now, there are some reasons to hope. We have a government which is starting to recognize that supporting families is not just about "welfare" but, for example, is also central to crime prevention. Consequently, the lead in family policy has been taken within the Home Office (the ministry covering policing and the prison service), where a new national childcare strategy is on the political agenda. Measures are being taken to address child poverty—compared with the rest of Europe, England's record here is scandalous. And it has become recognized that high-quality child care and family support are important for fostering social cohesion and quality of life.

There is certainly a will to change, and an acknowledgment that the present system is not working. The government review of research (Department of Health, 1995) explicitly recommended taking a wider perspective on child abuse—placing it in a context of mistreatment, and recognizing that abuse ranges from the minor to the severe. This wider perspective is one where the bulk of resources go into ensuring that children have good parenting, with deficits in their family being made up by high standards of supplementary child care. Whether, of course, the initiatives will deliver that is open to question. We can but hope that they will.

NOTE

1. The SPCC is a charitable body given special legal status empowering it to operate, in effect, like a state agency in respect to child protection.

REFERENCES

Adcock, M., White, R., & Hollows, A. (1991). *Significant harm: Its management and outcome*. Croydon: Significant Publications.

Corby, B. (1993). *Child abuse: Towards a knowledge base*. Buckingham: Open University Press.

Department of Health. (1991). *Working together under the Children Act 1989: A guide to the arrangements for inter-agency co-operation for the protection of children from abuse*. London: HMSO.

Department of Health. (1995). *Child protection: Messages from research*. London: HMSO.

Dingwall, R. (1992). Labelling children as abused and neglected. In W. Stainton Rogers, D. Hevery, J. Roche, and E. Ashe (Eds.), *Child abuse and neglect: Facing the challenge* (2nd ed.). London: Batsford.

Gibbons, J., Conroy, S., & Bell, C. (1995). *Operating the child protection system*. London: HMSO.

Giller, H., Gormley C., & Williams, O. (1992). *The effectiveness of child protection procedures: An evaluation of child protection procedures in four ACPC areas*. Manchester: Social Information Systems.

Glaser, D., & Frosh, S. (1988). *Child sexual abuse*. Basingstoke: Macmillan.

Hallett, C., & Osborne, A. (1992). Interagency work in child protection. In W. Stainton Rogers, D. Hevey, J. Roche, & E. Ash (Eds.), *Child abuse and neglect: Facing the challenge* (2nd ed.). London: Batsford.

Home Office. (1989). *Report of the Advisory Group on Video Evidence*. London: HMSO.

Inglis, R. (1978). *Sins of the fathers*. London: Peter Owen.

Jobling, M. (1978). Child abuse: The historical and social context. In V. Carver (Ed.), *Child abuse: A study text*. Milton Keynes: The Open University.

Newell, P. (1989). *Children are people too: The case against physical punishment*. London: Bedford Square Press.

Parton, N., Thorpe, D., & Wattam, C. (1997). *Child protection: Risk and the moral order*. London: Macmillan.

Stainton Rogers, W., & Roche, J. (1994). *Children's welfare and children's rights: A practical guide to the law*. London: Hodder and Stoughton.

Stainton Rogers, W., & Stainton Rogers, R. (1992). Taking the child abuse debate apart. In W. Stainton Rogers, D. Hevey, J. Roche, & E. Ash (Eds.), *Child abuse and neglect: Facing the challenge* (2nd ed.). London: Batsford.

4

INDIA

Uma A. Segal

PROFILE OF INDIA

The Republic of India, located in southern Asia and bordering the Indian Ocean, has an area of 3.3 million square kilometers. The capital is New Delhi. India's 952 million people (15 percent of the world's population) include Indo-Aryans, Dravidians, Mongoloids, and other ethnic backgrounds. The major religious groups include Hindus, Muslims, Christians, and others. A wide variety of languages is spoken in India, including Hindi, English, and fourteen other official languages. The infant mortality rate is 81 per 1,000, and the life expectancy is sixty-one years. Education is required between the ages of 8 and 14, and the literacy rate is 48 percent. The gross national product per capita in 1998 was $340 (U.S.). The Indian government is a federal republic with suffrage over the age of twenty-one. The form of government has some similarities with the British parliamentary system.

A CASE STUDY

Asha was eight years old when her parents "sold" her in Nepal for $175 to a "nice" man who promised to find her a good job in the bustling metropolis of Bombay (Mumbai). This was an unexpected opportunity for Asha and a relief to her overburdened parents, who have four other children. Thus, Asha obligingly accompanied the "nice" man. As she traveled by train across India, Asha marveled at the sights and vastness of the country. She was treated well, and while she missed her family, she was thrilled by the experience. Upon her arrival in Mumbai, she was placed in a house with several other young women and children. She was told that she would be working there, "caring" for men who visited the house in the evenings. Instead, she was physically and emotionally abused, as her tender young body was violated repeatedly each night. She sobbed uncontrollably and ached desperately for her family, but did not know how to return to Nepal or contact her parents. Over the next few months, Asha grew accustomed to these nighttime encounters. The woman who cared for the girls was not unkind, and Asha received sufficient food and adequate housing. The women made friends among themselves and developed a network of support, resigning themselves to their fate.

TYPES AND DEFINITIONS OF ABUSE

Child Abuse

In 1988, Finkelhor and Korbin proposed a universal definition of child abuse as "the portion of harm to children that results from human action that is *proscribed, proximate and preventable*" (p. 4). An action that is *proscribed* is one that is not acceptable; when it is *proximate*, it occurs within the immediate environment of the child; if it is *preventable*, it is an action that is within the control of the individual perpetrating it. This distinguishes the definition of child abuse from other social, economic, and health problems of international concern and allows its application to a range of situations and cultural contexts. Focus is on the perpetrator's intent and on social censure. However, in developing countries such as India, political, societal, economic, and health issues often contribute to the many forms of abuse that children suffer.

India is not indifferent to the abuse of children, as is exemplified by a number of child protection laws and a strong network of governmental and nongovernmental services for children. Nevertheless, because of limited resources and tradition, children continue to experience several forms of societal and parental abuse.

Societal Abuse

Societal abuse is perpetuated by society, through its culture and values, or by its tendency to passively accept abusive behavior. In India, concomitants of poverty, such as homelessness (street children), child labor, child beggary, child prostitution, and child marriage, are increasingly becoming recognized as abusive. All involve the exploitation of children by adults and deprivation of nurture necessary for healthy development.

The presence of street children in India is a major problem and has attracted the attention of numerous governmental and nongovernmental programs. In major Indian cities, the population of street children is believed to be over 100,000 (Mallik, 1994). Their sheer numbers have far-reaching implications for many other problems children face, as they are likely to be exploited by adults who induce them into working, begging, and prostitution (D'Sami, 1992). In addition, street children receive no education and can become involved in substance abuse and violent crime (Raj, 1992). These children are categorized into three groups: (1) children who work on the streets but have fairly strong family ties, (2) children who seek shelter and food from the streets and have infrequent contact with their families, and (3) abandoned children, who seek food, shelter, and companionship from the streets and whose familial bonds are completely severed. Street children generate suspicion and elicit little sympathy from the general population as they are usually strong-willed, self-reliant, and emotionally hardened (Raj, 1992). Despite this, they are often prey for adults, who use them for underpaid work, to beg, or for sexual gratification under the guise of providing them with work and/or food.

Child Labor

In response to national and international concern about child labor in the early 1980s, the Indian government passed the Child Labour (Regulation) Act of 1986, which regulates the conditions under which children can work. This law limits their working hours and prohibits them from working in hazardous occupations when they are under the age of fourteen years. Many activists are unconvinced of the effectiveness of the act, however, believing that the government is impotent to enforce it (Agnivesh, 1989). These concerns are warranted. India has the world's largest number of working children. Some accounts estimate 60 million (Pal, 1998), while others suggest 100 million (Butalia, 1997). However, it is clear from all reports that at least one-third of the world's child laborers are in India.[1] Of these, 10 million are slaves and another 15 million are bonded laborers (Pal, 1998).[2] Thus, despite a 1976 law prohibiting bonded labor and the 1986 Child Labour Act banning workers under the age of fourteen in hazardous occupations, child labor is still rampant in India. Child labor negatively impacts the health of the child, interferes with normal family life, and seriously hampers education, precluding the child's future ability to participate productively in society (Tagore, 1992). Child laborers are especially attractive to employers because they are vulnerable and dependent, and therefore will work long hours, under hazardous conditions, for subsistent benefits. Thus, as unemployment increases for adults in India, employment increases for children.

Although begging in general, and child begging in particular, are considered illegal (Indian Penal Code, Section 363A [Pande, 1988]), begging continues as a widespread form of child exploitation in India. It is correctly believed that almsgivers are more likely to be moved by children who are begging than by adults (Pande, 1988). Almsgivers view this activity as necessary for the child's survival, leading them to contribute more readily. As such, children are often recruited into the life of begging at an early age. While clearly a response to poverty, limited opportunities, and a sense of helplessness, begging has also become an organized trade in India, and children who are brought into the profession are subjected to cruelty, suppression, and indignity. Reports abound of children being sold, rented, and recruited as beggars (Chatterjee, 1997). To evoke sympathy, children with disabilities are often kidnapped to be used as beggars, and the able-bodied are maimed (R. R. Singh, 1988).

Child Prostitution

Young girls of lower socioeconomic levels who are lured to cities to escape abject poverty and deplorable conditions at home (Ashtekar, 1991) often find themselves sold into prostitution (Simons, 1994). Close to 20 percent of the prostitutes in Mumbai are minors for whom there is no dearth of clients (P. Singh, 1987). A widespread belief that sexual intercourse with a virgin will cure venereal diseases (including AIDS) ensures that increasingly younger girls are recruited and infected. Those who help adults procure child prostitutes between the ages of eight and thirteen emphasize that they are free of venereal disease (Simons, 1993).

In addition, children are often sold by their families and taken to the Middle East to work in brothels or to appear in pornographic films (Simons, 1993). Organized international gangs and smuggling rings have found that there is a substantial national and international market for young children, often as young as eight years of age (Mallik, 1994).

Abuses of the Female Child

Indian society and tradition have so denigrated the female that many parents, especially the poor and uneducated, are socialized to undervalue or reject their daughters.[3] Females are targeted for victimization from birth through death as a consequence of gender-selective abortion, infanticide, neglect, and child marriage. Most countries report a greater female to male ratio, yet India's 1991 census indicated a ratio of 92.2 females to 100 males (Mullatti, 1995). UNICEF reported that 25 percent of girls in India die by the age of fifteen (Crossette, 1990). Abortion, infanticide, and other practices harmful to females are clearly implicated (Kapoor, 1995).

Abortion

In an anonymous survey of attitudes toward prenatal diagnosis and gender selection of seventy-one medical geneticists in four developing countries,

52 percent in India indicated that they would perform prenatal diagnosis to select a male (Wertz & Fletcher, 1993). In Brazil, Greece, and Turkey, it was 30 percent, 29 percent, and 20 percent respectively. This reinforced UNICEF's observation that amniocentesis, designed to detect congenital abnormalities, was widely used in India to determine gender and abort the female fetus (Crossette, 1990). More recently, the availability of ultrasound technology is supplanting amniocentesis for gender selection, and a chilling UNICEF pronouncement about most of the female fetuses that survive was that "birth is the only equal opportunity they will ever get" (Crossette, 1990).

Infanticide and selective neglect are centuries-old vehicles for controlling the population of female, disabled, and unwanted children, especially when resources are scarce. Female infanticide is the practice of killing female children within hours or days of their birth (Crossette, 1990). Parents who engage in selective neglect favor their sons, who receive the best food, nurture, support, and health care. Consequently, undernourished female children often succumb to preventable and curable diseases (Burns, 1994). In 1993, the National Foundation of India estimated that 300,000 newborn girls die annually from gender discrimination, either as a result of being killed or dying from illness or starvation (Burns, 1994). In India, female infanticide and selective neglect are identified as the primary reasons for the low female to male ratio among children and youth.

Child Marriage

Child marriage has a long history in India, and until recently was not viewed pejoratively. Deeply rooted in a number of social, economic, and psychological factors (Rajyalakshmi, 1986), child marriage ensured that two well-acquainted families were joined for social and economic reasons. Traditionally, girls resided with their families of origin until they reached puberty, at which time they were considered the appropriate age for marriage. Now, girls move into their in-laws' homes soon after the marriage, relieving their biological parents of responsibility for them and providing the in-laws with extra workers. Although outlawed by the 1986 Marriage and Restraint Act, approximately 25,000 child marriages were known to have occurred in 1988 (Singh, 1988), and are still common (*World News*, 1998).

Many child advocates stress the harmful effects of child marriages, including enforced widowhood, inadequate socialization, deprivation of education, and health issues resulting from frequent pregnancies. Nevertheless, most communities that practice child marriage do not perceive it as being detrimental (Rajyalakshmi, 1986), especially when the marriage is between two young children. Recently, as a result of extreme poverty, another form of child marriage has become widespread. Specifically, hundreds of girls who are perceived as financial burdens are forced to marry fortune hunters or elderly men who sexually abuse them and often sell them to brothels (Sinha,

1992). Such marriages of girls at very young ages inevitably result in torture, exploitation, or death.

Parental/Caregiver Abuse

Sufficient literature exists to reinforce the frequently made assertion that child abuse by parents and/or caregivers has occurred since time immemorial and is known to exist across cultures (Finkelhor & Korbin, 1988). Yet relatively little is known about this phenomenon in developing countries such as India. Although many forms of societal abuse are destructive and dangerous to children, the dynamics that contribute to their perpetuation are often a result of poverty and societal norms. Other dynamics may account for maltreatment in the form of physical and emotional violence and purposeful neglect by caregivers. This author suggests that because an important function of caregivers is to protect children from harm, when abuse of children is perpetrated by the very adults responsible for their care, the long-term impact may be greater than when the perpetrator is outside the family.

In many nations, including India, traditional themes of the sanctity of the family, the privilege of parents, and children as parental property have protected abusive families from intervention by society (Menon, 1988). At the first National Seminar on Child Abuse in India, in 1988, the National Institute of Public Cooperation and Child Development (NIPCCD, 1988) reported a dearth of empirical data on the extent, nature, causes, and effects of different forms of child abuse, with practically no information on familial abuse. In 1992, the National Committee for the Prevention of Child Abuse (NCPCA, 1992) revealed no prevalence/incidence studies on child abuse in India. Although there is an official child abuse policy and a central registry for reports of child abuse and fatalities, there are no mandated reporters.

Physical Abuse

Although physical harm to a child should be both the least difficult to assess and the least controversial, this is often not the case. Except when physical child abuse results in death or disfigurement (Bhattacharyya, 1983), there is often disagreement about what constitutes abuse. Menon (1988) identifies physical abuse as "beating, fracturing, burning, scalding, belting, caning, and tying up" (p. 31). Since she omits slapping, punching, kicking, pulling hair, squeezing, and so on, should one assume that these are acceptable? Corporal punishment is prevalent and acceptable in India (NIPCCD, 1988), and there are many other types of abuses that children experience. Consequently, physical abuse of children by caregivers has not received much attention. Furthermore, although abuse may occur, it may not be so perceived, as those in positions to intervene are themselves products of the culture that sanctions it (R. R. Singh, 1988).

Sexual Abuse

Sexual abuse, defined as any sexual activity between an adult and a child (Rane, 1991), may include child prostitution, child marriage, child pornography, child molestation, incest, and rape of children. Child prostitution, child marriage, and child pornography are forms of societal abuses, but child molestation, rape, and incest are perpetrated on children by known adults, often caregivers. The sexual abuse of children, especially by parents and relatives, has always been considered very serious, particularly because of the violation of a major societal taboo against incest (Giovannoni & Becerra, 1979). The extent of the problem in India is unknown. Popular literature indicates, however, that it is more widespread than is currently acknowledged. Given the few studies that address the sexual abuse of children (Dave, Dave, & Mishra, 1982; Segal & Ashtekar, 1994), it appears that if childhood sexual abuse occurs at all in India, it is among the poor and uneducated. Contrary to this, Castelino's (1985) survey of 133 postgraduate students from various disciplines revealed that 26 percent of the respondents had been sexually abused when they were between the ages of three and twelve, with the mean age being nine years. Furthermore, only 16 percent had been victimized by strangers, reinforcing Western literature that the majority of perpetrators of sexual abuse are within the child's social/familial network.

PREVALENCE

More recently, a program of research, consisting of three studies, addressed three interrelated factors necessary for understanding child abuse. Specifically, the behavior of perpetrators, the effects on children, and the perception of observers (Mayhall & Norgard, 1983) were examined. Beginning with the belief that if abusive behavior is not perceived as such by society, the phenomenon becomes a non-issue, the first study compared social workers' perceptions of the seriousness of different forms of child abuse with those of the general population. Findings revealed that social workers were no more sensitized to the issue of child abuse in India than were non–social workers (Segal, 1992). Using Straus's (1979) definitions of different levels of abusiveness, a subsequent study of face-to-face self-reports of 313 college or graduate school educated middle-class professionals indicated that, in the previous year, 56.9 percent had engaged in "normal" corporal punishment, 41.9 percent in "abusive" forms of discipline, and a surprising 2.9 percent in "extreme" forms of violence with their children (Segal, 1995).[4] In a third study, 515 children were interviewed at intake to a detention center. Of these, 258 indicated that they had experienced physical violence from their parents, and 156 stated that they had run away when they could no longer tolerate the abuse (Segal & Ashtekar, 1994).

The latter studies reveal that child abuse by parents may be more prevalent than Indian society has been willing to recognize. That corporal punishment is acceptable was supported by its open acknowledgment in the face-to-face interviews (Segal, 1995) and the absence of attention to it by child advocates and researchers. While professionals who can intervene may not perceive corporal punishment as being destructive, many children who experience it find it intolerable and report running away from home. This is a significant finding that has implications for Indian society, but which has received little attention. While the public and social services are increasing outreach programs to the growing numbers of street children who become enmeshed in prostitution and other criminal activities, less effort appears to be placed on understanding what causes, besides poverty, contribute to their presence on the streets.

While Indian society appears to have little awareness of child abuse as it is known in the West, it realizes children's vulnerability and their value as the resources of the future. Therefore, although parental abuse has not been identified as a cause for alarm by many, the prevalence of societal abuses is apparent and has attracted the attention of legislators, activists, and service providers who have sought to address these forms of maltreatment.

LEGAL INNOVATIONS

In 1924, India passed the first Children Act, calling for the protection of children against cruelty and indignity. The first Children Act was found insufficient in detail, therefore the Central Government passed the Central Children's Act, in 1960, to protect children from assault, willful neglect, or harm that could cause unnecessary physical and mental suffering (Belavadi, 1989). In addition, the 1974 National Policy for Children underscores the nation's commitment to the protection of children from neglect, exploitation, and cruelty and stipulates the need to amend existing laws so that in all legal disputes involving children, the child's interest is paramount (Nath & Kohli, 1988).

In recognition that the Central Children's Act and the National Policy for Children needed further specificity, in the last two decades, several laws have targeted unique forms of abuse that are prevalent in India. The Sharda Act of 1929 was amended to become the Child Marriage Restraint Act of 1978, making marriages of females below the age of eighteen or males under age twenty-one criminal offenses. The 1986 National Policy on Education calls for the exclusion of corporal punishment from the schools, and the 1986 Child Labour Act prohibits the employment of children in hazardous occupations and regulates conditions of work in permissible occupations. Furthermore, Article 24 in the Indian Constitution gives every child between the ages of six and fourteen the right to education and seeks a ban on child labor. The Juvenile Justice Act of 1986 aimed to bring uniformity to the acts and served to provide separate administrative mechanisms to deal with destitute and delinquent children (Belavadi, 1989), who, heretofore, received the same services. Existing laws such as the Indian Penal Code and the Children Acts provide for the punishment of all offenses against children (Rane, 1991).

The Indian Penal Code

The sections of the Indian Penal Code focusing on offenses against children generally cover all societal abuses. Offenses that are specified are (a) infanticide and abandonment of infants, or children under the age of twelve, (b) use of children for begging, (c) kidnapping or maiming of children, (d) using them for prostitution, (e) engaging in sexual intercourse with children, or (f) selling of children. All are punishable by fines and/or imprisonment for up to ten years (Belavadi, 1989; Rane, 1991). To address problems in each of these areas, specific legislation was passed.

The 1960 Children Act

Passed to protect children against "cruelty and indignity," this act addresses the transportation or sale of children for the purpose of begging, exploiting them through employment, and subjecting them to "willful cruelty and neglect." Punishment in the form of fines and imprisonment is prescribed. Furthermore, the act indicates the necessity of providing for the protection and rehabilitation of neglected and abused children (Pande, 1988).

For several years, women's groups in India have been lobbying to protect female fetuses, female children, and women. The Indian Penal Code clearly specifies that although the killing of a child after birth is murder, "the causing of the death of a child in the mother's womb is not homicide" (Pande, 1988, p. 60). A major advance was seen when, in 1994, the Indian Parliament passed a new law providing criminal penalties for prenatal tests used solely to determine gender (Burns, 1994). However, some proponents of women's rights fear that curtailing prenatal tests will result in a reversion to female infanticide and selective neglect (Burns, 1994).

Impediments to Implementation

Clearly, the Indian government is concerned about the range and extent of abuses that children experience, and the numerous laws detailed above are indicative of this. Difficulties are experienced, however, in their implementation and enforcement. The country lacks the resources to ensure enforcement. In countries, such as India, where poverty is pervasive and even law enforcement officials are poorly paid, bribery and corruption are rampant. Thus, although the Indian Constitution has made provision for the protection of children, and the existing laws provide for the punishment of all offenses against children, these laws are rarely enforced. The most apparent reasons for this are the weak mechanisms of implementation and the absence of a child welfare orientation among officials, including those on the police force and in the judiciary system (Rane, 1991). News reports do indicate, however, that legislation is periodically implemented and adult perpetrators of violence against children are punished. In addition, in December 1997, the Indian Labour Minister optimistically promised that child labor will be abolished in India by the year 2002 (Pal, 1998).

There are, however, other dilemmas and inconsistencies that must be addressed. There is little social or legal consensus on who is a child. In some instances, it is an individual under the age of fourteen years, as defined by the Child Labour Act of 1986. In other instances, as in the Child Marriage Restraint Act, females are children under the age of eighteen and males under the age of twenty-one. In still other situations, as described in the Indian Penal Code, parents must care for children who are under the age of twelve years, yet boys under the age of sixteen and girls under the age of eighteen are considered minors. Taking a very pessimistic view of the effectiveness of legislation, Pande (1988) states that, given "the lack of political will on the part of those entrusted with the governance of polity . . . the constitutional mandate of economic equality and social justice remain mere epithets in the fact of stark poverty, increasing social violence and prevailing disparities" (p. 58).

Child witnesses are often used to prosecute adults in Western countries (see Bottoms & Goodman, 1996), yet there are currently no recommendations to include them in the Indian legal system. Children's testimony is not admissible in court, and they may not testify against adults, either on their own behalf or on behalf of others (Segal, 1996). A prevalent belief is that "expecting children to give evidence before strangers in a court room is . . . quite unrealistic" (R. R. Singh, 1988, p. 106). While this reinforces the lack of recognition of children's rights in India, it is also presented as a protection of children from further distress. Juvenile officers report what children have discussed with them, or parents of victims can press charges. Since definite evidence is often lacking, and hearing proceedings are interminably long, parents lose interest and cases are often dismissed (Ashtekar, 1991).

CHILD PROTECTION

Although several legislative mechanisms are faulty, several advocacy groups continue to seek to bring the plight of vulnerable children to the attention of policy makers and authorities. A number of programs exist to address the needs of street children. A number of church-sponsored residential programs are available for children to come and live, receive education and sustenance, and leave when and if they wish (Fonseca, 1992).

Other programs provide street-based (Ghosh, 1992), center-based, and community-based intervention (James, 1992). Aims of these programs are to provide education, rehabilitation, support, and guidance to encourage transition away from street life.

The Bonded Labour Liberation Front, a grass-roots advocacy group, is involved in the identification, release, and rehabilitation of child bonded laborers. The Bal Mazoor, a children's labor union, aims to win child laborers the same rights and protection as adult workers (Freedman, 1995). In Tamil Nadu, in response to the high rate of female infanticide, the state government instituted the Cradle Baby Scheme, allowing parents anonymously to place their unwanted children for adoption in cradles in hospitals, health clinics, and orphanages (Devapragasam, 1994).

With the size of the child population in India (340 million under the age of fourteen years [McDevitt, 1999]) and the number of children that live below the poverty line, the need for child welfare services is monumental, and the financial resources of the country are meager. India has been highly cognizant of the general plight of a large percentage of its children, and therefore has passed the many acts discussed above. However, with a lack of funds and training, these cannot be operationalized or applied. Although a highly sophisticated network of social services for children has been present in India throughout this century, most resources address the health, education, and survival needs of children and families. The most innovative and effective of these programs is the nationwide Integrated Child Development Services (ICDS), which provides prenatal care for pregnant women, nutrition, and health education for breast-feeding women, and immunizations, health care, and education for children to the age of six years.

The programs for children can be classified as statutory or nonstatutory, as institutional or noninstitutional; they may also be categorized as developmental, preventative, or rehabilitative services. Developmental services are the main focus of governmental intervention and target all children with an aim to promote health, nutrition, education, and recreation. Preventative services focus on preventing delinquency, vagrancy, and emotional distress, while rehabilitative services target physically disabled children and those subjected to societal abuse, neglect, or destitution (Segal, 1996).

Although the focus has primarily been on eradicating illiteracy, malnutrition, and disease and on providing safe housing for destitute, delinquent, and unwanted children, there now are major efforts by child advocates to address the societal abuse of children, specifically child labor and child prostitution. There is a scarcity of preventative programs directed toward educating parents to avoid traditionally sanctioned abusive practices. Although it has been a decade since the First National Seminar on Child Abuse and Neglect in 1988, there has been no second seminar. Few resources (human or monetary) are available to address parental abuses of children. That the child has a family at all is perceived a blessing by many social service workers!

CONCLUSION

While India has long been aware of the need to protect children and has several laws to guard their rights, most governmental and private social service agencies have, of necessity, focused on their basic survival needs. This chapter has provided an overview of some of the varied forms of abuse and exploitation children in India experience. Various components of the adult-child relationship are culturally, socially, and economically defined, and child maltreatment must be viewed within the national context. However, extreme cultural relativism must be avoided, and human service professionals in India must actively identify and denounce harmful behavior that is not proscribed by Indian society. Advocates for children must continue to lobby for the Rights of the Child (United Nations, 1990), the Children Act, the Juvenile Justice Act, the Child Labour Act, the Child Beggary Act, and the Child Marriage Restraint Act, and for the enforcement of the Penal Code to protect children from exploitation. They must call for the actualization of these acts, both within society and within the family unit. Professionals from the human services are most vital to the success of such endeavors and should be drawn from such fields as medicine, law, social welfare, education, and law enforcement. Human service workers in India may need to reassess long established perceptions of children, use of children, and child rearing practices. Emphasis may need to be placed on consciousness-raising efforts for the general population, for policy makers, for human service workers, and for families. It is only when the society truly believes the claim of the 1974 National Policy for Children, that children are the most precious resource and that their care and nurture is of utmost importance, that the Rights of the Child (United Nations, 1990) will receive more than lip service.

NOTES

1. A child laborer is a child under the age of fourteen who does not attend school and is compelled to work.

2. Slaves (here children) are owned by their masters and may have been sold into slavery by their parents. Bonded laborers are those people who are tied to their masters because of a debt. Regarding children, the debt may be inherited from parents. When a bonded parent dies, it becomes the child's responsibility to pay off the debt. Children may also be placed into bondage to pay off small loans their parents may have incurred.

3. While considered a form of parental abuse, for purposes of this chapter, child marriage and some of the extreme forms of rejection experienced by female children are categorized as societal abuse rather than parental abuse.

4. "Normal violence" includes socially acceptable methods of discipline, including slapping and shoving; "abusive violence" involves behaviors such as punching, kick-

ing, and hitting with an object; and "extreme violence" refers to behaviors such as burning, shooting, or cutting, or threatening to do so.

REFERENCES

Agnivesh, S. (1989). Foreword to S. Agnivesh (Ed.), *Into that heaven of freedom?* (pp. 1–2). New Delhi: Bonded Labour Liberation Front.

Ashtekar, A. (1991). Abused girls under statutory institutional care. In TISS Unit for Family Studies (Ed.), *Research on families with problems in India* (Vol. 2, pp. 472–482). Bombay: Tata Institute of Social Sciences.

Belavadi, R. N. (1989). The Juvenile Justice Act, 1986. *Indian Journal of Social Work, 50*, 239–243.

Bhattacharyya, A. K. (1983). Child abuse and neglect: Indian perspective. *Indian Paediatrics, 20*, 803–810.

Bottoms, B. L., & Goodman, G. S. (Eds.). (1996). *International perspectives on child abuse and children's testimony.* Thousand Oaks, CA: Sage.

Burns, J. F. (1994, August 27). India fights abortion of female fetuses. *New York Times*, Y5.

Butalia, U. (1997). So many Shivas. *Index on Censorship, 26*, 161–164.

Castelino, C. T. (1985). *Child sexual abuse: A retrospective study.* Bombay: Tata Institute of Social Sciences. Unpublished manuscript.

Chatterjee, P. (1997). Children for sale: For parents in eastern India, the only ticket out of poverty is "renting" a child for begging overseas. *Chicago Tribune*, Sec. 13, 1.

Crossette, B. (1990, October 5). 25% of girls in India die by age 15, UNICEF says. *New York Times*, A6.

Dave, A. B., Dave, P. B., & Mishra, K. D. (1982). Child abuse and neglect (CAN) practices in Durg District of Madhya Pradesh. *Indian Paediatrics, 19*, 905–912.

Devapragasam, S. (1994, September). *The Cradle Babies Scheme of Tamil Nadu—An Indian state's response to female infanticide.* Paper presented at the 10th International Congress on Child Abuse and Neglect, Kuala Lumpur, Malaysia.

D'Sami, V. (1992, August). *Street child—Unspoken victim of society.* Paper presented at the 9th International Congress on Child Abuse and Neglect, Chicago, IL.

Finkelhor, D., & Korbin, J. (1988). Child abuse as an international issue. *Child Abuse and Neglect, 12*, 3–24.

Fonseca, P. (1992, August). *A home away from home.* Paper presented at the 9th International Congress on Child Abuse and Neglect, Chicago, IL.

Freedman, S. (1995, March 24). Breaking poverty's cocoon. *Times Educational Supplement* (4108), 16.

Ghosh, A. (1992, August). *The Freedom School.* Paper presented at the 9th International Congress on Child Abuse and Neglect, Chicago, IL.

Giovannoni, J. M., & Becerra, R. M. (1979). *Defining child abuse.* New York: Free Press.

James, S. (1992, August). *Help them today to have a better tomorrow.* Paper presented at the 9th International Congress on Child Abuse and Neglect, Chicago, IL.

Kapoor, A. (1995, December 20). The girl child has a right to life. *Times of India*, 13.

Mallik, B. (1994, September). *Mainstreaming children of the street*. Paper presented at the 10th International Congress on Child Abuse and Neglect, Kuala Lumpur, Malaysia.

Mayhall, P. D., & Norgard, K. E. (1983). *Child abuse and neglect*. New York: Macmillan.

McDevitt, T. M. (1999). *World population profile: 1998*. Washington, DC: U.S. Bureau of the Census.

Menon, L. (1988). Understanding child abuse in Indian context. In National Institute for Public Cooperation and Child Development [NIPCCD] (Ed.), *National Seminar on Child Abuse in India*. New Delhi: NIPCCD.

Mullatti, L. (1995). Families in India: Beliefs and realities. *Journal of Comparative Family Studies, 26*, 11–26.

Nath, N., & Kohli, M. (1988). Child abuse in India: Some issues. In National Institute for Public Cooperation and Child Development [NIPCCD] (Ed.), *National Seminar on Child Abuse in India* (pp. 137–151). New Delhi: NIPCCD.

National Committee for the Prevention of Child Abuse [NCPCA]. (1992). *World perspectives on child abuse: An international resource book*. Chicago: NCPCA.

National Institute of Public Cooperation and Child Development [NIPCCD]. (1988). Main observations and suggestions. In NIPCCD (Ed.), *National Seminar on Child Abuse in India* (pp. 9–17). New Delhi: NIPCCD.

Pal, A. (1998). A trek against child labor. *The Progressive, 62*, 13.

Pande, D. C. (1988). Child abuse and the law. In NIPCCD (Ed.), *National Seminar on Child Abuse in India* (pp. 52–70). New Delhi: NIPCCD.

Raj, T. D. (1992, August). *Delinquency among street children*. Paper presented at the 9th International Congress on Child Abuse and Neglect, Chicago, IL.

Rajyalakshmi, C. (1986). Gurudakapu Movement: A model solution for child marriages. *Social Change, 16*, 10–13.

Rane, A. J. (1991). Research on child abuse in families. In TISS Unit for Family Studies (Ed.), *Research on families with problems in India* (Vol. 2, pp. 451–461). Bombay: Tata Institute of Social Sciences.

Segal, U. A. (1992). Child abuse in India: An empirical report on perceptions. *Child Abuse and Neglect, 16*, 887–908.

Segal, U. A. (1995). Child abuse by the middle class? A study of professionals in India. *Child Abuse and Neglect, 19*, 213–227.

Segal, U. A. (1996). Children as witnesses: India is not ready. In B. L. Bottoms & G. S. Goodman (Eds.), *International perspectives on child abuse and children's testimony* (pp. 266–282). Thousand Oaks, CA: Sage.

Segal, U. A., & Ashtekar, A. (1994). Detection of intrafamilial child abuse: Children at intake at a Children's Observation Home in India. *Child Abuse and Neglect, 18*, 957–967.

Simons, M. (1993, April 9). The sex market: Scourge on the world's children. *New York Times*, A15.

Simons, M. (1994, January 16). The littlest prostitutes. *New York Times Magazine*, 30–35.

Singh, P. (1987, June 7). The damned. *Illustrated Weekly of India*, 8–15.

Singh, R. R. (1988). Role of social workers and community in the prevention and management of child abuse. In National Institute for Public Cooperation and Child Development [NIPCCD] (Ed.), *National Seminar on Child Abuse in India* (pp. 93–120). New Delhi: NIPCCD.

Sinha, I. (1992, August). *The lost girlhood, the torture, the exploitation.* Paper presented at the 9th International Congress on Child Abuse and Neglect, Chicago, IL.

Straus, M. A. (1979). Measuring intrafamily conflict and violence: The Conflict Tactics (CT) Scales. *Journal of Marriage and the Family, 41*, 75–88.

Tagore, D. B. (1992, August). *Child labor—An abuse of society.* Paper presented at the 9th International Congress on Child Abuse and Neglect, Chicago, IL.

United Nations. (1990, October 1). Excerpts from the United Nations Declaration on Children. *New York Times*, A12.

Wertz, D. C., & Fletcher, J. C. (1993). Prenatal diagnosis and sex selection in 19 countries. *Social Science and Medicine, 37*, 1359–1366.

World News. St. Louis Post-Dispatch, (1998, April 24). A13.

5

IRELAND

Harry Ferguson

PROFILE OF IRELAND

Ireland, an island in northern Europe bordered by the Atlantic Ocean, has an area of 70,282 square kilometers. The capital is Dublin, and the country's 3.7 million people with an Irish or English background speak either English or Irish (Gaelic). The majority of the inhabitants are Roman Catholic (91.6 percent), but 2.5 percent are members of the Church of Ireland and 5.9 percent are of other religions. The infant mortality rate is 5.5 per 1,000, and the life expectancy is approximately seventy-two years for males and seventy-eight years for females. Children are required to attend school until the age of sixteen, which is reflected in a literacy rate of 98–99 percent. In 1998, the gross national product per capita was $18,340 (U.S.). The government is a parliamentary republic with a universal voting age of eighteen.

A CASE STUDY

"Mary" lived with her mother, father, and younger sister on a small farm in County Kilkenny, Ireland. Her father began abusing her when she was ten years old. He repeatedly raped and physically abused her over the next sixteen years. At various times, she was punched, beaten, flogged, and thrown out of the house naked. She experienced a horrendous catalogue of physical injuries, including being blinded in one eye, having her fingers broken with a hammer, and having several ribs broken. Her father impregnated her and at the age of fifteen she gave birth to his child. He also regularly beat Mary's mother, severely limiting her capacity to protect her daughter. The abuse finally stopped when Mary was helped to bring a complaint against her father at the age of twenty-six. This occurred after she experienced yet another serious assault that placed her in the hospital, where a woman police officer patiently obtained her case history. Thus, the evidence was finally gathered to charge her father.

On March 1, 1993, Mary's father was convicted and sentenced to seven years imprisonment. During the trial, it was disclosed that over the years that Mary was being abused, she had regular contact with health services, social services, and the police. Subsequently, Mary appeared on Irish television and blamed these professionals for failing to protect her. The public outcry that followed led to an inquiry by the Irish government. This was the first major inquiry into failures in the child protection system in Ireland. Within a week of Mary's father's conviction, the maximum penalty for incest was increased from seven to twenty years. The subsequent inquiry report (McGuinness, 1993) into the "Kilkenny incest case" began a process that radically raised public and political awareness of child abuse in Ireland and led to unprecedented developments in the Irish child protection system.

INTRODUCTION

The island of Ireland is made up of thirty-two counties, twenty-six of which comprise the Republic of Ireland as constituted by the formation of the Irish Free State in 1922 (hereafter referred to as "Ireland"). The other six counties remained under British rule in the United Kingdom and are not included in the analysis in this chapter. With a population of 3,626,000 (1996 census), Ireland is a small country. Yet as we begin a new millennium, public interest in the social problem of child abuse in Ireland has reached extraordinary levels. While the fact that children are abused and neglected is nothing new, the history of child welfare in Ireland is one of public neglect. This is epitomized by the fact that until the 1990s, child care was still administered under the 1908 Children Act, a piece of legislation enacted under British rule. The voluntary sector, principally through the work of the Irish Society for the Prevention of Cruelty to Children (ISPCC), carried administrative responsibility for child protection for much of the twentieth century. It has only been since the late 1970s that the Irish state has taken on primary responsibility for child care policies and that distinct child protection procedures and practices have been implemented by state agencies (Ferguson, 1996a).

The emergence of the "battered child syndrome" (Kempe, Silverman, Steele, Droegmeuller, & Silver, 1962) and reconceptualization of "child cruelty" in terms of "non-accidental injury" and "child abuse" have been at the heart of these developments. The implementation of a new Child Care Act (1991) and new church and state child protection guidelines in the

1990s (Department of Health [DoH], 1987, 1995, 1999; Irish Catholic Bishops' Advisory Committee, 1996) have meant that there have been more developments in childcare and protection law, policy, and practice over the past decade than occurred in Ireland in the previous eighty years (Ferguson & Kenny, 1995; Richardson, 1999). Major transformations in public awareness of child abuse and protection have occurred through a series of public disclosures of serious cases of child abuse. These cases have included sexual violence and physical abuse and neglect which have focused unprecedented public and political attention on the problem and, in particular, on the failures of the system to protect children known to be at risk (DoH, 1996; Keenan, 1996; McGuinness, 1993; Moore, 1995; North Western Health Board, 1998).

As I show in what follows, this has had two main consequences. First, it has led to the development of a more bureaucratic, procedurally led system for responding to child abuse, greatly increasing the level of accountability of the state and professionals for achieving effective child protection. Second, and somewhat paradoxically, it has resulted in decreased confidence in the ability of the state to protect children and in a severe weakening of the power and moral authority that the Catholic Church has traditionally held in Ireland. This is primarily because the church failed to bring many known clerical child abuse perpetrators to justice or to prevent the systematic abuse of children cared for in residential institutions run by religious orders (Ferguson, 1995a). A remarkable feature of this increased awareness of abuse has been the role that adult survivors of child abuse have played in speaking out about their abuse and the failure of the system to protect them (C. Buckley, 1996; Fahy, 1999; McKay, 1998). The situation in Ireland exemplifies the huge significance that child abuse has as a social problem in the "reinvention" of late-modern politics and processes of "detraditionalization" (Beck, Giddens, & Lash, 1994). Child protection is at the heart of a reconstruction of the traditional relationship between the child, the family, the individual, the state, and other authorities, such as the church (Ferguson, 1997).

HISTORY

Child Abuse and the Development of the Child Protection System in Ireland

As a modern problem, child abuse must be analyzed as a social construction that has relied historically on a process of recognition, identification, and labeling by expert systems (Dingwall, Eekelaar, & Murray, 1983; Gelles, 1975). The beginning of modern child protection in Ireland is found in the formation of a Dublin branch of the National Society for the Prevention of Cruelty to Children (NSPCC) in 1889, whose headquarters was in London.

Irish branches remained under the administrative control of the NSPCC's central office in London until 1956 and the founding of a self-governing Irish Society (Allen & Morton, 1961). The 1889 Prevention of Cruelty to Children Act (PCC) criminalized child cruelty and gave NSPCC inspectors new power to remove cruelly treated children from parental custody (Behlmer, 1982). The provisions of the PCC Acts of 1889, 1894, and 1904 were extended into the Children Act of 1908, which provided the statutory basis for child protection in Ireland until the recent full implementation of the 1991 Child Care Act in 1996. In addition, the 1908 Punishment of Incest Act criminalized incest for the first time in Irish society.

From the outset, rather than being about child "rescue," preventing cruelty to children fell heavily on parents, and mothers in particular. The primary objective of the child protection movement was not to relieve parents of the care of their children, but rather to enforce parental responsibilities as conceived by the state. In the early years, prosecution was a key strategy toward this objective, with the incarceration of parents in prisons being the main reformative resource utilized. After 1908, this punishment-centered approach was replaced by a casework ideology and practice based on the supervision of parent-child relations in their homes. A new optimistic professional ideology lay at the foundation of the "rehabilitative ideals" of modern welfare states (Garland, 1985) which, in child protection, primarily extolled the moral reformation of deviant parents (see Ferguson, 1992, pp. 163–165; 1996b; Gordon, 1989). This orientation was further consolidated with the establishment of the Irish Free State through the profound influence on social policy of Catholic social teaching and the 1937 Constitution (Whyte, 1980). Article 41 "recognizes the Family as the primary and fundamental unit group of Society, and as a moral institution possessing inalienable and imprescriptible rights, antecedent and superior to all positive laws" (Bunreacht na hEireann, 1937). The use of discretionary powers to protect children was often in opposition to the principle of minimum intervention into the family prescribed by the Constitution (ISPCC, 1954, p. 7). The proportion of children removed from home was quite small relative to the numbers worked with, amounting to between 1 and 2 percent per year (Ferguson, 1996a). Tragically, however, intervention also fell heavily on those children removed from parental custody who were placed in Ireland's large network of industrial schools run by religious orders, where many experienced horrendous abuse, which is only now beginning to be disclosed (Raftery & O'Sullivan, 1999).

During the years that Ireland was managed by the UK Society, "no fewer than 478,865 children were helped by the NSPCC in the Republic of Ireland" (Mayo & District Branch NSPCC, 1955, p. 2). From the outset, "neglect" predominated in agency classifications such that, by the 1930s, it was actually being stated that "cruelty is little known in Ireland" (Mayo & District Branch NSPCC, 1938). This meant that recognition of physical abuse was comparatively rare, while child neglect cases accounted for almost 90 percent of casework until the 1950s and 1960s (see ISPCC, 1957, p. 11). Recognition of sexual offenses against children remained virtually nonexistent, at well under 1 percent of cases.

During the 1970s, the professionalization of welfare services and a series of national and international developments provided the context in which the problem of child "cruelty" underwent a process of (re)definition and "diagnostic inflation" into child "abuse" (Dingwall, 1989) which led to the development of coherent Irish child protection policies. The 1970 Health Act established eight health boards, called Community Care teams, through which the state took over primary responsibility for child care and protection from the ISPCC (McGinley, 1995). In addition, policy was shaped by the work of government-sponsored committees, in particular the *Kennedy Report* (1970) and the *Final Report* of the Task Force on Child Care Services (1980). The creation of health boards greatly expanded the expert system to include such pivotal child welfare positions in Community Care teams as social workers (who were given the primary responsibility for investigating cases), public health nurses, area medical officers, and the senior management position of Directors of Community Care/Medical Officers of Health (Kelly, 1995). Developments in Ireland to some extent mirrored those in the United States and the UK, where more sophisticated models of program coordination between various agencies were established from the early 1970s (Hallett & Stevenson, 1980; Nelson, 1984), arising out of the work of Henry Kempe and his medical colleagues and their construction of the battered child syndrome (Kempe et al., 1962). The ISPCC took the lead in making knowledge of the battered child syndrome and highly publicized system failures in the United Kingdom more widely available in Ireland (Colwell Report, 1974) and engaged with the Department of Health on the development of appropriate policies (ISPCC, 1974, p. 18).

A new emphasis was placed on the child protection *system* as being the crucial variable in the effective management of what were now known as non-accidental injury (NAI) cases. In March 1977, the first formal guidelines on the abuse of children were issued to professionals by the Irish government (DoH, 1977), followed by revised guidelines in 1980, 1983, and 1987. Prior to 1987, guidelines dealt only with physical abuse and neglect, but the 1987 guidelines included emotional abuse and also gave systematic recognition to child sexual abuse on the basis that it "has particular features which require special attention" (DoH, 1987, p. 23). Arising from this, specialized child sexual abuse assessment units were established around the country (McGrath, 1996). These units deal almost exclusively with assessment and reflect how the institutional development of the Irish system has, until recently at least, favored the allocation of resources to investigative responses to child sexual abuse. This has resulted in a failure to develop long-term therapeutic and preventative services that might address problems such as neglect and the broader range of adversities affecting children's lives (Ferguson, 1995b; McElwee, 1996; M. Murphy, 1996).

INVESTIGATION

Since the early 1990s, childcare services have focused more *explicitly* on child protection. The administrative structures for dealing with cases have been tightened up through new official guidelines that require health board staff and gardai (the Irish police) to notify one another of all suspected cases of child abuse (DoH, 1995, 1999). These procedures arose after inquiries into system failures where the absence of communication between the police and social workers played a crucial role in the failure to protect at-risk children (McGuinness, 1993). More formalized child protection notification systems have also been introduced in which interdisciplinary management groups now meet regularly to process "notified" referrals and cases and monitor their progress.

In effect, the 1990s have seen a dramatic shift in the degree of accountability expected of Irish professionals in responding to child abuse, reflecting the impact of how the Child Care Act was implemented under the pressure of child abuse inquiries and disclosures of system failures. The role of the state in child welfare and protection has been clearly specified through the implementation of the Child Care Act (1991). Under the 1908 Children Act, intervention was framed in reactive terms as a requirement merely to respond to possible criminal offenses against children. Under the 1991 legislation, for the first time since its foundation, the Irish state has been given powers and responsibilities to be proactive in promoting the welfare of children at risk. The series of clerical scandals and child abuse inquiries that have occurred have involved every aspect of the child care and protection system. This process began with the Kilkenny incest investigation—the case scenario featured at the head of this chapter—that examined why action was not taken sooner by the health services to halt the serious physical and sexual abuse of a girl by her father over a sixteen year period from 1976 to 1992 (Ferguson, 1994; McGuinness, 1993). Virtually every aspect of policy and the child abuse guidelines, most particularly interagency and interprofessional coordination, have become the subject of critical analysis and recommendations for change, leading to more comprehensive revised child abuse guidelines in 1999 (DoH, 1999). Proposals have also been made for constitutional reform to specify more clearly the rights of children (McGuinness, 1993), and there has been vigorous debate about how best to identify abused children. After a lengthy consultation process and much prevarication, the Irish government finally committed itself in 1998 to introducing mandatory reporting of child abuse by 2001 (DoH, 1996).

Table 5.1
Reported and Confirmed Cases of Child Abuse in Ireland, 1984–1997

Year	Total reports received	Cases confirmed
1984	479	182 (38%)
1985	767	304 (40%)
1986	1,015	495 (49%)
1987	1,646	763 (46%)
1988	2,673	1,243 (47%)
1989	3,252	1,658 (51%)
1991*	3,856	1,465 (38%)
1992	3,812	1,701 (45%)
1993	4,110	1,609 (39%)
1994	5,152	1,868 (36%)
1995	6,415	2,276 (35%)
1996**	7,732	2,270 (29%)
1997**	7,312	2,659 (36%)

*No figures available for 1990. **Southern Health Board not included in these figures.

PREVALENCE

Trends in Child Abuse and Child Protection Practices in Ireland

The impact of policy developments and changing definitions of child cruelty, non-accidental injury, and abuse is clear in the number and nature of cases being reported. During the 1980s, the number of child abuse referrals made to health boards increased almost tenfold, from 406 cases in 1982 to 3,859 in 1991. There was, however, no corresponding growth in staff to respond to increasing referrals, such that these referrals were investigated by a more or less fixed number of social workers. Little wonder, then, that preventative work suffered. Reports of child abuse have grown relentlessly in the 1990s as public awareness has increased, and interagency cooperation has been strengthened in the light of child abuse inquiries (see Table 5.1). The referrals have increased from 3,856 in 1991 to 7,312 in 1997 (the last year that national figures are available), an increase of almost 90 percent. Significantly, the rate of confirmation of abuse has declined as the number of reports has increased, from a high of 51 percent in 1989 to as low as 29 percent in 1996. This may suggest that practitioners have raised the threshold of what "confirmed" abuse is judged to be as the system strains to respond to an increased number of cases (Thorpe, 1997). Increases in reported child abuse cases also reflect the availability of more staff and services to report suspected cases and to respond to them. Nationally, some 900 additional posts in childcare services have been created in professional and administrative areas since the implementation of the Child Care Act (DoH, personal communication, 1997), which constitutes significant development in a small country like Ireland. In a real sense, it is only now just about possible to speak of Ireland as having the human resources, decent offices, and general infrastructure needed to constitute a modern child protection system (Walsh, 1999).

In line with changing definitions, recognition of different forms of child abuse has also changed considerably, especially with respect to child sexual abuse. The Department of Health has not produced up-to-date figures on the forms of abuse identified by health boards during the 1990s. But in 1989, 34 percent of the confirmed cases dealt with involved child sexual abuse; 8 percent involved emotional abuse, and 11 percent physical abuse, while neglect was the highest category, identified at 47 percent. In the area of child sexual abuse, the number of cases confirmed by health boards suggests that at least one in every 1,000 children is sexually abused in Ireland (McKeown & Gilligan, 1991). Around 90 percent of child sexual abusers are men. Fathers are the abusers in 35 percent of confirmed cases as compared to 3 percent of cases perpetrated by mothers. The remaining categories of abusers tend not to be immediate family members and include babysitters, distant relatives, and neighbors. One-third are adolescent males (McKeown & Gilligan, 1991). The situation with regard to physical abuse and neglect is quite different, with mothers being just as likely as fathers to be accountable (Ferguson & O'Reilly, 2000). A striking feature of such cases is the *absence* of resident fathers. Single-parent mothers are overrepresented in child protection cases in Ireland, and high proportions of these women have experienced addiction problems and other indicators of vulnerability, such as social isolation, poverty, and disadvantage (Buckley, Skehill, & O'Sullivan, 1997; Ferguson & O'Reilly, 2000). A significant correlation is also emerging in Irish research between domestic violence against women and other forms of child abuse, especially maternal neglect, where the woman's capacity to parent is weakened by violence from her partner (Ferguson & O'Reilly, 2000).

A great deal of child protection work is focused on children and families who are well known to the system and experiencing multiple problems. In one Irish study, almost half of the families had previous contact with social work services (Buckley et al., 1997). In my own research, as many as 70 percent of substantiated child protection cases were previously known to the social work department for childcare concerns (Ferguson & O'Reilly, 2000). The most frequent length of past involvement was between two and six years (28 percent), while 16 percent were known for over six years. A relatively small number of cases involve actual harm to children from sexual and physical abuse—meaning that, however great its impact on public awareness and policy, cases of the severity of the Kilkenny incest case are, thankfully, exceptional. Most involve neglect, poor parenting competencies and resources, domestic violence, and the legacy of emotional trauma that these and other developmental and relationship problems bring for children. The nature of the adversity for these children and families is often extreme because of the presence of multiple problems of a long-standing nature.

CHILD PROTECTION

Post-Investigative Services Provided for Affected Children and Families

In the early 1990s, Irish research suggested that the impact of greater proceduralization and accountability in child protection was that a relatively small proportion of children reported to health board Community Care teams ended up receiving services of any kind, as cases were screened out at every stage through the system (H. Buckley, 1996). This trend seemed consistent with international research findings (e.g., Besharov, 1985; Gibbons et al., 1995; Parton, Thorpe, & Wattam, 1997; Thorpe, 1994) where referrals were being prematurely defined as child protection and children in need were being screened out of the system having received little more than an investigation. Meanwhile, referrals that did not fit the child abuse categories set by the agency did not even receive an investigation. Some researchers have argued that such trends are presently sustained in Ireland (Buckley et al., 1997; Thorpe, 1997). This perspective is, however, questionable in that it relies too heavily on paradigms for understanding the nature of "child protection" developed outside of Ireland, and is not sensitive enough methodologically to capture the dramatic changes that have occurred in childcare services since the early 1990s.

TREATMENT

My own research suggests that the concept of child protection that is now operating in Ireland includes a notion of family support—one that does not appear to exist to the same extent in many other Western nation-states. This reflects how notions of the integrity of the family are still powerfully enshrined culturally and in Irish social policy. Thus, relatively speaking, significant services are now being offered in substantiated child abuse cases. While there remains considerable room for improvement, this is a product of the changing consciousness surrounding child welfare and the system development that has occurred under the implementation of the 1991 Child Care Act (Ferguson & O'Reilly, 2000). My research sampled 319 referrals reported to three Community Care social work teams in 1996 and tracked them for twelve months into late 1997 (Ferguson & O'Reilly, 2000). Results revealed that a complex division of labor now exists in the provision of post-investigative services, with social work having a core coordinating function. Social workers have no active case work role at all or play solely a case management role in 40 percent of substantiated cases, while the primary therapeutic and support work is done by other professionals. Nevertheless, social workers continue to provide meaningful protection and welfare services in 60 percent of cases, usually in combination with other services. Clinical services like psychiatry and child psychology are provided in 39 percent of substantiated cases and are particularly active in cases where young people are in distress and manifesting serious behavior and control problems. Family support workers and community childcare workers employed by health boards play an invaluable role in some 30 percent of substantiated cases, by helping vulnerable families to develop parenting skills and by doing direct work with children, especially in long-term neglect cases. Meanwhile, 21 percent of substantiated cases are provided with a care-based service, most of it voluntary and short-term in nature, of which foster care is the most common form of placement, followed by residential care. Cases involving parenting difficulties, control and behavior problems in children, neglect, and addiction problems predominate, accounting together for 67 percent of referrals that result in children entering care. Thus, despite the positive service development that has occurred, there remains a serious shortfall in support and therapeutic services that can prevent childhood adversity and prevent children from ultimately being received into care (Ferguson & O'Reilly, 2000).

LEGAL ISSUES

Child Protection and Legal Processes

The law has come to play a much greater role in child welfare and protection in Ireland through the 1991 Child Care Act and institutionalization of the role of the police through the Department of Health's 1995 *Guidelines for the Notification of Suspected Cases of Child Abuse Between Health Boards and Gardai*, which requires both agencies to share all suspected cases of abuse with one another. Research suggests that just over half (54 percent) of all referrals to health boards in Ireland are formally notified to the police under the 1995 guidelines (Ferguson & O'Reilly, 2000). A quarter of these notifications (26 percent) are actually directly investigated by the gardai. However, just 13 percent of investigated cases actually result in prosecutions, of which only a handful result in successful convictions. While the law is playing an increasingly significant role in child protection, its impact is not equal across all forms of child abuse. Direct use of the law only has a direct relevance to physical abuse, neglect, and emotional abuse in extreme cases where applications are made for care orders or supervision orders, while the use of the criminal law in such cases is extremely rare. Most cases are not serious enough to warrant consideration of criminality as such, and conceptualizing them in criminal/punitive terms goes against the kind of therapeutic/welfare approach which has come to characterize models of good practice in responding to children's and parents' needs. Domestic violence is more directly subject to legal intervention, and while very effective co-ordinated interventions by the police and social workers do occur, health board professionals are often perplexed by the *under*-use of the law by the gardai in terms of a perceived reluctance in some cases to arrest and prosecute suspected offenders (Ferguson, 1997b). Intervention programs based on group work with violent men have been developing in Ireland since the late 1980s (Ferguson & Synott, 1995; O'Connor, 1996). As well as a new Domestic Violence Act (1996), a Government Task Force on Violence Against Women has set out core principles for best practice that have now become government policy in this area (Task Force on Violence Against Women, 1997).

With child sexual abuse, however, social workers and other childcare professionals, as well as nonabusing parents, feel hugely constrained by the operation of the legal system. Major efforts are expended gathering evidence that is forensically sound with minimal beneficial outcomes for children and families. Intervention even makes matters *worse* in some child sexual abuse cases, as the children and (nonabusing) parents are left (alone) to carry the burden of cases that take an extremely long time to process through the criminal justice system and rarely end in prosecutions. Parents are, rightly, perplexed at the extreme caution with which the legal system and the health boards approach suspected abusers and the fact that little seems to be done to protect the children with whom they continue to have contact. Social workers fear being perceived as having interfered with correct forensic in-vestigative procedures by saying the wrong thing to a child and "contami-nating" evidence by rendering the child's statement inadmissible in court. Consequently, they do not really engage with children or support their par-ents. In fact, some social workers who specialize in child sexual abuse as-sessments are so concerned about how to conduct interviews in a legally acceptable way that they even feel restricted in offering comfort to suspected abused children (Ferguson & O'Reilly, 2000).

Decisions regarding all prosecutions by the state are made by the Director of Public Prosecutions (DPP). The low prosecution rate of confirmed child sexual abuse cases arises from decisions by the DPP not to proceed in a large number of cases. The precise reasons for these decisions are rarely publicly disclosed, as the DPP's office is not obliged to be publicly accountable be-cause it has been given complete administrative and political independence. It is known, however, that most of the cases that are prosecuted rely on guilty pleas from the accused. In defending his office from criticism of its failure to prosecute more cases where the offense is denied by the accused, the DPP has argued that the conditions of his role preclude him from pros-ecuting any case unless a conviction is a likely outcome and that the adver-sarial nature of the criminal justice system is "singularly unsuited" to dealing with child sexual abuse cases (McGrath, 1996, p. 66). The major issue here is whether the legal system is anti-child, or at least pro-adult. This includes the presumption of unreliability on the part of children in giving evidence, particularly in cases involving alleged sexual offenses. Even attempts to empower children as witnesses through the use of video links to courtrooms have been frustrated by a constitutional challenge to such practices by a defendant. In reality, children are no less reliable witnesses than adults and are in many respects more reliable informants because of their less developed ability to lie or deceive (McGrath, 1996).

The net result is that not only is justice not served, but many sex offenders remain free and untouchable in the community. This has huge implications for child protection since this is a compulsive form of behavior which offenders don't give up voluntarily (Finkelhor, 1986). Few attempts are even being made to work with *known* offenders, especially those who have been imprisoned for such offenses. It is now broadly accepted within the professional community that sanctions and treatment programs are the only way to stop abuse and protect future victims. Yet, treatment programs for sex offenders of all types are scandalously underdeveloped in Ireland. This is despite the best efforts of frontline professionals such as probation officers and psychologists who are working with offenders and who advocate the extension of treatment facilities (Cotter, 1999; Geiran, 1996; Murphy, 1998). Approximately one-third of child sex abusers in Ireland are adolescents, for whom just one treatment project exists, the highly effective Northside Inter-Agency Project in Dublin. This treatment is a community-based group-work intervention focused on adolescent male sex offenders. Just one Irish program has official backing at a central policy level. It is located at Arbour Hill Prison in Dublin and is jointly run by the Probation and Welfare and the Psychological Service of the Department of Justice. It was created in June 1994 and caters to a mixed group of imprisoned sex offenders. While there are some 300 sex offenders in Irish prisons at any one time, just 10 of these at a time participate in the Arbour Hill program (Geiran, 1996). Participation in the program is voluntary, leaving it to offenders themselves to decide whether they wish to seek rehabilitation. Unless participation is made mandatory, large numbers of known sex offenders will continue to be released into the community without any real attempt to directly address their offending behavior. In August 1998, the Irish government did, however, announce plans to introduce a register of convicted sex offenders designed to monitor perpetrators after release from custody. In demonstrating such administrative irrationality and failure to even attempt rehabilitation, responses to sex offenders merely exemplify how the Irish criminal justice system works (or fails to work) in general (McCullagh, 1996).

CONCLUSION

As I have shown in this chapter, responses to child abuse and childcare policy in Ireland have developed in an ad hoc and reactive fashion, although there are signs that the 1991 Child Care Act is bringing about more accountability and planning and a greater commitment to advancing children's rights (Richardson, 1999). The child protection system has developed significantly in terms of service provision and has become more accountable and proceduralized, with mixed results for vulnerable children and caregivers. Yet to fully appreciate the changing profile of child abuse in Ireland it is important to also consider its meaning and impact at a cultural level. The social problem of child abuse has come to occupy an extraordinarily powerful new position in Irish society, where the problem and responses to it are now routine subjects for media discussion and professional and lay debate. Child abuse has taken on a profound sociological significance in processes of "de-traditionalization" and liberalization of Irish society. Recent disclosures of clerical child sexual abuse have shattered the sacred trust of lay people in the Catholic Church. The hegemony of that institution in Irish society, its patriarchal power over women and children, and its apparent lack of compassion for child victims and survivors of abuse have been profoundly challenged, resulting in all priests and members of religious orders being tarnished with the label of pedophile and viewed with suspicion (Ferguson, 1995a). Publication of child protection guidelines by the Church in 1996 reflects attempts to restore the trustworthiness of that institution (Irish Catholic Bishop's Advisory Committee, 1996).

Social relations and identities in Irish society are being reconstituted in post-traditional forms where citizens no longer simply refer (or *de*fer) to external authorities such as the Church. The self has become a "reflexive project" as individuals take much more responsibility for decisions and the management of their lives. "Active" citizens now construct their identities and conduct their life-planning in ways in which trust in the Church and other forms of authority and expertise may or may not have significance. Post-traditional relations between experts and lay people are much more contingent and open to negotiation and determined by the perceived trustworthiness of experts (Giddens, 1990, 1994). The paradox of this reconstruction of trust relations is that, at a time of crisis in the delivery of effective child protection services, more and more citizens—in particular women and children themselves—are reporting child abuse and domestic violence cases and using social work and other forms of therapy to find protection and get support in life-planning and healing (Ferguson, 1997). Central to these processes has been the extraordinary role played by adult survivors of childhood abuse in courageously coming out publicly and challenging the state and church institutions that failed to protect them. The (re)awakening of public consciousness has been further advanced by the publication by survivors like

Bernadette Fahy and Sophia McColgan of best-selling books on their lives (Fahy, 1999; McKay, 1998) and by television documentaries which have had such an impact that they have become extraordinary cultural phenomena (C. Buckley, 1996; Raftery, 1999). The television series *States of Fear*, about the abuse of children in care institutions in twentieth century Ireland, was broadcast in April/May 1999 and culminated in the Irish government offering a formal apology to survivors of institutional abuse and the creation of the Commission on Child Abuse to examine the problem and hear publicly the testimony of survivors. The government has also made available a whole new package of resources to create counseling services within the health boards to respond specifically to the needs of adult survivors of institutional and other forms of abuse. Such justice seeking by survivors is a compelling example of the genuine possibilities that the reflexive nature of late-modern social relations create for the reappropriation of power by individuals and groups who were abused and marginalized by traditional society (Giddens, 1991). In this manner, child protection survivors are helping to "reinvent" politics by making the state accountable and changing institutions in significant ways. Thus, in a late-modern era, it is not sufficient to interpret the nature and meanings of child abuse and protection systems simply "from above" in terms of what the state is doing to respond to the problem. It is also necessary to take account of perspectives "from below" in how lay people are today increasingly active in constructing their lives and influencing the shape of effective protection policies and practices (Ferguson, forthcoming). The onset of such dynamic new politics of child protection, fueled by highly publicized system failures and child abuse inquiries, should not simply be seen as reflecting declining professional standards. While problems undoubtedly persist at every level of the system, the paradox of Irish child protection at the beginning of the new millennium is that public perceptions of the effectiveness of professionals' work with child abuse have never been lower at a time when standards of service have never been higher.

REFERENCES

Allen, A., & Morton, A. (1961). *This is your child: The story of the National Society for the Prevention of Cruelty to Children*. London: Routledge.

Beck, U. (1992). *The risk society*. London: Sage.

Beck, U., Giddens, A., & Lash, S. (1994). *Reflexive modernization*. Cambridge: Polity.

Behlmer, G. K. (1982). *Child abuse and moral reform in England, 1970–1980*. Stanford: Stanford University Press.

Besharov, D. J. (1985). "Doing something" about child abuse: The need to narrow the grounds for state intervention. *Harvard Journal of Law and Public Policy, 8*, 539–589.

Buckley, C. (1996, February 26). *Dear daughter.* RTE television documentary.

Buckley, H. (1996). Child protection guidelines in Ireland: For whose protection? In H. Ferguson & T. McNamara (Eds.), *Protecting Irish children: Investigation, protection and welfare,* special edition of *Administration* (pp. 37–56). Dublin: Institute of Public Administration.

Buckley, H., Skehill, C., & O'Sullivan, E. (1997). *Child protection practices in Ireland: A case study.* Dublin: Oaktree Press.

Bunreacht na hEireann. (1937). *Constitution of Ireland.* Dublin: Government Stationery Office.

Colwell Report. (1974). *Report of the Committee of Inquiry into the care and supervision provided in relation to Maria Colwell.* London: HMSO.

Cotter, A. (1999). The criminal justice system in Ireland: Towards change and transformation. In S. Quin, P. Kennedy, A. O'Donnell, & G. Kiely (Eds.), *Contemporary Irish social policy.* Dublin: University College Dublin Press.

Department of Health. (1977). *Memorandum on non-accidental injury to children.* [Booklet]. Dublin: Department of Health.

Department of Health. (1987). *Child abuse guidelines: Guidelines on procedures for the identification, investigation and management of child abuse.* [Booklet]. Dublin: Department of Health.

Department of Health. (1995). *Guidelines for the notification of suspected cases of child abuse between health boards and gardai.* [Booklet]. Dublin: Department of Health.

Department of Health. (1996). *Putting children first: Discussion document on mandatory reporting.* [Booklet]. Dublin: Department of Health.

Department of Health. (1999). *Children first: National guidelines for the protection and welfare of children.* [Booklet]. Dublin: Department of Health.

Dingwall, R. (1989). Some problems about predicting child abuse and neglect. In O. Stevenson (Ed.), *Child abuse: Public policy and professional practice* (pp. 28–53). Brighton: Wheatsheaf.

Dingwall, R., Eekelaar, J., & Murray, T. (1983). *The protection of children: State intervention and family life.* Oxford: Blackwell.

Fahy, B. (1999). *Freedom of angels: Surviving Goldenbridge Orphanage.* Dublin: O'Brien Press.

Ferguson, H. (1992). Cleveland in history: The abused child and child protection, 1880–1914. In R. Cooter (Ed.), *In the name of the child: Health and welfare, 1880–1940* (pp. 146–173). London: Routledge.

Ferguson, H. (1994). Child abuse inquiries and the report of the Kilkenny incest investigation: A critical analysis. *Administration, 41,* 385–410.

Ferguson, H. (1995a). The pedophile priest: A deconstruction. *Studies, 84,* 247–256.

Ferguson, H. (1995b). Child welfare, child protection and the Child Care Act 1991: Key issues for policy and practice. In H. Ferguson & P. Kenny (Eds.), *On behalf of the child: Child welfare, child protection and the Child Care Act 1991* (pp. 17–41). Dublin: A. & A. Farmar.

Ferguson, H. (1996a). Protecting Irish children in time: Child abuse as a social problem and the development of the Irish child protection system. In H. Ferguson & T. McNamara (Eds.), *Protecting Irish children: Investigation, protection and welfare,* special edition of *Administration* (pp. 5–36). Dublin: Institute of Public Administration.

Ferguson, H. (1996b). The protection of children in time: Child protection and the lives and deaths of children in child abuse cases in socio-historical perspective. *Child and Family Social Work*, 1, 205–217.

Ferguson, H. (1997). Protecting children in new times: Child protection and the risk society. *Child and Family Social Work*, 2, 221–234.

Ferguson, H. (forthcoming). Social work, individualization and life politics. *British Journal of Social Work*.

Ferguson, H., & Kenny, P. (Eds.). (1995). *On behalf of the child: Child welfare, child protection and the Child Care Act 1991*. Dublin: A. & A. Farmar.

Ferguson, H., & O'Reilly, M. (2000). *Keeping children safe? Child abuse, protection and the promotion of welfare*. Dublin: A. & A. Farmar.

Ferguson, H., & Synott, P. (1995). Intervention into domestic violence in Ireland: Developing policy and practice with men who batter. *Administration*, 43, 57–81.

Finkelhor, D. (1986). *A sourcebook on child sexual abuse*. London: Sage.

Garland, D. (1985). *Punishment and welfare: A history of penal strategies*. Aldershot: Gower.

Geiran, V. (1996). Treatment of sex offenders in Ireland: The development of policy and practice. In H. Ferguson & T. McNamara (Eds.), *Protecting Irish children: Investigation, protection and welfare*, special edition of *Administration* (pp. 5–36). Dublin: Institute of Public Administration.

Gelles, R. J. (1975). The social construction of child abuse. *American Journal of Orthopsychiatry*, 45, 363–371.

Gibbons, J., Conroy, S., and Bell, C. (1995). *Operating the child protection system*. London: HMSO.

Giddens, A. (1990). *The consequences of modernity*. Cambridge: Polity.

Giddens, A. (1991). *Modernity and self identity*. Cambridge: Polity.

Giddens, A. (1994). *Beyond left and right: The future of radical politics*. Cambridge: Polity.

Gordon, L. (1989). *Heroes of their own lives: The history and politics of family violence, 1880–1960*. London: Virago.

Hallett, C., & Stevenson, O. (1980). *Child abuse: Aspects of interprofessional cooperation*. London: Allen & Unwin.

Irish Catholic Bishops' Advisory Committee. (1996). *Child sexual abuse: Framework for a church response*. [Booklet]. Dublin: Veritas.

Irish Society for the Prevention of Cruelty to Children [ISPCC]. *Annual Reports*. 1954, 1956, 1957, 1974, 1976. Dublin: ISPCC.

Keenan, O. (1996). *Kelly: A child is dead*. Interim report of the Joint Committee on the Family. Dublin: Government Publications Office.

Kelly, A. (1995). A public health nursing perspective. In H. Ferguson & P. Kenny (Eds.), *On behalf of the child: Child welfare, child protection and the Child Care Act 1991* (pp. 186–202). Dublin: A. & A. Farmar.

Kempe, C. H., Silverman, F. N., Steele, B. F., Droegmeuller, W., & Silver, H. K. (1962). The battered child syndrome. *Journal of the American Medical Association*, 181, 17–24.

Kennedy Report. (1970). *Reformatory and Industrial Schools Systems Report*. Dublin: Stationery Office.

Kenny, P. (1995). The Child Care Act, 1991 and the social context of child protection. In H. Ferguson & P. Kenny (Eds.), *On behalf of the child: Child welfare, child protection and the Child Care Act 1991* (pp. 42–59). Dublin: A. & A. Farmar.

Mayo and District Branch NSPCC. (1938; 1955). *Annual Report*. London: NSPCC Archives.

McCullagh, C. (1996). *Crime in Ireland: A sociological introduction*. Cork: Cork University Press.

McElwee, C. N. (1996). *Children at risk*. Waterford: StreetSmart Press.

McGinley, M. (1995). A programme manager perspective. In H. Ferguson & P. Kenny (Eds.), *On behalf of the child: Child welfare, child protection and the Child Care Act 1991* (pp. 145–157). Dublin: A. & A. Farmar.

McGrath, K. (1996). Intervening in child sexual abuse in Ireland: Towards victim-centered policies and practices. In H. Ferguson & T. McNamara (Eds.), *Protecting Irish children: Investigation, protection and welfare*, special edition of *Administration* (pp. 57–72). Dublin: Institute of Public Administration.

McGuinness, C. (1993). *Report of the Kilkenny incest investigation*. Dublin: Government Stationery Office.

McKay, S. (1998). *Sophia's story*. Dublin: Gill and Macmillan.

McKeown, K., & Gilligan, G. (1991). Child sexual abuse in the Eastern Health Board Region of Ireland in 1988: An analysis of 512 confirmed cases. *Economic and Social Review, 22*, 101–134.

Moore, C. (1995). *Betrayal of trust: The Father Brendan Smyth affair and the Catholic Church*. Dublin: Marino.

Murphy, M. (1996). From prevention to "family support" and beyond: Promoting the welfare of Irish children. In H. Ferguson & T. McNamara (Eds.), *Protecting Irish children: Investigation, protection and welfare*, special edition of *Administration* (pp. 73–101). Dublin: Institute of Public Administration.

Murphy, P. (1998). A therapeutic program for imprisoned sex offenders: Progress to date and issues for the future. *Irish Journal of Psychology, 19*, 190–207.

Nelson, B. (1984). *Making an issue of child abuse: Political agenda setting for social problems*. Chicago: University of Chicago Press.

North Western Health Board. (1998). *Report of the inquiry into the West of Ireland farmer case*. Manorhamilton, Co. Leitrim, Ireland: North Western Health Board.

O'Connor, C. (1996). Integrating feminist and psychological systemic approaches in working with men who are violent towards their partners: The Cork Domestic Violence Project. *Feedback, 7*, 2–6.

Parton, N., Thorpe, D. & Wattam, C. (1997). *Child protection, risk and the moral order*. London: Macmillan.

Raftery, M. (1999a, April 24, May 4, May 11). *States of fear*. RTE television broadcasts.

Raftery, M. (1999b, May 11). Are the children of today at last safe in the care of the state? *Irish Times*, p. 18.

Raftery, M., & O'Sullivan, E. (1999). *Suffer the little children: The inside story of Ireland's industrial schools*. Dublin: New Island Books.

Richardson, V. (1999). Children and social policy. In S. Quinn, P. Kennedy, A. O'Donnell, & G. Kiely (Eds.), *Contemporary Irish social policy* (pp. 174–200). Dublin: University College Dublin Press.

Task Force on Child Care Services. (1980). *Final report.* Dublin: Government Stationery Office.

Task Force on Violence Against Women. (1997). *Final report, Office of the Tanaiste.* Dublin: Government Stationery Office.

Thorpe, D. (1994). *Evaluating child protection.* Milton Keynes: Open University Press.

Thorpe, D. (1997). Regulating late-modern childrearing in Ireland. *Economic and Social Review, 28,* 63–84.

Walsh, T. (1999). Changing expectations: The impact of "child protection" on social work in Ireland. *Child and Family Social Work, 4,* 33–42.

Whyte, J. H. (1980). *Church and state in modern Ireland, 1923–1979* (2nd ed.). Dublin: Gill and Macmillan.

6

ISRAEL

Tamar Cohen

PROFILE OF ISRAEL

The state of Israel, located in the Middle East and bordering the Mediterranean Sea, has an area of 20,325 square kilometers. The capital is Jerusalem, in which a variety of religious sects are found, including Judaism, Islam, Christianity, and Druze. The population consists of 4.7 million Jewish citizens and 1.2 million non-Jewish citizens who speak Hebrew, Arabic, Russian, and English. The infant mortality rate is 7.4 per 1,000 and the life expectancy is 79.5 years for females and 75.5 years for males. Formal education is free and required from the ages of five to sixteen. The literacy rate for Jewish citizens is 97 percent. The Arab literacy rate is 90 percent. In 1998, the gross national product per capita was $15,940 (U.S.). The government is a parliamentary democracy in which the age of suffrage is eighteen.

A CASE STUDY

A three-year-old girl was sexually abused by her father for several months. Her nursery school teacher suspected abuse, consulted with her supervisor, and was told to report her suspicions to the girl's mother and to the child protection service. A complaint was then registered with local police, the child's father was arrested, and the case was referred to Meital: Israel Center for Treatment of Child Sexual Abuse, where both the girl and her mother received individual therapy. Meanwhile, criminal proceedings were initiated against the father, leading to his imprisonment. Therapy during this period focused not only on the abuse, but also on the father's sudden absence from the home and its effect on the child and mother. While in prison, the girl's father requested that he be allowed to have visits with his daughter, and the court requested input from all relevant agencies.

The child protection service called several joint meetings with Meital's therapists, the community social worker, and the social worker from prison. The meetings were difficult and, at times, stormy, mirroring the power issues of the family (Furniss, 1991). The mother's therapist represented her need for a total disconnection from her husband; the father's social worker insisted on his right to maintain contact with his daughter; and the child's therapist conveyed the child's fear, as well as longing, related to her father. The final recommendation was to allow supervised visits in a neutral place, with close evaluation of their effects on the child. Two and a half years later both the mother (who subsequently divorced her husband) and the child ended therapy. The child's father is still in prison. A community social worker continues to supervise visits between the child and her father, and also provides periodic support.

INTRODUCTION

Child abuse and neglect have been recognized as a societal problem in Israel over the last few decades. This chapter describes the relevant social and cultural aspects of Israeli society and the ways in which they relate to the problem of child maltreatment. It also presents recent changes in the Israeli legal system and social services, highlighting some evolving ethical questions and identifying needs that remain unmet.

Empirical studies of various forms of child maltreatment suggest that their immediate and long-range consequences seriously interfere with and negatively affect the physical, intellectual, and psychosocial development of victimized children (Kempe & Kempe, 1978; Mullen, Martin, Anderson, Romans, & Hubison, 1993), and that the financial cost of both short- and long-term care for victims is high. In addition, many studies indicate that child maltreatment is likely to be carried over from one generation to the next (Cohen, 1995; Coohey, 1995; Egeland, Jacobvitz, & Papatula, 1987; Rutter, 1993; Zuravin, McMillan, DePantilis, & Risley-Curtis, 1996).

It must be emphasized that abusive and negligent behavior of parents and other adults toward children is, to an extent, culturally defined. What constitutes an abusive behavior in one society may be accepted as normative along the continuum of child-rearing practices in another culture. Severe corporal punishment is one example that illustrates this point. Indeed, some of the most powerful risk factors for child abuse and neglect are those specific to the given culture or society in which the family lives. For example, values associated with children in general, minority children, and disabled children, and the existence of gender inequalities all impact abusive and neglectful behavior toward children. Equally important is the extent to which violence is socially acceptable in a given culture. These observations are not intended to justify abusive behavior or to minimize its negative effect on child victims. Rather, they are intended to emphasize the need for those who deal with prevention, detection, evaluation, and intervention of child abuse and neglect to be culturally sensitive.

HISTORY

Israeli society is a complex mixture of past and present, of old traditions and very advanced technology. Although Israel is a relatively young country (it was established as a democratic state only in 1948), the tradition of its people goes back thousands of years. Its neighboring states—all Muslim countries—are Lebanon, Syria, Jordan, and Egypt. Prior to 1948, the Jewish population in the region was indeed small in numbers—about 717,000. However, since 1948, the country has experienced large waves of immigration. The aftermath of World War II, with its Holocaust, brought Jewish refugees from eastern and western Europe. The establishment of a Jewish state enabled the immigration of whole communities (especially from Islamic countries such as North Africa, Iraq, and Yemen) who had suffered persecutions in other parts of the world. Jews from the United States, Canada, South America, and South Africa immigrated to Israel out of idealism. Over the years, the population of Israel has grown to 5.5 million citizens, 2 million of which are children. In addition, during the last decade, the country has absorbed a significant number of immigrants from the former USSR and Ethiopia. The existence of Arab minority groups (e.g., Muslims, Druzes, and Christians) needs to be stressed as well.

The first priority of the young state of Israel was the quick absorption of the masses of immigrants. Emphasis was placed on education and health. During the first decade of its existence, Israel established universal services for its children in the field of education (e.g., compulsory education) and health (e.g., "well baby" clinics). Formal social services also paid attention to child neglect, especially in terms of hygiene and health (Rosenfeld & Kedem, 1998).

Attitudes Toward the Problem of Child Abuse

Historically, Israeli society has been prone to several myths that sustained denial of the child abuse problem in Israel. The first myth is the widespread view of the Jewish family, which was, and is, perceived as a perfect social framework whose main concern is the child's welfare. These values contributed to a common denial: "It can't happen to us."

The second myth stems from the pre-state ideology of the country's founding fathers. They strove to create a model society in Israel free from the social ills they had known in the Diaspora. Such an ideology prevented the recognition of child maltreatment as a social problem. Finally, the third myth was that of the sanctity of the family. An important social value in Israel was attached to the family as a unit that should not be tampered with.

These three myths focused the attention of Israeli society and the individual Israeli family on the child, the future generation, and hampered the acknowledgment of child maltreatment problems. It was inconceivable that the Jewish family in Israel, an entity that should provide the child the greatest nurturance, comfort, and protection, might pose the greatest danger.

As a whole, Israeli society during the early days of the country looked upon cases of child maltreatment as bizarre and isolated phenomena. Physical and emotional abuse of children by families was not acknowledged, or, at best, abusive practices were viewed as educational methods used by parents of certain ethnic groups. Sexual abuse of children was totally ignored. Social services intervened only in extreme cases of incest, and the usual solution was to remove the child from his or her family.

Additional issues relating to incest and child sexual abuse deserve attention. The incest taboo, which exists almost universally throughout human history and in all communities, is often coupled with another, more subtle, social prohibition against its revelation. Denial, disbelief, and minimization are common reactions in the face of suspicion or discovery of sexual abuse of children, and may in fact be an expression of this second revelation taboo. Israeli society is not different from other societies in this respect.

Further, Israeli attitudes toward sexuality are generally fraught with contradiction and ambivalence. In the ancient Jewish tradition, sexual relations were allowed only between married couples, following the Biblical blessing of "be fruitful and multiply." However, Western influence, advanced medical technology, and liberal thinking have altered this old "puritanical" stance. Thus, a tension still exists in Israel today between old mores and new approaches with regard to sexuality.

Even in its attitudes toward children, which are generally positive and protective, Israeli society exhibits mixed messages. On the one hand, like many developed countries, Israel has laws that protect children, mandate their education, and provide for their health through universal health services. On the other hand, the legal definition of a "child" varies significantly depending on the specific issue at hand. For example, the voting age is eighteen, but compulsory education only applies to children up to tenth grade. In criminal proceedings, a child under age twelve is considered a minor, and thus is not punishable by law. However, other court proceedings, especially in family matters of custody and visitations, are more flexible and the child's age is less important than his or her developmental maturity (Morag & Elkashan, 1996).

LEGAL INNOVATIONS

Legal Framework Relating to Child Maltreatment

During the last fifteen years, Israel has experienced a growing recognition and concern about the existence and prevalence of child abuse and neglect, and the severe consequences that accompany them. This concern and recognition of child abuse and neglect as a social problem have been shared by the general public and by professionals of different disciplines who took actions to bring about necessary social changes. These efforts culminated in 1989, when the Knesset (the Israeli parliament) passed an amendment to the existing Penal Code. This amendment (Amendment 26, 1989) became known as the Law for the Prevention of Abuse of Minors and the Helpless.

One part of the 1989 amendment imposes a mandatory reporting requirement on professionals who have either knowledge or suspicion of child abuse. The requirement is imposed on all professionals who come in contact with children as part of their work (i.e., teachers, social workers, counselors, mental health workers, physicians, psychologists and psychiatrists, public health nurses, etc.). These individuals are given the alternative of reporting either directly to the police or to the child protection service. Failure to report child abuse is punishable by six months in prison.

The second part of the 1989 amendment relates to incest and child sexual abuse. Until 1989, incestuous abuse of children received inadequate legal attention as it related only to father-daughter intercourse. Other sexual acts involving a father and a daughter, or severe sexual abuse involving other relatives, were not considered incestuous.

The law identifies sexual abuse of children (or the helpless) as a separate crime, and makes sexual abuse a particularly serious felony when committed by a parent, a family member, or a person responsible for the child. The specific sexual acts and behaviors that constitute this felony were expanded and punishments were increased. Prior to the amendment, a child abuser would usually receive a light punishment, such as a prison term of a few months. Recent amendments have stiffened potential penalties, which may now run as long as ten to fifteen years in prison if the circumstances of abuse are severe.

The 1989 amendment was an important addition to the Law of Evidence which was originally enacted in 1955 and amended in 1983 (Law of Evidence—Child Protection, 1983). This unique law (perhaps the only one of its kind in the world) provides that a child under fourteen who is believed to have been a victim of abuse shall be investigated by a special investigator (not a policeman or a police official) and shall not be required to testify against the perpetrator in court. Instead, the special investigator is allowed to testify on the child victim's behalf. These investigators, who work for the Ministry of Welfare, are specially trained and appointed for this purpose.

Table 6.1
Youth Investigations Concerning Child Maltreatment, 1990–1996

Year	Numbers of Cases
1990	1,647
1991	2,049
1992	2,722
1993	3,252
1994	3,412
1995	4,218
1996	3,808

Source: Adapted from *The State of the Child in Israel: A Statistical Abstract* (p. 265), edited by A. Ben-Arieh, 1998. Jerusalem, Israel: The National Council for the Child (in Hebrew).

The mandatory reporting requirement of the 1989 amendment is an important development that resulted in a significant increase in the reported cases of various forms of child maltreatment. Soon after, however, came the realization that existing social services for handling and treating victimized children and their families were inadequate. Furthermore, professionals began to experience and to identify new moral and ethical dilemmas that were directly connected to the process of treatment under the new law.

PREVALENCE

The Rise in Reported Cases of Child Abuse and Neglect

To illustrate the process mentioned above (i.e., the rise in reported cases of abuse and the realization that existing resources were inadequate) summaries of reported cases of child maltreatment over a period of several years are presented in Table 6.1, which shows the total number of youth investigations conducted during the period from 1990 to 1996. As mentioned earlier, these investigations generally take place after the police officially receive a complaint relating to a child under fourteen years of age. It is clear that the number of these investigations has risen. In fact, between the years 1990 and 1995 the number of reports increased 156 percent.

We also looked at the categorical distribution of these child investigations,

Table 6.2
Police Status of Children Investigated (under Age 14) in 1996

Police Status	Percent of Child Investigations
Child victims of incest and sexual abuse	44.4%
Child victims of physical and emotional abuse by family	41.9%
Child witnessing sex offenses	7.8%
Child suspected of committing sex offenses	5.9%

Source: Adapted from *The State of the Child in Israel: A Statistical Abstract* (p. 269), edited by
A. Ben-Arieh, 1998. Jerusalem, Israel: The National Council for the Child (in Hebrew).

according to their status with the police. Table 6.2 provides the distribution
for the year 1996. The fact that over 80 percent of the child investigations
are related to sexual abuse and physical abuse may reflect the severity with
which Israeli society views such offenses.

It is important to stress that not all cases of child maltreatment come to
the attention of the police. Many such cases are known to the country's
various welfare departments and are treated without police involvement. In
1996, close to 300,000 of the 2 million children in this country were considered to be at risk for maltreatment.

CHILD PROTECTION

Children who are known or suspected to be suffering direct abuse are
usually referred to the child protection service (CPS), which operate in most
local departments of welfare. The treatment offered by CPS includes various
methods of intervention, including an official report to the police and other
potential legal steps, such as removing a child to an emergency shelter. Table
6.3 presents the total number of children through age eighteen who were
referred to CPS in the years from 1994 to 1997. Table 6.3 reflects an obvious increase in referrals. However, when we compare the number of children who were known to be exposed to direct risk of abuse in 1996 to the
referrals to CPS in that year, we find that only 13 percent of the victimized

Table 6.3
Referrals to Child Protection Services, 1994–1997

Year	Number of Referrals
1994	16,342
1995	16,815
1996	18,605
1997	20,989

Source: Adapted from *The State of the Child in Israel: A Statistical Abstract* (p. 286), edited by
A. Ben-Arieh, 1998. Jerusalem, Israel: The National Council for the Child (in Hebrew).

children were referred. This gap may well reflect the slow allocation of resources to child protective services in Israel.

A more detailed look at the CPS statistics for 1997 revealed that only 4.7
percent of the referrals turned out to be false reports of abuse, and that 43.5
percent of the referred children were girls and 56.5 percent were boys. We
also checked the nature of the abuse reported during that year and found
the categorical distributions shown in Table 6.4.

The referrals to CPS may come from various sources and include referrals
from the health system, particularly from emergency rooms. In 1997, there
were a total of 1,692 such referrals from twenty-five hospitals. These referrals
reflect an increase when compared to the two previous years. In 1996, there
were 1,106 health system referrals, while there were only 898 in 1995. Table
6.5 shows the distribution of referrals from the health system in 1997, according to the nature of abuse and the age of the victimized children.

An examination of Tables 6.1 through 6.5 reveals several discrepancies
between data collected from the various sources. Data from the police department show a high proportion of child sexual abuse cases as compared
to other forms of child maltreatment. On the other hand, the large proportion of child emotional abuse and child neglect found in the CPS data
does not appear at all in the data from the police.

These discrepancies may reflect a lack of generally accepted definition of
child maltreatment among the disciplines and systems that deal with the
problem. They may also reflect a general attitude in Israel toward different
forms of child maltreatment: physical and sexual abuse of children is looked
upon very severely and is treated through criminal proceedings and by punitive measures, whereas neglect and emotional abuse of children are allocated to the social services domain and are treated with quite different
interventions.

Table 6.4
Nature of Child Abuse in 1997

Nature of Abuse	Percent of Reported Cases
Physical abuse	33%
Severe neglect	31%
Emotional abuse	29%
Sexual abuse	7%

Source: Adapted from *The State of the Child in Israel: A Statistical Abstract* (p. 286), edited by A. Ben-Arieh, 1998. Jerusalem, Israel: The National Council for the Child (in Hebrew).

INVESTIGATION

Treating Child Maltreatment: Issues and Dilemmas

A number of major issues and dilemmas concerning child abuse and neglect in Israel exist against the complex backdrop just described.

Mandated reporting

The mandatory reporting requirement creates a therapeutic dilemma for professionals who work with abused children. Reporting abuse exposes the abuse, and may protect the child, but it may create a serious breakdown in the family structure and additional traumatic experiences for the child. Family members may blame the child and isolate him/her in order to keep the family intact. The family may even break up after the report, leaving the child to feel guilty and responsible for the breakup. Therapists must keep these and other negative consequences in mind when fulfilling their reporting duty. Blind and rigid adherence to the reporting requirements, without taking steps to enlist the support and understanding of the victim's family, may result in additional and unnecessary trauma to the child. Of course, these kinds of negative outcomes may occur during *or* after professional intervention, but the process of family evaluation and counseling can minimize the risk of additional, secondary trauma to the child.

Therapists must also keep in mind that once they report the sexual abuse of their client, other social systems will become involved in the case. Therapists need to educate themselves to become cognizant of these systems and foresee their potential effects on the child. For example, the criminal proceedings in Israel are strongly based on clear evidence. However, cases of child sexual abuse often do not present definitive evidence, such as physical

Table 6.5
Referrals from Hospitals to Child Protection Services in 1997

Nature of Abuse	Age 0-5	Age 6-14	Age 15-18	Total
Physical abuse	258	220	117	595 (35%)
Sexual abuse	56	122	57	235 (14%)
Neglect	400	105	46	551 (33%)
Other	138	81	92	331 (18%)
Total	852	528	312	1692

Source: Adapted from *The State of the Child in Israel: A Statistical Abstract* (p. 293), edited by
A. Ben-Arieh, 1998. Jerusalem, Israel: The National Council for the Child (in Hebrew).

injuries, medical proof, or corroborating eyewitnesses. Consequently, police
may decide not to open a file, or a prosecutor may decide to close the case
against the suspected perpetrator without even bringing him to trial. The
victimized child may then feel betrayed by the entire adult world.

The professional's dilemma with regard to the mandated reporting requirement can be expressed in the following way. On the one hand, reporting abuse may result in a negative outcome and cause the child to feel
deep disappointment and betrayal toward the therapist. On the other hand,
withholding a report may allow the abuse to continue while the child is in
therapy, potentially making the therapist feel like, and perhaps be perceived
by the child as, either an abuser or as a nonprotective "parent."

Therapists in Israel are beginning to recognize these implications and their
potential negative impact on the child, and find it increasingly difficult to
report abuse. Their ambivalence is becoming evident in the relative decrease
of reported cases to the police during the last two years (see Table 6.1).

TREATMENT

Services Following Reporting and Investigation

As mentioned earlier, once the Israeli police receive a complaint about
child sexual abuse, a specially trained social worker who is not a police official will investigate the allegation. Child investigators are trained and qualified social workers who are employed by the Ministry of Welfare. These
investigators must complete specialized training to conduct child investigations. Their role is to conduct the investigation therapeutically and bring

it to its conclusion as quickly as possible. Many of these investigators see that children feel a great deal of relief after disclosing their abuse during the investigation, and mistakenly believe that the child will cope with the trauma without further intervention. As a result, there is often no referral for an additional, more comprehensive assessment of the child's needs. When this occurs, the child may develop subsequent symptomatology that ultimately results in a referral, albeit late.

Such delayed referrals ultimately make it more difficult for a therapist to evaluate the meaning of the child's presenting symptomatology. The therapist, and the client's family, may find it quite easy to relate the current symptomatology to the past trauma. However, the current symptomatology may be based on subsequent developments, and not the initial trauma.

The story of Sarah F., the daughter of a religiously orthodox family, illustrates this point. Sarah was sexually abused by a neighbor. Because Sarah's investigator found Sarah to be verbal and cooperative during the investigation, the investigator did not recommend a referral for counseling. Sarah was referred to therapy several months later when she began to display a number of behavioral difficulties. At first, the therapist tried to relate the current symptomatology to Sarah's past abuse. Sarah resisted this approach, and it was only later in the relationship that the therapist discovered that Sarah's presenting symptoms were caused predominantly by two current events. First, Sarah was anxious about meeting the perpetrator, who had returned to the neighborhood while awaiting trial. Second, Sarah's parents had inadvertently caused Sarah to repeatedly relive the original trauma by inviting a religious person into their home on a bi-daily basis for approximately two months to ask Sarah about the details of her sexual abuse. (The family was eager to know the details of the abuse because the nature of the sexual activities Sarah had engaged in could affect her marriage prospects within the orthodox community.) Fortunately, after discovering the additional factors, the therapist was able to respond successfully to the present stressors and refocus the therapy away from the original trauma. Had Sarah been referred to therapy immediately after the investigation, she would have received better treatment for the initial trauma, and her subsequent complications might have been avoided.

Treating Children over Fourteen

As mentioned above, the Law of Evidence provides special protections for victimized children under age fourteen. It does not, however, provide the same protections for older children. Cases involving older children are investigated by police youth officers, not trained investigators, and, more important, such children are required to testify in court in the presence of their abuser. This procedure produces a different set of problems for older abused adolescents. Older adolescents frequently recant disclosures that they originally gave during police investigations, succumbing to family pressure, fear of facing their abuser, and anxiety about court proceedings. The longer the period of time between the investigation and trial, the stronger the pressures and fears described above become. There is a need to extend to older adolescents the legal and evidentiary protections afforded to children under the age of fourteen and to speed up the legal process and reduce the delay between reporting and trial.

The Need to Improve

There is no doubt that the various governmental systems in Israel that are responsible for solving the problem of child maltreatment are limited in their abilities. The functions of prevention, detection, validation, and intervention are spread among several ministries, mainly social services, the police and judicial system, education, and health. Each of these agencies is responsible for one aspect of the problem, and they do not coordinate their efforts or cooperate very well. Furthermore, these various agencies seem to lack a unified definition of the problem, which would help in getting a clearer picture about the scope of the problem.

Although Israel is currently trying to develop a comprehensive national policy, decisions have not yet been reached. For example, the current system places great emphasis on detecting and reporting abuse, especially child sexual abuse, and on punishing the abuser. However, the state is still not committed to, or responsible for, the long-term treatment of victimized children and their families after the abuse is discovered. In addition, Israel currently lacks community treatment programs for perpetrators during the pretrial period, after release from prison, or as an alternative to prison.

There also are no local interdisciplinary teams to evaluate each case and collectively determine a course of action for intervention and treatment. Instead, there are localities in Israel where social workers, whose caseloads are already overburdened, must shoulder the added responsibility of protecting children from abuse. Moreover, there are some communities where the child protection function is totally nonexistent.

Another difficulty in Israel is the absence of a national registry of known cases of child maltreatment or a hospital network of information about children brought to emergency rooms who are suspected of being abused. Instituting these mechanisms naturally raises questions concerning citizens' and children's rights to privacy, as well as the ethical issue of confidentiality. But such a registry may facilitate follow-up of identified cases, possibly preventing further maltreatment.

There is also an urgent need in Israel for mandatory basic training about child maltreatment in the professional studies of medicine, nursing, social work, psychology, education, and law. Presently, whether a course will be offered is determined by the individual interest of teachers/lecturers in the various academic institutions. However, further ongoing training within and between the various disciplines is also needed.

There are signs that national policies are moving in the right direction, toward comprehensive training and education about child maltreatment. At the grade school level, the Ministry of Education has introduced compulsory courses on "life skills," which are adapted to different grade levels. The Ministry of Welfare is involved in creating community-based committees that are responsible for assessing the needs and services of the child protection system. The media have also been active in reporting about child maltreatment and creating public pressure for changes in national policy. There is more awareness about child maltreatment and a rise in reported cases, but it is difficult to ascertain whether these recent developments are the result of a changed public attitude toward child maltreatment or a fear of growing violence in general.

CONCLUSION

Treating child maltreatment stands at the intersection of the individual, family, and social systems. Thus, it presents a complex and intricate challenge. The diversity of social and cultural attitudes toward child abuse that exists among different groups in Israel, and the "conspiracy of denial" that remains, make it difficult to reach a shared workable definition of the problem. This lack of a shared definition hampers attempts to (a) study the problem's true prevalence in this country, (b) identify its characteristics and risk factors, and (c) understand the ways in which these characteristics and risk factors operate.

Israeli society has taken significant steps toward recognizing and dealing with the problem of child maltreatment. Laws have been amended to protect children from abuse, professionals of various disciplines are now committed to recognizing, detecting, and reporting suspected cases, and the important role that the child protection system plays in the treatment of these cases has been expanded.

Presently, Israel has a social framework and legal structure aimed at protecting children. However, additional resources are required to make this structure work. Israel needs to develop and expand a continuum of services with a clear commitment to making those services available to maltreated children, for as long as those children need them.

REFERENCES

Ben-Arieh, A. (Ed.). (1988). *The state of the child in Israel: A statistical abstract.* Israel: National Council for the Child. (in Hebrew).

Cohen, T. (1995). Motherhood among incest survivors. *Child Abuse and Neglect, 19*, 1423–1429.

Coohey, C. (1995). Neglectful mothers, their mothers, and parents: The significance of mutual aid. *Child Abuse and Neglect, 19,* 885–895.

Egeland, B., Jacobvitz, D., & Papatola, D. (1987). Intergenerational continuity of abuse. In J. B. Lancaster & R. J. Gelles (Eds.), *Child abuse and neglect: Biosocial dimensions* (pp. 255–276). New York: Aldine de Gruyter.

Furniss, T. (1991). *The multi-professional handbook of child sexual abuse.* London: Routledge.

Garbarino, J. A. (1976). A preliminary study of some ecological correlates of child abuse: The impact of socioeconomic stress on mothers. *American Journal of Orthopsychiatry, 47,* 372–381.

Gil, D. B. (1970). *Violence against children: Physical child abuse in the United States.* Cambridge, MA: Harvard University Press.

Israel Penal Code, Amendment #26 (1989). (in Hebrew).

Kempe, C. H., Silverman, F. N., Steele, B. F., Droegmeuller, W., & Silver, H. K. (1962). The battered child syndrome. *Journal of the American Medical Association, 181,* 105–112.

Kempe, R., & Kempe, C. H. (1978). *Child abuse.* London: Fontana Open Books.

Law of Evidence, 1955, Revision, Protection of Children. (1983). In Israeli Laws Concerning Children and Youth, State of Israel, Ministry of Labor and Social Affairs, Department of International Relations, 53–57.

Law of Evidence, Revision, Protection of Children. (1991). In Selected Israeli Laws Concerning Children and Youth, Ministry of Labor and Social Affairs, Department of International Relations, 66–69.

Morag, T., & Elbashan, Y. (Eds.). (1996). *The law and the child—A collection of laws.* Tel Aviv, Israel: Hagigim Publishers.

Mullen, P. E., Martin, J. L., Anderson, J. C., Romans, S. E., & Hubison, G. J. (1993). Childhood sexual abuse and mental health in adult life. *British Journal of Psychiatry, 163,* 721–732.

Rosenfeld, J. M., & Kedem, A. (1998). Betwix and between the "Generation of the desert" and the "Children of the dream": Fifty years of social work in child welfare in Israel. In F. M. Lowenberg (Ed.), *Meeting the challenges of changing society—Fifty years of social work in Israel.* Jerusalem, Israel: Magness Press.

Rutter, M. (1993). Intergenerational continuities and discontinuities in serious parenting difficulties. In D. Cicchetti & V. Carlson (Eds.), *Child maltreatment: Theory and research on the courses and consequences of child abuse and neglect* (pp. 317–348). New York: Cambridge University Press.

World Health Organization. (1999). *Report of the consultation on child abuse prevention.* Geneva: World Health Organization.

Youth Care and Supervision Law. (1990). In Selected Israeli Laws Concerning Children and Youth, Ministry of Labor and Social Affairs, Department of International Relations, State of Israel, 66–69.

Zuravin, S., McMillan, C., DePantilis, D., & Risley-Curtis, C. (1996). The intergenerational cycle of child maltreatment: Continuity versus discontinuity. *Journal of Interpersonal Violence, 7,* 471–489.

7

JAPAN

Akihisa Kouno and Charles Felzen Johnson

PROFILE OF JAPAN

Japan, an East Asian archipelago bordered by the Sea of Japan and the Pacific Ocean, has an area of 377,765 square kilometers. The capital is Tokyo and the population of 126.2 million consists of Japanese and Korean ethnic backgrounds. The primary language is Japanese and the major religious followings are Buddhist and Shinto with a small Christian population (1 percent). The infant mortality rate is 4 per 1,000 and the life expectancy is seventy-seven years for males and eighty-three years for females. In 1998, the gross national product per capita was $32,380 (U.S.). Public schooling through junior high school is free for all children, with almost 90 percent of students completing high school. The literacy rate is 99 percent and the universal age of suffrage is twenty. The government is a constitutional monarchy with a parliamentary system.

A CASE STUDY

In 1998, on a cold evening in early spring, a subway stationmaster noticed what sounded like the weak cry of a baby coming from a coin-operated locker at the train station. He opened the locker with his master key and was shocked to find a five-month-old male baby. The baby was benumbed with cold, but appeared safe. The next day, a nineteen-year-old mother declared at a police station, "My lovely baby was kidnapped by someone! Please search immediately." Apparently, she had divorced her husband three months prior to this. Further, she had gone to a restaurant with her new boyfriend the night that the baby was found and had spent the night in this man's room. She insisted that she had intended to use the coin-operated locker box as a temporary nursery during her secret meeting and had not intended to abandon her baby completely. The scandal was widely reported throughout Japan as an example of childhood neglect, young marriage and divorce, and child abandonment.

HISTORY

Japan's historical background and present social situation influence the manifestations of child abuse and neglect that currently occur within Japan. The first record of child trafficking appears in Japan's first formal history, which was recorded in the seventh century by the command of the fortieth emperor, Tenmu (720). In addition, ancient folktales such as "Issun—Boushi and Sansyou—Dayuu" also describe child maltreatment (Ikeda, 1987; Miura, 1999). These folktales record instances of child trafficking, kidnapping, sexual abuse, physical abuse, infanticide, and neglect. These "classical" types of abuse are recognized in Japan and have existed in Japan up to the modern age.

Up through the mid-nineteenth century, child maltreatment was found frequently among the lower classes of society, who suffered severe poverty as one result of a punitive system of taxation that existed before the Meiji revolution in 1867. After these excessive taxes were collected, large extended families did not have sufficient resources to feed themselves, making it difficult for a family to raise more than one or two children. This financial stress resulted in a variety of serious, even deadly, consequences for children. In fact, the relatively stable population of Japan prior to 1868 may have been due to infant mortality from infectious diseases and infanticide. Many newborns were killed during this period by asphyxiation, decapitation, and crushing injuries. Although these acts are considered inappropriate and illegal today and were considered criminal at that time, they were nevertheless culturally accepted. This was due in part to extreme poverty among the lower classes that made elimination of children by one means or another necessary in order for other family members to live. Child maltreatment by the master of a brothel or a lower-class feudal lord was caused by the same situation. The *kokeshi* doll found in northeastern Japan, now considered a souvenir, was once displayed as a memory to children who died from this classical type of child maltreatment (Kouno & Johnson, 1995).

The 1867 Meiji revolution and World War II brought a number of drastic changes to Japanese society that contributed to and set the stage for current forms of child maltreatment and abuse. Japanese social systems changed drastically during these periods, and a high standard of living developed rapidly. Moreover, Western ideals influenced the Japanese lifestyle and changed traditional culture and value systems. Contrary to expectations, as a result of these "civilizing" influences, the number of children suffering from child maltreatment has increased.

World War II influenced an entire generation of Japanese children, subjecting them to conditions of maltreatment that grew worse day by day from 1942 to 1945. Many students and children had to leave the city and live away from their parents in the relative safety of the countryside. Many of their parents died as the result of carpet-bombing and the two atomic bombs used by the Allied forces. More than a million civilians, including 300,000 children and infants, were killed. During the 1940s and 1950s, many war orphans lived in big cities like Tokyo and Osaka (Hayashi, 1968). These parentless children grew up to become the future generation of parents.

The "classical" types of child maltreatment, such as child trafficking, kidnapping, sexual abuse, physical abuse, infanticide, and neglect, which were motivated primarily by poverty, were seen in Japan until the end of World War II. This poverty-related maltreatment was effectively eliminated by countermeasures initiated by the Allied forces, such as the dissolution of the plutocracy (*zaibatsu—kaitai*) and agrarian reform (*nochi—kaikaku*). These measures eliminated the centralization of wealth and emancipated the lower class of farmers. The Korean and Vietnamese wars benefited the Japanese economy and also decreased child maltreatment cases caused by poverty.

But Japan's economic successes produced new social pressures that influenced the well-being of Japanese children. Japan's industrial structure was reformed and the working population rapidly moved to the big cities. Japanese industry demanded skilled workers. Competition for limited positions in high-quality schools increased, and Japan became a "credential society" (*juken—sensou*). Examinations became very competitive, resulting in a new crisis for Japanese children. Many children dropped out of school as a result of fierce competition, and others attempted suicide or participated in antisocial crimes. Competition for a limited number of positions has created antisocial reactions known as *ijime* (persecution) or *hikou* (delinquency by students) (Kinoshita, 1998).

Although movement to the big cities increased living standards, it also caused disintegration of the nuclear family as many wives joined the work force and a bustling economy resulted in more overtime work. As a result, friendly neighborhood associations declined and finally collapsed. Child care and parent support previously provided by elders in the community decreased. Ties with the extended family began to loosen and an increased consciousness about privacy developed. Individuals who moved into cooperative housing often did not know their neighbors. Under these situations, violence that occurred behind closed doors increased. The weakening of the nuclear family was associated with an increased incidence of abusive acts that were previously visible to, and possibly prevented by, the extended family (Kouno & Johnson, 1995).

The increasing number of parents under the age of twenty-five also had a negative effect on the well-being of children. Because young parents may not have adequate knowledge of child development, child rearing, and child health, they may have been more likely to use inappropriate and harmful discipline (Johnson, Loxterkamp, & Albanese, 1982). A 1999 report from the Association for the Prevention of Child Abuse and Neglect in Tokyo recently indicated that one out of ten mothers in Japan have neglected or physically punished their children. These acts included physical abuse, neglect, and sexual abuse. Some accidents, such as asphyxia and dehydration, may actually be due to neglect (Nakata, Kouno, & Nakayama, 1996; Nasuno, Terayama, Kouno, & Nakayama, 1998; Okamoto, 1999).

In sum, child maltreatment and abuse appear throughout Japan's history, but the factors causing and contributing to maltreatment and abuse have changed. Prior to the Meiji revolution, child maltreatment and abuse were primarily caused by extreme poverty, which prompted families to neglect, sell, or even murder their children. Japan's economic success since the Meiji revolution, and the increasing influence of Western countries such as the United States, the United Kingdom, Germany, and France, have decreased these pressures, but have brought with them other influences, including the breakdown of the nuclear family, the disintegration of community ties, the increasing privacy of family life, and pressures due to competitive struggles for economic status and success. These factors all contribute to the current manifestations of child maltreatment and abuse.

FORMS AND PREVALENCE OF CHILD ABUSE

Physical Abuse and Neglect

In Japan, suspicions of child neglect and physical and sexual abuse are based on history and physical findings. A child who has many unexplained old and new injuries or who is malnourished should be suspected to be suffering from abuse or neglect. Developmental delays or an unkempt appearance may also suggest neglect.

Accurate statistics about the incidence or prevalence of physical abuse and neglect in Japan are notably lacking. Local data from Osaka indicate that there are approximately 2–5 cases per 100,000 children, but the number of reported cases has been increasing each year (Furuya & Funayama, 1993; Izumi, 1993; Kouno, Matoba, & Shikata, 1989; Naya, Suzuki, & Kobayashi, 1995). Approximately 5,000 abuse cases occur in Japan each year. In 1996, eighty-four victims died because of physical abuse or neglect as diagnosed by medico-legal examinations (Japanese Society of Legal Medicine, 1997). In contrast, there were 2.9 million cases of child abuse and 1,261 child abuse deaths reported in the United States in 1992 (Kouno, Okamoto, & Johnson, 1994). The disparity between prevalence rates of reported abuse cases in the United States and Japan may be the result of differences in lifestyle and reporting laws between Western countries and Japan. It may also be due to differences in definition, reporting propensities, availability of services, or changes in societal value systems.

Sexual Abuse

Until recently, it has been rare to find cases of sexual abuse in Japan. Naya reports seven cases of suspected sexual abuse in 1995 (Naya et al., 1995). There were 10 cases of sexual abuse identified among 316 abuse reports made in Osaka prefecture from 1983 to 1987. The youngest victim was three years old and the oldest was over fifteen years old. In two cases, the child was pregnant. Five children had injuries to their genitalia.

These data probably do not reflect the full extent of abuse in Japan because it is an oriental country in which there is reluctance or taboo about discussing the existence of sexual abuse. It is therefore difficult to discover such abuse as it tends to be hidden.

The reluctance within Japanese society to discuss sexual abuse is even more acute when the abuse involves a foreigner. Because Japan was largely closed to foreigners prior to the nineteenth century, sexual intercourse between Japanese and foreign individuals was very rare. Because rape by a foreigner touches a significant taboo within Japanese society, it is unlikely that it will be discussed openly (Amino, Tsukamoto, & Yokoi, 1987). This situation differs significantly from that in the United States or Europe, where diverse races have a long history of interacting with each other.

Well-publicized events occurring over the last few years have highlighted the existence of sexual abuse by foreigners. After World War II, the Allied forces located many military bases within Japan. Since that time, rape of Japanese civilians by American soldiers occurred but was hidden by American military authorities as well as the Japanese, who hid them due to social taboos. However, in 1995, a twelve-year-old Japanese girl was raped by three American soldiers in Okinawa, where the largest American base in Asia was located. This crime sparked many protests against the Allied forces. These protests led the United States to agree to reduce the number of military bases in Japan. In addition, the three soldiers involved were sentenced under Japanese judicial law.

Infanticide and "Coin-Operated Locker Babies"

As mentioned earlier, infanticide occurred in Japan before the Meiji revolution because parents suffered deprivations due to severe taxation. Despite subsequent legal prohibitions, infanticide continued in Japan until after World War II, when systems of child welfare were introduced. Although acts against children that were associated with poverty decreased after the institution of these measures, the tendency to kill babies persisted. Poverty continued to be one reason for infanticide, but a growing acceptance of premarital sex, especially by young people isolated from their families, resulted in more unwanted pregnancies and subsequent infanticide.

During the last three decades, the manifestation of infanticide in Japan has taken a new form, the so-called coin-operated locker babies. Beginning in the 1970s, as facilities for railways and airplanes developed, coin-operated lockers were placed in railway stations and airports for storage of luggage and packages. Unfortunately, this equipment, intended to provide security for travelers, also provided secure storage for illicit materials such as firearms, drugs, smuggled goods, and explosives. Additionally, it provided a hiding place for unwanted and murdered infants. The prevalence of these abandoned and murdered infants had become a serious social problem by 1975, when the term "coin-operated locker baby" was first applied (Kouno & Johnson, 1995).

In the case of coin-operated locker babies, it was difficult to locate parents or assailants. Only occasionally would a gynecologist examine a postpartum woman whose baby had strangely disappeared and report her to the police. Most infants appeared to have died of asphyxiation, and their bodies, generally wrapped in plastic, were discovered one to three months after death.

As with any infant found dead in the immediate neonatal period, it is important to know whether the baby was born alive or stillborn. Hydrostatic lung, stomach, and bowel tests can be performed by medical examiners or forensic pathologists to determine this. If, however, the body is examined one to three months after death, it may be impossible to ascertain the cause of death because of decomposition (Kouno, Matoba, & Shikata, 1989).

When a time and cause of death of an infant can be determined, the case is classified as follows. Cases involving stillborn children are not considered abuse. Cases involving babies who were born alive are generally classified in one of three ways. If the baby was killed soon after birth and abandoned, the case is considered homicide. If the baby was killed after several days of life, the case is considered neglect and homicide. If the baby was abandoned in a locker but found alive, the case is considered severe neglect.

Approximately 300 infanticide cases are reported in Japan every year, and at least until 1981, approximately 7 percent of infanticides were coin-operated locker babies. The number of such deaths decreased rapidly from 1980 to 1989, along with the number of infanticides. This was apparently due to a number of countermeasures taken in 1981, such as locker relocation and locker inspection (Kouno & Johnson, 1995). In addition, the problem of coin-operated locker babies was widely publicized and became recognized by the general population. Further, education about contraception was provided to a wider number of people, in an effort to decrease the number of unwanted babies. These actions reduced the number of reported coin-operated locker babies from approximately forty cases in 1980 to only seven cases in 1990. Unfortunately, the decrease in the number of coin-operated locker babies has been countered by increases in other types of abuse.

Shaken Infant Syndrome

There have been only a few reports of shaken infant syndrome in Japan. According to an American pediatrician, some reports of subdural hematomas in infants made by neurocerebral surgeons are suspected to be cases of shaken infant syndrome (Aoki & Masuzawa, 1984). However, the term "shaken infant syndrome" was introduced in Japan only several years ago, and it is suspected that the number of reports will increase (Furuya & Funayama, 1993; Kouno, Okamoto, & Johnson, 1994; Ueda, Oka, Ishii, & Kiya, 1998).

Munchausen Syndrome by Proxy

There have been four reports of Munchausen syndrome by proxy in Japan. The term was introduced by Nagahata in 1983 but is still uncommon in Japan. The actual number of cases of the syndrome is considered to be larger (Kouno, Nakayama, & Matoba, 1995; Tahira, 1995).

Medical Neglect and Newly Established Religious Organizations

The recent establishment of nearly 200 new religious parties has raised new concerns about child maltreatment and abuse in Japanese society. These religious parties are loosely divided into three groups derived from traditional animism, Buddhism, and Christianity. Some of these religions spread a special dogma that denies general medical treatment or compulsory education to children. For example, the Honmichi is a new branch of traditional animism that rejects general medical treatment for diseases. The Jehovah's Witnesses, a branch of Christianity, reject blood transfusion, and the AUM, a new branch of Buddhism, rejects compulsory education and performs nonmedical treatments on its followers.

The AUM provides a particularly disturbing example of the potential risks to children within these new religious organizations. More than eighty children have been harmed by AUM's practices. Some of these children were confined by their parents to church dormitories or separated from their parents in these dormitories by the group's founder. Some were not fed enough food and not properly educated, being "educated" instead by electric shock and subliminal stimulation methods. Some girls were enslaved by executives of the group. Some girls were raped because it was proffered that sexual intercourse and ejaculation by the founder of the sect constituted a "holy ceremony of energy filled with god's power." In addition, there is concern that children born of the founder may subsequently be rejected by the general society.

Most of these children have been rescued from the group, although many still remain confined in their dormitories. These remaining children are difficult to remove because the sect claims that these children are protected by their parents, and Japanese society strongly protects parents' authority over their children. Meanwhile, rescued children have experienced extreme difficulty adjusting to Japanese society due to the effects of conditioning. They mistrust general society. Their average educational level is three to five years behind average based on their age (Kinoshita, 1998).

Emotional Abuse and *Ijime* Persecution

Japanese society is a typical "credential" society. Education is compulsory for nine years (six years for elementary school and three years for junior high school). Over 90 percent of students who graduate from junior high school attend a school of higher education. Of these, over 60 percent go on to attend a college or university (Yano, 1996). However, among these students it is unusual to find many with a real interest in their studies. Japanese children are severely pushed to compete for admission to good schools, and this pressure to succeed may begin in infancy. Their first examination occurs at age two or three in order that they may enter a preparation school for a quality kindergarten. In order to enter a quality elementary school, junior high school, senior high school, and university, children are required to pass other difficult entrance examinations.

In response to this intense pressure to succeed, many children drop out of the education system altogether. Those who have dropped out sometimes attempt suicide or become involved in drug abuse, illegal smoking, illegal drinking, or shoplifting, or become members of a *yakuza* (Japanese gang) or an American-derived gang such as Bosozoku (Hell's Angels) (Kinoshita, 1998). From ten to twenty years of age, many children become depressed and lose self-esteem. Suicide is the most common cause of adolescent death in Japan, with hanging or leaping from buildings being the most common forms of such suicide (Nasuno et al., 1998).

Social changes have caused another unique social problem for children called *ijime* (Kinoshita, 1998). The term refers to the persecution of school-age children by other children. It is most common in adolescence. The *ijime* victim is generally a disliked or unpopular student. Although such harassment has occurred in the past (approximately one-third of all children claim to have been persecuted by someone during school), previous forms of harassment were generally minor and transient. The problem with the present situation is the apathy of the assailants, the atrociousness of their behavior, and the increasing sensitivity of the sufferers. Kinoshita (1998) reported that criminal cases involving children have been changing from repeated minor offenses (e.g., shoplifting) to more serious crimes (e.g., armed robbery and homicide).

A shocking homicide case that occurred in Kobe in 1997 provides a striking example of the *ijime* phenomenon. A thirteen-year-old male student killed an eleven-year-old boy, cut off his head, and displayed it at the front of the school gate. The victim was autistic and a playmate of the offender. The offender had apparently been pushed by his parents to go to a higher level school, resulting in overwhelming stress.

Ijime may even lead victimized children to commit suicide in order to escape persecution. This persecution goes beyond traditional bullying and may be considered a type of child abuse or assault that is neglected by the community (Kinoshita, 1998).

INVESTIGATION

In Japan, there are no standardized ordinances that address child abuse and neglect. Everyone is required to report abusive acts to the police or a child protection center, but there are no penalties for nonmedical professionals failing to report abuse. If, however, a doctor documents or suspects physical abuse or neglect, he/she is mandated to report this to law enforcement officials within twenty-four hours (Sasaki, 1998).

It is usual for suspicions to arise based on unkempt children, suspicious injuries, or the neglectful and dangerous lifestyles of parents. Occasionally, a public health nurse will discover abuse during a home visit, or an elementary school or kindergarten teacher may suspect abuse. It is likely that most cases of child maltreatment go unreported in Japan. Modern Japanese do not want to become involved in what they see as others' problems. In addition, it is unlikely that a verbally abused child would report his or her own abuse. In fact, some victims prefer to defend their assailant(s).

If information about suspected abuse comes to the attention of a child protection center or regional welfare center, these organizations have the authority to investigate the case. They may do so by working with law enforcement officers or lawyers. However, a parent's authority may overrule the actions of these organizations, as parental authority is often given higher priority than children's rights. Given this, evaluations and investigations of suspected abuse in Japan may be superficial, unless stronger laws are enacted to investigate and protect children.

PROTECTION OF VICTIMS

At present, it is very difficult to protect maltreated children in Japan. Child protection agencies try to isolate children from suspected assailant(s) by placing them in childcare centers or in hospitals. However, these children may be removed from protection by the assailant(s) because in almost all cases, the assailant is one of the child's parents and, as mentioned previously, parental authority is well protected under Japanese law. There are some other methods that are used to protect children in Japan (Sasaki, 1998; Tuzaki, 1992). For example, child protection services offer home-based services to families, including childcare and lifestyle counseling. Such home-based guidance is useful for the daily detection of child abuse risk factors and allows provision of services that may prevent abuse.

A number of temporary procedures exist for protecting children who may be abused. If the child protection service or regional welfare center encounters an emergency case, it can protect the child from the assailant by admitting the child to a temporary protection center. With the parent's consent, a child protection service or the regional welfare center may place the child in an orphanage or daycare nursery school for educational protective admission.

In an appropriate case, compulsory protective action may be sought by the director of a child protection center or regional welfare center by bringing an allegation of protective admission under the Twenty-Eighth Child Welfare Act. To obtain compulsory protective action, the director must present the family court with evidence of child abuse. If the family court finds the evidence sufficient and approves the allegation, the child is sent to a compulsory protective institution. In 1991, only thirteen cases of abuse were alleged, and only nine of these were approved by family court (Ministry of Health and Welfare, 1992).

A similar procedure is used for compulsory suspension of a parent's authority by the family court. If a relative of the abused child, a public prosecutor, or a director of a child protection center/regional welfare center documents severe parenting problems, he/she can allege a compulsory suspension of the parent's authority. If the family court finds the evidence sufficient and approves the allegation, deputy parents are selected. Only eleven compulsory suspension cases were alleged in Japan during the period 1982–1991. Of these eleven cases, eight were approved or supported (Ministry of Health and Welfare, 1983, 1984, 1985, 1986, 1987, 1988, 1989, 1990, 1991, 1992).

Finally, if the assailant is recognized as a substance abuser (including alcohol) or is emotionally disturbed, and three psychiatrists or psychologists confirm this diagnosis, then the assailant will be forcibly admitted to a mental hospital. This separates the child from the assailant and provides the child with some protection from further abuse.

TREATMENT

Japan does not have very many useful resources for providing remedial services to children and families affected by maltreatment or abuse. As the number of abuse cases increases, this absence of resources is becoming a social problem. As in the United States, the variety of types of maltreatment and the complex social issues associated with abuse make it difficult to provide a standardized protection system. To date, the Japanese government has not been able to provide a successful task force to solve these issues.

However, in Osaka prefecture, several teams of doctors, public health nurses, and child protection workers are meeting to discuss abuse cases. One of the most active teams, the Sensyu Society for Prevention of Child Abuse and Neglect, meets every two months to review cases. These teams visit problematical families with the intent of establishing communication with the families and uncovering the most severe cases as soon as possible. The teams are operated privately, with some financial support from the prefectural government. An abuse hot line, which is fully operated by private volunteers, is also available in Osaka. Tokyo, the capital city of Japan, is becoming another active child protection region. In many cases, a family in which abuse has been established will escape from the region and the child will be victimized in a different region of the country. Members of these protection teams nonetheless try to use family guidance and hot lines to protect potentially abused children within their community (Hirata, 1995; Kato, 1993; Sasaki, 1998; Tuzaki, 1992).

LEGAL INNOVATIONS

Laws for the Protection of Children

As mentioned previously, Japan does not have a cohesive, integrated system of child protection. However, a number of governmental and private organizations provide important services that help to protect children in Japan from abuse and maltreatment. The Ministry of Health and Welfare maintains public health centers that provide health screenings of infants, childcare guidance, and home visiting services by public health nurses (Sasaki, 1998). Child protection services and regional guidance centers provide child protection services, conduct case investigations, and present potential cases of abuse to the family court for judicial resolution (Sasaki, 1998; Takai, 1993). The Medical Center and Research Institute for Maternal and Child Health develops regional childcare systems and provides medical treatment to abused children (Naya, 1995). The Ministry of Education also provides some educational services to parents related to child care.

Of course, entities within the legal system also have child protection duties. The National Police maintain a Department of Boys and Girls Guidance that provides a general social patrol intended to prevent violence and child crimes. In addition, the police are responsible for arresting assailants, investigating cases, and presenting evidence and charges to the Public Prosecutor's Office. The Public Prosecutor's Office investigates child abuse cases and presents them in family court. The family court can take away the abusive parent's authority, issue arrest warrants, place assailants in jail, or mediate a childcare case plan with parents and public organizations (Sasaki, 1998). As mentioned previously, a number of nongovernmental organizations also provide child protective services, such as telephone hot-line services for children and parents or preventative materials designed for general audiences (Hojo, 1993; Kato, 1993). Finally, the Japanese Society for Prevention of Child Abuse and Neglect, organized in 1998, organizes child abuse conferences in Japan.

There are three primary sources for the laws governing child protection: the Child Welfare Act, the Civil Code, and the Criminal Code. The Child Welfare Act contains most provisions concerning the authority and responsibilities of the child protection and regional welfare centers. The 2nd code of the Child Welfare Act requires that all people who notice an abused or neglected child report it to the child protection center or regional welfare center. The 28th code provides for protective admission to an institution under the guidance of the director of a child protection center/regional welfare center by the family court. The 33rd code provides for an emergency temporary protective order by the director of the child protection center without approval by the family court. The 6th article in the 33rd code provides for suspension of a parent's authority under the 834th code of the Civil Code by the director of the child protection center as made to family court.

The Civil Code provides for the family court's authority in child abuse cases. For example, the 834th code provides for compulsory admission of a parent's authority by the family court, and the 819th code provides for the selection of a deputy parent or relative.

The Criminal Code contains most of the compulsory procedural devices used to protect children from abuse and maltreatment. For example, the 29th code provides for compulsory hospitalization of patients who have been diagnosed by three psychiatrists with alcohol or drug abuse or a dangerous psychiatric condition. The 230th code and 232nd code provide that allegations of suspected child abuse or neglect can be made by relatives to law enforcement officials or the prosecutor's office. The law also provides for the arrest of the assailant.

Justice for Assailants in Japan

The Japanese judicial administration uses old laws with new interpretations for abuse cases. The Child Abuse Prevention and Child Relief Act was established in 1933 to protect children under fourteen years of age. The Mother and Child Protection Act was established in 1937. These acts targeted the "old" types of child abuses, including selling of children, childhood prostitution, and mother-child suicides. The Child Welfare Act of

1947 expanded existing policies to protect the welfare of all children. A Child Abuse Protection and Child Relief Act was included in the thirty-fourth article of the new constitution. However, this act is outdated and does not adequately address current maltreatment concerns. The Civil Code, the Criminal Code, and the Child Welfare Act govern the prosecution of child maltreatment in the following manner:

Homicide

If an assailant kills a child and it is proven that the act was premeditated or planned (i.e., first degree murder in the United States), the assailant is charged with murder. Murder is punishable by death by hanging. If it is established that the assailant suffers from psychological illness, he or she will not be sentenced, but rather placed in a psychiatric hospital.

Bodily injury resulting in death

If it cannot be proven that the assailant intended to kill the child, the assailant is charged with bodily injury resulting in death (i.e., unpremeditated murder). The most severe penalty for this is a sentence of life imprisonment. If psychological illness is present in cases of unpremeditated injury or death (i.e., second degree murder in the United States), the assailant is not sentenced to jail, but is placed instead in a psychiatric hospital.

Bodily injury

If the child victim is injured, the assailant is charged with bodily injury (i.e., child abuse in the United States). The most severe consequence for this is imprisonment with several years hard labor. Again, if some psychological illness is present, the assailant is not sentenced, but is placed in a psychiatric hospital.

Neglect

If the victim is killed as the result of neglect, the assailant is charged with abandonment of parental caretaking responsibility resulting in death. The most severe legal consequence of this is imprisonment with several years hard labor. If some psychological illness or special situation (such as a lack of resources or restraint by another person) is present, the assailant is not sentenced. It is very difficult to punish an offender who does not have the ability to maintain an acceptable standard of life. Many neglect cases have been caused by limited offenders (such as the mentally retarded), or by offenders forced to neglect a child by others. This usually occurs in the context of newly risen religious groups, such as the AUM.

Infanticide or coin-operated locker baby

If a dead baby is determined to have been born alive and the mother is identified, the mother is investigated for charges of homicide and abandonment of a corpse. If the dead baby is proven to have been stillborn, the mother is investigated on a charge of abandonment. However, if the assailant is discovered to be the mother of the baby, she is rarely sentenced because she is considered to have been in a "mentally unusual situation" during and after the pregnancy.

Sexual abuse

If the victim is under thirteen years of age, the assailant is investigated on charges of sexual violation of a child. Such cases are usually punished by imprisonment with hard labor for several years. If the victim is over thirteen years old, it is difficult for the court to prove that the sexual activity was not consensual, and the court requires that victims prove the assailant violated them. This is considered a sexual scandal and is still a social taboo in Japan. Therefore, the victim generally does not want to make the sexual violation public. When the violation is made public the trial may be quite stressful to the victim, and thus the victim may refuse to testify or may abandon the charges.

PREVENTION

There are no effective systematic or universal prevention measures applied in Japan that are known to reduce the incidence of abuse. For example, schools do not teach students about child maltreatment, as they do in many school districts in the United States. The curriculums in many Japanese professional schools do not address child maltreatment. Recently, however, the mass media have presented information to the public on child abuse (Kawana, 1990; Takemura, 1989), and the Japan Medical Association published a special issue on child abuse and neglect in 1990 (Ohkuni, Ikeda, & Naitow, 1990). In addition, several special books on child abuse and neglect have been published, and papers on these issues have been increasing in the pediatric and social science journals (Ikeda, 1987; Kobayashi, 1996; Kouno, Matoba, & Shikata, 1989). However, these books and papers are primarily about physical abuse or neglect; sexual abuse and psychological maltreatment have not been adequately recognized in the society.

As mentioned previously, private networks that diagnose, treat, and prevent child abuse have been established in large cities such as Osaka and Tokyo. The government of Osaka prefecture organized a group specifically designed to deal with the detection and protection of child abuse and neglect in Osaka, and in 1993 this group published a manual on how to manage an abused child. The manual was revised in 1996 (Kobayashi, 1996). The manual defines child abuse and neglect in Japan and describes the legal basis for dealing with abuse cases, case reports, and legal procedures. New responsibilities are being developed for the protection of Japanese children by the community and welfare organizations (Izumi, 1993).

Despite these measures, there is much to be done to improve the detection, reporting, and protective services needed to fully serve children.

The Effectiveness of Social and Legal Policies

The problem of child abuse and neglect is just being recognized in Japan. At present, the number of abuse cases is still relatively small when compared with other developed countries. Japanese citizens believe that child abuse is unusual and more common to other societies and countries. As a result, child abuse legislation is a low government priority. More public and professional education is needed to increase concern for this important cause of child morbidity and mortality. The hot line established in the Osaka prefecture is one of the more successful systems for increasing the public's awareness of abuse and protecting child victims. At present, there are approximately 10 consultation cases a day, and from 1990 to 1995 there were more than 10,000 consultations. Publishing an account of a case of child abuse in a monthly women's comic magazine was another successful education method. Japanese citizens do care for the welfare of children. Small family size may place increased value on Japanese children. The industrialization of Japan has, as in Western society, decreased the potential "services" that children once provided to families, such as on farms. This industrialization, including movement to large cities, has weakened the protection of the nuclear family and increased abuse risk factors. Until the identification and reporting of cases approach the actual prevalence, it will not be possible to determine if Japanese culture provides relatively more protection to its children than other countries. If the prevalence of abuse is truly lower than in other advanced societies, these societies may learn valuable prevention methods from Japan. Japan must learn about how risk factors in other countries, such as teenage pregnancy, substance abuse, domestic violence, animal violence, and single-parent families, can be prevented.

REFERENCES

Amino, Y., Tsukamoto, M., & Yokoi, K. (Eds.). (1987). Senmin To Oken [Emperor's authority and the lowly]. *A history of Japan*, 7 (76) 290–320. Tokyo: Asahi Shinbunsha Press.

Aoki, N., & Masuzawa, H. (1984). Infantile acute subdural hematoma. *Journal of Neurosurgery, 64*, 273–280.

Furuya, T., & Funayama, M. (1993). Autopsy cases of battered child syndrome in Hokkaido in 1980–1991. *Research and Practice in Forensic Medicine, 36*, 291–297.

Hayashi, S. (1968). *A history of Japan: The Pacific War, 25*, 374–416. Tokyo: Chuo-Koronsha Press.

Hirata, Y. (1995). A report of hot-line consultation of child abuse and neglect cases in Osaka. *Japanese Journal of Pediatric Medicine, 27*, 123–127.

Hojo, M. (1993). The role of child protection house. In Jido-Gyakutai Boushi Seido Kenkyuukai (Ed.), *Kodomo-no Gyakutai Boushi* (pp. 113–124). Osaka: Toki-Shobo Press.

Ikeda, Y. (1987). *Jido-Gyakutai* [Child abuse and neglect]. Tokyo: Chuo Koronsya Press.

Izumi, K. (1993). Jido-gyakutai to shinken [Child abuse and parental authority]. *Liberty and Justice, 42,* (2), 22–27.

Japanese Society of Legal Medicine (Ed.). (1997). *Houi kantei-rei gaiyou* [An annual report of legal autopsy cases in Japan]. Tokyo: Japanese Society of Legal Medicine.

Johnson, C. F., Loxterkamp, D., & Albanese, M. (1982). Effect of high school students' knowledge of child development and child health on approaches to child discipline. *Pediatrics, 69,* 558–563.

Kato, Y. (1993). A hot-line activity on child abuse and neglect. In Jido-Gyakutai Boushi Seido Kenkyuukai (Ed.), *Kodomo-no Gyakutai Boushi* (pp. 125–138). Osaka: Toki-Shobo Press.

Kawana, K. (1990). *Oyani-narenai* [I can't be a parent]. Tokyo: Asahi Synbunsya Press.

Kinoshita, T. (1998). Persecution and antisocial crimes. *Journal of Japanese Medical Association, 119* (11), 1783–1787.

Kobayashi, M. (Ed.). (1996). Jido-Gyakutai boushi manual. Osaka: Prefectural Government of Osaka.

Kodomo-no gyakutai junin ni hitori. (1999, April 22). *Nihon—Keizai—Shinbun,* p. 39.

Kouno, A., & Johnson, C. F. (1995). Child abuse and neglect in Japan: Coin-operated locker babies. *Child Abuse and Neglect, 19,* 25–31.

Kouno, A., Matoba, R., & Shikata, I. (1989). A medico-legal and socio-medical report on maltreated children. *Japanese Journal of Pediatrics, 42,* (11), 163–170.

Kouno, A., Nakayama, M., & Matoba, R. (1994). Sudden infant death syndrome. *Japanese Journal of Pediatrics, 47* (2), 7–16.

Kouno, A., Nakayama, M., & Matoba, R. (1995). SIDS or child abuse? *Japanese Journal of Pediatric Medicine, 27* (11), 79–85.

Kouno, A., Okamoto, N., & Johnson, C. F. (1994). Clinical aspects of child abuse and neglect in the United States of America. *Research and Practice in Forensic Medicine, 37,* 403–410.

Ministry of Health and Welfare. (1983, 1984, 1985, 1986, 1987, 1988, 1989, 1990, 1991, 1992). *The annual report on the Administration of Health and Welfare.* Tokyo: Kosei-Tokei Kyokai Press.

Miura, S. (Ed.). (1999). *Dowa-tte honto wa zankoku* [The real horrible meaning of fairy tales]. Tokyo: Futami-syobo Press.

Nakata, K., Kouno, A., & Nakayama, M. (1996). An epidemiologic study of 280 unexpected death cases in infancy. *Japanese Journal of Pediatrics, 49* (8), 105–110.

Nasuno, A., Terayama, M., Kouno, A., & Nakayama, M. (1998). A case report of 101 child unexpected deaths in Osaka prefecture. *Japanese Journal of Pediatrics, 51* (7), 141–146.

Naya, A., Suzuki, A., & Kobayashi, M. (1995). A case report on sexual abuse cases. *Journal of Osaka Pediatricians Association, 12* (3), 14–15.

Ohkuni, M., Ikeda, Y., & Naitow, M. (1990). Jido-gyakutai [Child abuse and neglect]. *Journal of Japan Medical Association, 103* (9), 1437–1516.

Okamoto, N. (Ed.). (1999). *A handbook for sudden infant death syndrome.* Osaka: Prefectural office of Osaka.

Osaka Medical Examiner's Office. (1999). *An annual report on the cause of death.* Osaka: Osaka Medical Examiner's Office Press.

Sasaki, K. (Ed.). (1998). *Kodomono Gyakutai Boushi Hoteki Jitumu Mannual* [A manual for prevention of abusive acts on children]. Tokyo: Akashi Shoten Press.

Shinbun, N. K. (1999, April 22). One of ten parents have experiences of abusive act for their children in Japan, recently. *Kodomo-no gyakutai junin ni hitori* [newspaper], p. 39.

Tahira, K. (1995). Munchausen syndrome by proxy. *Japanese Journal of Pediatric Medicine, 17* (11), 95–99.

Takai, Y. (1993). The role of child guidance section of regional welfare center. In Jido-Gyakutai Boushi Seido Kenkyuukai (Ed.), *Kodomo-no Gyakutai Boushi* (pp. 89–101). Osaka: Toki-Shobo Press.

Takemura, T. (1989). *Kizuno-Fukasa Naze-Wagako-no-Gyakutai-wo? Kodomono Jinkenwa-Ima.* Osaka: Liberty Booklet Press.

Tenmu, Emperor (Ed.) (720). *Kojiki* [An official history of Japan before the eighth century].

Tuzaki, T. (1992). *Kodomo-no Gyakutai* [Child abuse and neglect]. Osaka: Toki-Shobo Press.

Ueda, O., Oka, T., Ishii, N., & Kiya, T. (1998). A case report of whiplash shaken infant syndrome victim. *Journal of Child Health, 57* (2), 153.

Yano, I. (Ed.). (1996). *Nihon Kokusei Zue* [A charted survey of Japan]. Tokyo: Kokusei-sya Press.

8

KENYA

Philista P. M. Onyango and Victoria W. M. Kattambo

PROFILE OF KENYA

The Republic of Kenya borders the low coastal plain of the Indian Ocean to the east and the mountain plains of Lake Victoria to the west, and has an area of 582,646 square kilometers. The capital is Nairobi and the 28 million inhabitants speak English, Swahili, and over forty other local ethnic languages. Their religious followings vary, with 40 percent Protestant, 30 percent Catholic, 20 percent Muslim, and 10 percent indigenous beliefs. The ethnic groups present in Kenya include African groups such as Kikuyu (21 percent), Luhya (14 percent), Luo (13 percent), Kalenjin (11 percent), Kisii (11 percent), and Meru (5 percent) and non-African groups of Asians, Europeans, and Arabs (1 percent). The infant mortality rate is 58 per 1,000 and the life expectancy is fifty-eight years. Education is not required for children, but the first eight years of primary school are provided through payments by both the parents and the government. Kenya has a primary school attendance of 83 percent and an English literacy rate of 59 percent. The gross national product per capita in 1998 was $330 (U.S.), with a primarily agricultural workforce. The government is a republic in which the president is elected by Kenyans over the age of eighteen.

A CASE STUDY

An employer (a distant relative) brought Jane, age ten, from her rural home to work in Nairobi. The employer had negotiated a salary of KShs. 600 (U.S. $8) per month with her mother, and promised Jane free education in

Nairobi. On arrival, Jane found that the employer had five children of her own, three of whom were attending school. Jane had to take care of the employer's two small children who were not at school while doing other household chores. The work proved too much for Jane, and the employer beat her when she did not perform as expected. Jane ran away and went to the police for help because she wanted to go back to her rural home and go to school. Jane had heard on the radio that child labor was bad and that children should go to school.

When she realized the police could not help her, she wandered the streets, and fortunately some girls from a nearby rescue center found her. Jane stayed at the center for some time before being returned to her family. When Jane was found, she was reported to be ten years old, but she looked six.

A visit to Jane's home revealed that she had four sisters, none of whom were attending school and two of whom were working for other people. Her father was in his thirties, and her mother was twenty-six years old; both were unemployed, and both had dropped out of school. Jane and three of her sisters had attended a nearby primary school in the past, using a neighbor's name to avoid paying school levies, but all the children had been forced to drop out of school in 1997 when the neighbor could not pay the levy for his own children. After leaving school, Jane and two of her siblings began to work. Jane had worked for two other employers before coming to Nairobi.

Jane was lucky to reach the rescue center, and now she is back at school. Many other children such as Jane are not so fortunate. They suffer all types of abuse while working as domestic workers or living as street children.

HISTORY

The value of children in traditional Africa is well documented. In all African societies children are expected to contribute to family labor both agriculturally and domestically. Traditionally, care of aged parents, as well as extended family and kin, is often left to children.

Historically, in most African societies, the care and protection of children were collective responsibilities mainly entrusted to families. At the birth of a child, if a mother did not have a child of her own who was old enough to assist, she was assigned a babysitter. With time, the support of other members of the household was elicited, and anybody living in the household lent a hand (Kayongo-Male & Walji, 1984; Lambo, 1969). The mother, nonetheless, remained the key caregiver and protector.

At three to four years of age, the child was introduced to the extended family. The child could be fed, disciplined, or assigned errands by relatives. Nicknames were assigned to the child to demonstrate appreciation and love. Sleeping arrangements also changed at this point. Initially, an infant slept next to the mother in the same bed. At age four, the child joined others in the grandparents' house or in a sleeping place earmarked for children. At this time, the children also began their education through storytelling, and the entire family taught the child the proper way to behave with both relatives and strangers (Nzewi, 1989). Throughout these changes, the child was introduced to relatives who could be trusted and called upon in times of trouble or need.

The value placed on children, and a rather organized family-centered system of caring for and protecting children, rendered concepts such as abuse and neglect unnecessary. How could one think of abusing a treasured person? Acts that could appear abusive were seen as helping children grow up properly (Kayongo-Male & Onyango, 1991). For example, physical punishment, whether excessive or light, was and is still seen as a method of disciplining children. The majority of parents know no better way of restraining children from doing wrong things, especially when verbal restraints have failed. Adults do not necessarily view this as abuse, in part because they recall with nostalgia how the canings they received as children made them better persons.

Removing children from school to babysit or herd animals for family or other relatives is still considered normal in rural Kenya (Kayongo-Male & Walji, 1984). Similarly, sending children to live with their relatives is normal. Informal fostering is seen as a way of reciprocating favors and an extension of generosity to relatives. Studies done on child labor show that the majority of domestic child workers were brought into employment by their relatives (Bwibo & Onyango, 1987; Onyango & Orwa, 1991). Whatever forms of abuse these children face in work situations are seen as a process of socialization. Further, while many relatives promised children free education, often the children received no education. Although the children were very disappointed and felt deceived, the parents had no complaints, as the children were obtaining food and clothing, which the parents could not provide.

Historically, even practices such as female genital mutilation and child marriages were considered noble cultural practices. Both were considered virtues; a circumcised girl was believed to be protected from becoming promiscuous, and those marrying early were protected from teenage pregnancy. Thus, these traditions, which many would consider to be abuse, were practiced to protect the most valued people in African society, that is, the children.

Sexual abuse and abandonment of children have never been condoned in African society. In situations when they occurred, they were made scandalous within the family circles. African society considered an adult who sexually molested children to be an abnormal person who should not be allowed to be near children, and children were warned about such a person.

Abandonment and neglect of children was rare since childless relatives were entitled to receive and care for other relatives' children. Hence, the burden of raising children could easily be shared by relatives with no children of their own who desired companionship and services (Kilbride & Kilbride, 1994).

Unfortunately, disabled children did not have an acceptable place in African society. Because children were valued for their services, these children were considered bad omens that needed to be disposed of. Such children were either killed at birth or neglected until they died (Kayongo-Male & Onyango, 1991).

In conclusion, while African children did not necessarily experience many types of abuse as typically defined in Western literature (e.g., neglect, sexual abuse), especially intrafamilial abuse, they did experience other types of maltreatment (e.g., forced labor, child marriage, and genital mutilation). Thus, the maltreatment of children in African society did exist historically.

CHILD ABUSE IN PRESENT-DAY KENYA

In modern Kenya, all types of child abuse are found. The local newspapers in Kenya report many cases of child maltreatment. Many children have been abandoned by their mothers, while others have been thrown into dustbins and left to die. Children have been abducted either for prostitution or child labor. Three studies done by the African Network for the Prevention and Protection Against Child Abuse and Neglect (ANPPCAN) in Kenya reveal that a large number of both children and adults have seen or experienced acts of child abuse (ANPPCAN, 1994a, 1994b, 1997). Local papers also frequently report cases of children severely beaten by parents, and the four reporting desks for cases of abuse created by the Coalition on Child Rights and Child Protection in Kenya receive at least five reports of child abuse per day.

A 1997 study conducted in a slum community in Nairobi found that the majority of respondents were aware of the existence of some form of child abuse. Respondents identified physical, sexual, and emotional abuse, with physical abuse being the most often mentioned (ANPPCAN, 1997).

A 1994 ANPPCAN study assessing adults' views about child abuse in both rural and urban communities suggested that child abuse was quite common. This study defined child neglect as occurring when caretakers failed to provide food, education, or medical care; if children were forced to work instead of going to school; or if they were mistreated. Physical abuse was defined as any time a child had injuries due to beatings, neglect, or abandonment. Sexual abuse occurred when one talked to a child using vulgar language, touched the private parts of a child, had sexual contact with a child, or when rape and defilement occurred. Finally, emotional abuse was defined as occurring when a caretaker told a child that he or she was worthless, failed to show affection, verbally abused or threatened a child, refused to interact with a child, did not show the child that he or she was loved, or failed to congratulate a child for positive performance. (ANPPCAN, 1994a, 1994b).

In the 1997 ANPPCAN study, 60 percent of the respondents reported having either witnessed child abuse or having been a victim of child abuse. Similarly, in the 1994 study, a large proportion of children and adults (63 percent and 68 percent, respectively) reported witnessing situations where children were being abused.

In Kenya, physical abuse is manifested through beating of children, both in families and institutions of learning, such as schools. Physical punishment is seen as an acceptable way of disciplining children. In the 1994 study, a large proportion of respondents (62 percent) considered physical punishment as necessary if used for disciplinary purposes. Only 28 percent of respondents felt that physical punishment was a poor method of disciplining children.

Kenyans consider depriving children of food and education as the worst forms of child abuse. School dropout rates are very high in Kenya, especially at the primary level. According to available information, school enrollment of children aged six to thirteen years dropped from 94 percent in 1987 to a mere 76 percent in 1995 (Government of Kenya, 1997). Children who are not in school tend to end up in the streets begging or working. The majority of children who become child workers end up being overworked. Studies indicate that these children endure long hours of work and abuse. Similarly, other children do many family chores in addition to attending school, and this interferes with their learning (Bwibo & Onyango, 1987; Kayongo-Male & Onyango, 1982; Kayongo-Male & Walji, 1984; Onyango & Orwa, 1991).

Incidents of sexual abuse have increased tremendously over the last few years, according to newspaper reports. For example, fifteen cases of sexual abuse were reported in one daily between March and October 1999 (Bikuri, 1999). In a recent follow-up study on child abuse in Kenya done by ANPPCAN, 3 percent of 501 children interviewed reported having been sexually abused, while 12 percent of these children reported knowing a child who had been sexually abused (ANPPCAN, 2000). This clearly demonstrates that sexual abuse is on the increase in Kenya.

CAUSES OF CHILD ABUSE

Poverty

In Kenya, economic problems are a major contributing factor to child abuse (ANPPCAN, 1994a, 1994b, 1997). While not all poor families abuse their children, it is apparent that incidents of child abuse are frequent in families living in slums and rural Kenya. For example, cases of children being abandoned are associated with living in slum communities (ANPPCAN, 1994b), as well as having mothers who are imprisoned for petty offenses of an economic nature (Muli-Musiime & Kilonzo, 1985). Cases of children burnt by caretakers have also been related to situations in which a single parent could not afford an adult babysitter and had to resort to using a child or adolescent (Onyango, 1983).

Harsh punishment is also related to poverty. In rural Kenya, parents frequently tie and burn the hands of children who have stolen a few shillings. In some cases, children have been severely beaten and maimed for eating the only food the family had saved for supper. This demonstrates how family poverty can lead to abuse.

The occupations and earnings of parents of most street children demonstrate further the economic difficulties such families face. Onyango, Suda, and Orwa (1991) found that the majority of parents of street children and child workers are from low-earning occupations such as hawking, peasant farming, bar attendance, and prostitution. Most of these parents had either no or little education and no developed skills. Furthermore, street children primarily come from single-parent homes where mothers are trying to survive in a very competitive urban life. Both street children and child workers come from very large families without sufficient income (Onyango, Suda, & Orwa, 1991).

Kenya has been suffering severe economic difficulties since 1983. Because of these difficulties, the government initiated reductions of public expenditures and support given to poor families. The government also shifted the cost of education and health care to parents. As such, parents had to start paying school fees and other school levies (taxes) for things such as building classrooms. This added a large burden to families who were already finding it difficult to support themselves (UNICEF, 1989). The impact of these adjustments has been grave on children. For example, many children have been forced to leave school because their parents could not afford the tuition and related school levies (Government of Kenya, 1996).

Historically, the government has been the major employer in Kenya. Unfortunately, the country's economic difficulties have resulted in the retrenchment of civil service positions and a freeze on new posts. The small and underdeveloped private sector simply could not absorb the huge labor force. This has created a high level of unemployment, making it difficult for many families to earn an income. Further, changes that have been taking place in African families have exacerbated the situation for individual families. For example, support from extended family members is often no longer available.

Family Instability

Other factors that contribute to child abuse are found within the family itself. Family instability, substance abuse (i.e., alcohol and drug abuse), large families, single parenthood, unwanted pregnancies, and health problems are all related to child abuse and neglect. The traditional African family has changed over the years. With the onset of urbanization, many families moved into urban areas to benefit from the better living conditions offered there. In most cases, however, many family members are left in the rural areas since it is very expensive to bring the entire family into towns (Mbithi, 1969).

Often men who migrate to towns leave their wives and children in their rural homes. Due to long distances and the cost of travel, the fathers can only visit their homes periodically, and are essentially strangers to their children. This has resulted in a significant number of single-parent households headed by mothers, forcing the African family to change not only in structure, but in function as well (Government of Kenya, 1998). There are a large number of children being brought up by mothers who are alone in rural Kenya.

NATURE OF THE CHILD PROTECTION SYSTEM IN KENYA

Protection and care of children fall under different departments, namely, the judiciary, labor, education, police, health, children, and social services. Among these, only one department has been assigned the mandate to protect children through an act of Parliament. This is the Children's Department of the Ministry of Home Affairs, Culture and Social Services. The department has children's officers, some of whom are children's inspectors and prosecuting officers. Cases of child abuse are reported to children's officers at district, provincial, and headquarters levels. When the cases are dealt with, children are offered appropriate services, including removal of the child from home, family counseling, and material support to prosecute perpetrators. The majority of children's officers are professional social workers. In addition to government agencies, a few nongovernmental organizations (NGOs) also deal with cases of child abuse in Kenya.

Cases of abuse are reported by neighbors, other children, parents, abused children themselves, teachers, and through print media. Children's officers, at times, find it difficult to protect children effectively due to a lack of appropriate skills needed for such work. The police encounter many abused children, but are not trained to work with such children. Children in institutional care also experience forms of abuse from caretakers. Services provided to abused children are at times uncoordinated, although NGOs are attempting to improve the services by forming coalitions.

THE RESPONSE OF KENYAN LAW TO CHILD ABUSE

Kenyan law has not explicitly defined the concept of child abuse. What constitutes child abuse is a matter of interpretation of the statutes that deal with physical, sexual, and mental injury, resulting from a variety of actions and circumstances.

In spite of the difficulty presented by a lack of definitions, Kenyan law describes behavior that constitutes physical, mental, and sexual injury to children. Kenya has also ratified the Convention on the Rights of the Child and has gone further and drafted a Children's Bill in which issues related to child abuse and neglect have been addressed.

The main provisions of existing Kenyan municipal law on child abuse are embodied in the Constitution, the Children and Young Persons Act (Chapter 141—Laws of Kenya), the Penal Code (Chapter 163—Laws of Kenya), and the Employment Act (Chapter 226—Laws of Kenya).

The Constitution

The Constitution of Kenya addresses the rights of children in several respects. It prohibits torture and inhumane and degrading treatment of individuals, thus laying a firm basis for other statutory provisions relating to children. The most comprehensive provisions are to be found in the Children and Young Persons Act and the Penal Code.

The Children and Young Persons Act

This act was passed principally for the protection and discipline of children. It sets up an institutional framework through which a child can be afforded protection by both governmental and nongovernmental institutions. The government responses are channeled through the Children's Department in the Ministry of Home Affairs, Culture and Social Services, which derives authority under the act to intervene in a variety of situations involving children.

The main thrust of the protections provided by the act is to safeguard interests of children who are in need of discipline and those who are in undesirable or difficult circumstances that expose them to harm. The distinction between children "in need of discipline" and those "in need of protection" is obscure and sometimes operates as an obstacle to the development of focused programs to address different forms of child abuse. An ongoing law review exercise aims, among other things, to tackle this anomaly.

The process of invoking the protective provisions of the act involves police officers, administration officers, children's officers, chiefs, and other approved officers. These officers may apprehend a child found to be in need of protection and bring him or her before a juvenile court for appropriate orders. They are also empowered to take a child to a "place of safety," including any mission, hospital, or other suitable place. A juvenile remand home or a police station may also be used as a place of safety.

In addition to governmental institutions that are used as places of safety, many communities and nongovernmental organizations have established rescue centers for children in need of protection. A number of the NGOs have long-term prevention and reintegration programs that focus on the family environment of the child in need of protection.

Many children end up in the juvenile court, which is empowered to exercise a wide range of options to safeguard their welfare. These options include supervision orders, committal orders in which a child is committed into an approved school run by the government or an organization.

The protective measures provided by the act have been used over the years to aid abused children, particularly children whose survival and developmental needs have been at stake. There are, however, some limitations to the act. The act mainly concerns itself with the child in trouble and pays little attention to the circumstances of his or her family, even though the family system has contributed to the problem. Furthermore, the act has a punitive orientation in cases where deliberate neglect is proven. For example, when a parent fails to provide a child with food, clothing, medical aid, or lodging, the parent becomes liable to prosecution. Unfortunately, in a predominantly poor country such as Kenya, the line between intentional neglect and unavoidable neglect is a thin one. Finally, protective measures in the act that proscribe intentional assaults and ill treatment of children are difficult to implement because they are not supported by efficient reporting and investigation mechanisms.

The Penal Code

There is a tendency by law enforcement agencies to rely on Penal Code provisions in cases involving physical and sexual abuse. The code makes it an offense to fail to provide the necessities of life to a dependent when one has a specific duty to do so. Common assaults, assaults causing bodily harm, and unlawful acts or omissions that cause harm to any person are also offenses punishable under the code.

There are extensive provisions on various forms of sexual abuse involving children. These include provisions on defilement of girls less than fourteen years of age; rape of girls above fourteen years of age; incest; homosexuality; and living on the earnings of prostitution. In spite of these extensive provisions, enforcement remains problematic for a variety of reasons. First, provisions on defilement, when examined broadly in the cultural context, often present contradictions. The Constitution acknowledges the application of different family law systems, some of which (Islamic and customary) permit child betrothals and marriage of children as young as twelve years old. Thus, there is a double standard when one has a legal system that condemns sexual relations with a girl child below the age of sixteen years, while at the same time the system condones child marriage. There is a need for uniformity, and it is now accepted that uniformity of the definition of a child will facilitate the reality of protecting all children, irrespective of their cultural backgrounds. This may indeed be the genesis of challenging, and providing alternatives to, traditional practices that can no longer be condoned in view of their detrimental impact on the welfare of children.

Second, there are bottlenecks in the administration of the law. These include, among others, ignorance of the law among the people, inadequate facilities and specialized services to deal with special cases, poor infrastructure in rural areas, and lack of skilled professionals to handle cases of abuse. Coupled with the above are cultural and social practices that negate proper handling of the cases. These include taboos relating to discussions of sex, fear of police, stigma attached to sexual offenses, fear of retribution by perpetrators, and extrajudicial settlements (Kattambo, 1996). Removal of these bottlenecks will inevitably involve legal and nonlegal interventions.

The Employment Act

The Employment Act applies to employment situations involving children, except employment of children as apprentices or indebted learners. The act is complemented by the Regulation of Wages and Conditions of Employment Act, which provides various terms and conditions of employment applicable to all employees, including children. Applied together, these laws have the potential to provide a large measure of protection to child workers.

Generally speaking, the main thrust of employment legislation is to prohibit employment of children in activities that are dangerous to their lives, health, or morals. The Regulation of Wages and Conditions of Employment Act dictates various conditions for the employment of children. These include the number of hours of work allowed, a minimum wage for children, weekly rest time, required holidays, acceptable housing, safety issues, medical care, and provisions for children's health and general welfare. For example, employers must provide an acceptable level of food, clothing, and lodging when these are part of the contract of employment.

Through a wide network of inspectors, the Ministry of Labor endeavors to ensure that employment law is enforced. Labor officials have wide powers to terminate contracts of employment when an employer is found to be an undesirable person or if the nature of employment is dangerous, immoral, or likely to be injurious to the health of a juvenile (i.e., persons below sixteen years of age).

These laws have been enforced effectively in the formal sector. Unfortunately, children are exposed to abusive situations in the informal sector that are difficult to identify. Studies have shown that many children employed in the domestic and agricultural sectors are exposed to various forms of abuse that are difficult to detect due to the secluded nature of the work environments. Thus, in spite of an elaborate legislative and administrative framework, many children may remain at risk.

THE INVOLVEMENT OF CHILDREN IN THE LEGAL SYSTEM

The participation of children within the legal system has two main dimensions. Children may be involved either as victims or as witnesses of offenses committed by other persons. In both circumstances, the law treats them with caution and suspicion. It is therefore becoming increasingly necessary to revisit the general approach of the law toward the involvement of children, in an effort to make it friendly. A few NGOs have initiated a number of significant programs aimed at involving and educating children about their rights (Lynch & Onyango, 1998). There is also debate on revising the school curricula nationwide to include awareness of children's rights.

When legal action is instituted, the most critical factor, especially in sustaining a prosecution, is the availability of admissible evidence. Unfortunately, legal requirements for admitting children's evidence present serious obstacles to an otherwise sustainable prosecution. In general, evidence provided by a child of tender years is not currently trusted in Kenya's judicial system. When a child of tender years is required to give evidence, section 124 of the Evidence Act demands that such evidence be treated with caution and in fact demands that the evidence be corroborated by material evidence. This requirement for corroboration has resulted in much injustice, especially in cases of sexual abuse in which the victim (child) is often the only witness.

Further, although the act does not define a child of tender years, it has been argued that according to the Age of Majority Act corroboration should be required for any witness below eighteen years of age (Walekwa, 1990). This situation is being addressed in the current Children's Bill, which contains provisions to protect children adequately and allows for child participation. The bill also incorporates provisions from the UN Convention on the Rights of the Child and the African Charter on the Rights and Welfare of the Child regarding child protection.

LEGAL INNOVATIONS AND LEGISLATIVE REFORMS

The issue of child abuse forms an important part of the agenda of many children's rights organizations, some of which have been formed specifically to tackle child abuse and neglect. Among these is the African Network for the Prevention and Protection Against Child Abuse and Neglect (Kenya Chapter). The issue has also featured prominently in recent studies and workshops organized by various organizations and professional groups in collaboration with state institutions. In Kenya the process of reviewing laws affecting children started in 1991 and was completed in 1995. This culminated in the drafting of a Children's Bill, which has been discussed and revised by different interested groups and is awaiting presentation to Parliament for discussion and enactment.

LEGAL RAMIFICATIONS FOR PERPETRATORS OF CHILD ABUSE

Perpetrators of various forms of child abuse are subject to legal sanctions such as fines and imprisonment. Unfortunately, the wide discretion exercised by the courts, which has been central to the controversy regarding sentencing of sexual offenders in general, has resulted in major variations in the punishment meted out to perpetrators. When the victim is a child, the perpetrator is often subjected to lesser punishment than that meted out to the perpetrator of a similar offense against an adult. This inequity is being addressed in the Children's Bill awaiting presentation to Parliament.

CONCLUSION

In conclusion, while historically abuse and neglect of children were not expected by the society at large in Kenya, forms of child abuse, such as female genital mutilation, forced labor, physical punishment, and child marriage existed. Incidents of child abuse and neglect such as sexual abuse, abandonment, neglect, and child prostitution have emerged recently and are increasing rapidly.

Such incidents have been attributed to many factors ranging from poverty to changes taking place in families in Kenya. To respond to this, programs spearheaded mainly by NGOs have been initiated. The legal response to incidents of child abuse has been limited. However, the Children's Bill waiting presentation in Parliament, if enacted, stands to provide some hope to child protection in Kenya.

REFERENCES

ANPPCAN. (1994a). *A follow up study on views regarding child abuse in Kenya.* Nairobi: ANPPCAN.
ANPPCAN. (1994b). *Study of awareness and views on child abuse and neglect in Kenya rural and urban.* Nairobi: ANPPCAN.
ANPPCAN. (1997). *Baseline survey on child abuse and neglect in Korogocho slum.* ANPPCAN-Kenya Chapter. Nairobi: ANPPCAN.

ANPPCAN. (2000). *A survey of awareness and views regarding child abuse and child rights in selected communities in Kenya*. Nairobi: ANPPCAN.

Bikuri, K. (1999). Newspaper review on violence against adolescents in Kenya. Unpublished report. Nairobi: ANPPCAN.

Bwibo, N. O., & Onyango, P. (1987). *A report to WHO on child labor and health research*. Nairobi: University of Nairobi.

Government of Kenya. (1965). Penal Code. Nairobi: Government Printers.

Government of Kenya. (1996, 1997, 1998). National Development Plan. Nairobi: Government Printers.

Kattambo, V. W. M. (1996). *Violence against the girl child: A report prepared for research consortium on sexual harassment and abuse*. Nairobi: Public Law Institute.

Kayongo-Male, D., & Onyango, P. (1982). Psychological effects of child labor. In N. O. Bwibo & P. Onyango (Eds.), *Child labor and health: Proceedings of a WHO and University of Nairobi workshop on child labor* (pp. 15–20). Nairobi: City Printers.

Kayongo-Male, D., & Onyango, P. (1991). *The sociology of the African family* (3rd ed.). New York: Longman.

Kayongo-Male, D., & Walji, P. (1984). *Children at work in Kenya*. Nairobi: Oxford University Press.

Kilbride, J. E., & Kilbride, P. L. (1994). To have and to share culturally constituted fostering in familial settings. In J. Blacher (Ed.), *When there is no place like home* (pp. 307–310). Baltimore: Paul Books.

Lambo, T. A. (1969). *The child and the mother-child relationship in major cultures of Africa. Assignment* (pp. 612–674). New York: UNICEF.

Lynch, M., & Onyango, P. (1998). Planning and implementation of health programmes for working children. In C. Baris, G. K. Lieten, F. C. de Waal, & B. E. Wittenman al-Zwaini (Eds.), *Child health and child labor* (pp. 16–21). Amsterdam: Het Spinhuis.

Mbithi, P. M. (1969). *Rural level of living in eastern Kenya*. Unpublished master's thesis, Cornell University, Ithaca, NY.

Muli-Musiime, F., & Kilonzo, F. D. (1985). The conditions of children in adult penal institutions in Kenya. In N. O. Bwibo & P. Onyango (Eds.), *Children in especially disadvantaged circumstances: Proceedings of a regional workshop* (pp. 12–16). Nairobi: City Printing Press.

Nzewi, E. N. (1989). Effects of traditional and Western patterns of child-rearing on behaviour manifestations of Nigerian children. *Journal of African Psychology, 1*, 15–19.

Onyango, P. (1983). The working mother and the housemaid as a substitute: Its implications on the children. *Journal of Eastern African Research and Development, 13*, 24–31.

Onyango, P. (1996). *A review of commercial sexual exploitation in Kenya*. Nairobi: Child Welfare Society of Kenya.

Onyango, P., & Orwa, K. (1991). *A report to ILO on sample survey on child labor in Kenya*. Nairobi: University of Nairobi.

Onyango, P., Suda, C., & Orwa, K. (1991). *A study on street children in Kenya*. Report submitted to the Attorney General's Office. Nairobi: ANPPCAN.

UNICEF. (1989). *A report of proceedings of the Workshop on the Impact of Structural*

Adjustment on the Well-Being of the Vulnerable Groups in Kenya. Nairobi: UNICEF Country Office.

Walekwa, R. N. (1990). Background to legislation. In *A report of proceedings of the Workshop on the Rights of the Child* (pp. 26–31). Nairobi: ANPPCAN.

9

MALAYSIA

Mohd Sham Kasim

PROFILE OF MALAYSIA

Malaysia, encompassing 329,749 square kilometers and located in Southeast Asia, is comprised of thirteen states. The capital city is Kuala Lumpur. Malaysia is divided into two distinct peninsulas separated by the South China Sea: Peninsular Malaysia and East Malaysia. The government is a federal parliamentary democracy with a constitutional monarch. The population of Malay, Chinese, Indian, and indigenous tribes totals 22.2 million with an annual growth rate of 2.3 percent. The people of this country speak Malay, Cantonese, Hokkienese, Mandarin Chinese, English, Tamil, and several indigenous dialects. A number of religions are practiced, including Islam, Buddhism, Confucianism, Taoism, Christianity, Hinduism, Sikhism, and the Baha'i faith. The infant mortality rate is 9.7 per 1,000, and life expectancy is 68.9 years for males and 73.5 years for females. The country has compulsory education until the age of nine and a literacy rate of 93 percent. The gross national product per capita in 1998 was $3,600 (U.S.).

A CASE STUDY

A three-year-old boy was found abandoned and unconscious in the corner of the waiting room at the casualty department of a hospital. He was brought into the intensive care unit of the hospital and was intubated and ventilated immediately, as his breathing was irregular. He was also given blood, as he was very pale. There were bruises and scars over various parts of his body. Additionally, his anus was grossly dilated, and the edges were swollen and inflamed. The local TV crew took pictures of him and splashed them across the local newscasts a few hours before he died. Postmortem examinations showed that he had massive intraabdominal hemorrhages due to ruptures in the descending aorta, an artery that supplies blood to the lower part of the body and the lower limbs. Meanwhile, someone reported that she knew the child. Apparently, she had witnessed the child being abused by her neighbor, a thirty-year-old man who was looking after this child and his eight-year-old sister while the mother worked as a prostitute. The man was arrested and the sister was brought to the hospital because she also displayed visible signs of physical abuse. The doctors immediately recognized her because she had been admitted to the hospital previously due to suspicions that she was being abused. Eventually, the man admitted that he had shoved a metal rod into the boy's anus when he soiled his clothes. He reported that he was a drug addict who lived with the children's mother, who was also an addict and a prostitute. He was dependent on the money paid to him by the children's mother to sustain his addiction but claimed that when she could not pay him and failed to visit them, he became angry and began to abuse the children.

HISTORY

Child abuse and neglect in their modern context have a relatively short history in Malaysia. However, the passage of the Children and Young Persons Ordinance in 1947 suggests that the existence of child abuse must have been recognized in the country at that time. This ordinance, which was passed by the British colonial administration upon reassuming power over Malaysia from the Japanese Occupation Force after World War II, mainly emphasized detection and protection from childhood physical abuse and neglect. In addition, the ordinance addressed the issue of child labor. Children below the age of eight years were not permitted to work, and there were limitations on how long older children could work each day. However, no penalties were imposed on any person found to have maltreated a child or forced him/her to work beyond the period allowed for child labor. Little information is available regarding implementation of this ordinance in the first thirty years of its existence. The publication of Henry Kempe's article on the battered child syndrome in the *Journal of the American Medical Association* in 1962 led to interest about abuse among local pediatricians (Kempe, Silverman, Steele, Droegemuller, & Silver, 1962).

It was not until 1974 that the first article was published describing a series of child abuse cases detected at the University Hospital Kuala Lumpur (Woon, Chin, & Lam, 1974). Interest in abuse initially waned; however, few cases were reported from this hospital (Nathan & Woon, 1981), and those who discovered the abuse either retired or moved on to other disciplines in the hospital. Fortunately, due to an increasing number of cases identified in other parts of the country, the National Department of Social Welfare Services was persuaded to keep annual records of child abuse throughout the country, even though no clear definition of child abuse existed at that time (Children Protection Division, Department of Welfare Services, Malaysia 1997). During the first year of data collection, a total of eighty-nine cases were detected. The number of identified abuse cases remained about the same for the next few years, until 1990, when there was a sudden increase of reported cases to 511. The number of cases continued to escalate in the following years, with the total number of detected cases at 1,006 in 1996. The turning point occurred when Balasundram, a three-year-old child who was admitted with severe abuse, died due to his injuries. The highlighting of this case in the print and electronic media, and the subsequent release of information that other children had died prior to Balasundram also as a result of physical abuse prompted the authorities to become more vigilant.

In 1991, Malaysia passed the Child Protection Act, which made it mandatory for doctors to report abuse cases seen at their hospitals or clinics, either confirmed or suspected. Reported types of maltreatment of children included physical, sexual, and emotional abuse, and physical and emotional neglect. The most cases were reported by the Federal Territory, which includes the capital city of Kuala Lumpur, Selangor, and Penang. These states have a very high proportion of the population living in urban areas. In contrast, the states with few reported cases of child abuse, such as Terengganu, Perlis, and Kelantan, were those with a high proportion of the population living in rural areas. Although the rate of child abuse cases was low in comparison to developed countries, there was a high incidence in urban areas. Unfortunately, the data do not differentiate rates for different types of abuse. It appears, however, that most are cases of physical abuse, probably because the Children and Young Persons Ordinance of 1947 mentioned physical abuse and neglect, but not sexual abuse.

PREVALENCE

Another reason why child abuse received increased attention was the establishment of the Suspected Child Abuse and Neglect (SCAN) Team in 1985 at Hospital Kuala Lumpur, the biggest public hospital in Malaysia. Although it is located in the Federal Territory, it also serves surrounding areas of other states and caters to the health needs of low- and middle-income groups. As a result of developing the SCAN Team, the number of detected abuse cases at the hospital increased from 24 in 1985 to 140 in 1989 and 270 in 1993. By the end of 1996, a total of 1,872 cases were identified, including 970 cases of physical abuse, 328 cases of sexual abuse, and 520 cases of neglect and abandonment. Further, 45 percent (n = 836) of all cases were children below five years of age, including 23 percent (n = 435) who were one year of age, revealing that many small children were abused or neglected. The majority of the 970 physically abused children had mild injuries, including bruising and scars. However, many children were burned or scalded, or had cigarette burns, bone fractures, or even intracranial hemorrhaging. In a small number of cases, physical findings strongly suggest that these were cases of "shaken baby syndrome." Features of childhood sexual abuse were equally shocking. Specifically, many children presented with evidence of trauma on their external genitalia. Other children had gonorrhea or other sexually transmitted diseases, while a small minority was pregnant.

There are several reasons why the number of cases detected by the SCAN Team increased dramatically over time. There is a central casualty department where children are admitted to Hospital Kuala Lumpur and then sent to many different departments of the hospital. The employment of one full-time staff member to document and collate all cases of child abuse allowed more cases to be detected. Further, interest created by the SCAN Team led pediatricians in other public hospitals around the country to identify and document cases of child abuse as well. This resulted in an increased number of child abuse cases reported throughout the country, particularly in states with big urban populations.

Despite the success of SCAN, it was still felt that the 1947 ordinance was inadequate to deal with the extent of childhood abuse. This led to the promulgation and passage of the Child Protection Act in 1991, which gave very clear definitions of what constituted physical, sexual, and emotional abuse. In addition to mandating that doctors must report all confirmed or suspected cases of child abuse, it was determined that failure to do so would lead to a monetary fine. Others, such as teachers, childcare workers, and even members of the public, were encouraged to report suspected abuse. Social welfare officers were appointed as child protection officers to receive reports and document cases of child abuse and to place children in a place of safety if needed. The registry of child abuse cases was revamped to include more details about each case, allowing medical practitioners to retrieve information about suspected cases. The act also established a Child Protection Council who would advise the Department of Social Welfare Services to ensure effective implementation of the act. Child protection teams at state, district, and community levels were also formed to ensure continued protection of abused children. Even though SCAN Teams were not mandated under the new act, an increasing number of teams were created, such that most general hospitals have their own SCAN Teams.

DEFINITIONS

The Children and Young Persons Ordinance of 1947 gave no clear terminology of abuse except to define it loosely as "being assaulted, ill-treated or neglected." The Child Protection Act of 1991 gave very clear definitions of what constituted abuse, and this made reporting of cases easier. The various definitions of abuse are as follows: (a) Physical abuse occurs when there is substantial and observable injury to any part of the child's body as a result of the non-accidental application of force or an agent to the child's body that is evidenced by, among other things, a laceration, a contusion, an abrasion, a scar, a fracture or other bone injury, a dislocation, a sprain, hemorrhaging, the rupture of a viscus, a burn, a scald, the loss or alteration of consciousness or physiological functioning, or the loss of hair or teeth; (b) sexual abuse occurs when a child has taken part, as a participant or an observer, in any activity which is sexual in nature for the purposes of any pornographic, obscene, or indecent material photograph, recording, film, or videotape or for the purpose of sexual exploitation by any persons or another person's sexual gratification; and (c) emotional abuse occurs if there is substantial and observable impairment of the child's mental or emotional functioning that is evidenced by, among other things, a mental or behavioral disorder, including anxiety, depression, withdrawal, aggression, or delayed development (Laws of Malaysia, 1991).

Child abuse was initially considered a Western disease that was not expected to occur in Malaysia due to the strong family ties and caring attitudes shown by parents toward their children (Nathan & Woon, 1981). It was also thought that members of the extended family, as is a common practice in many Asian countries, would provide added support to parents in caring for their children. Thus, initial reports of child abuse were treated with disbelief and skepticism or considered isolated incidents. However, many did not realize that the rural-urban migration led to significant disintegration of the extended family, leaving nuclear families to cope without additional support in caring for their children.

With more cases of abuse being reported and with the realization that Malaysian society suffers from problems similar to those found in the West, it is now acceptable to acknowledge that child abuse occurs in Malaysia. As had happened in the West, physical abuse was recognized initially, and it was only later that cases of sexual abuse were identified. Thus, the SCAN Team of Hospital Kuala Lumpur (1996) reported twenty-four cases of physical abuse but only one case of sexual abuse in 1985, its first year of operation, whereas by 1996 more than a third were cases of sexual abuse. Politically, there was initial resistance to accepting abuse as a societal problem, especially sexual abuse. But when data showed increasing numbers of cases being reported, the government decided it was more pragmatic to devise strategies to prevent abuse than to ignore it altogether.

INVESTIGATION

Investigating Allegations of Child Abuse

The Child Protection Act of 1991 established a National Child Protection Council to coordinate an overall program for the identification and reporting of cases of child abuse and for provision of services for children in need of protection. The council consists of the Director General of the Department of Social Welfare Services and other members who are professionals in the fields of social work, education, medicine, law, and law enforcement.

Child protection teams headed by social welfare officers are formed at state and district levels to ensure that the activities designed are carried out. Other team members include individuals from nongovernmental organizations and the community. One problem with such volunteers, however, is that many have not been trained in counseling and are not allowed to do home visits to counsel parents and provide protection for children. Consequently, a few members have resigned from the child protection teams.

As discussed previously, doctors are mandated to report cases of suspected or confirmed child abuse to the social welfare department, and failure to do so could make them liable to a fine. In most public hospitals, pediatricians, obstetricians, psychiatrists, acute emergency department staff, and medical social workers are trained in the detection and management of abuse. The child suspected of being physically abused or neglected may be brought into the emergency or outpatient department by parents, social workers, teachers, police, or neighbors. Once abuse is confirmed, the child will be admitted to the hospital, unless the injuries are very mild, in which case the child may be discharged. In cases of suspected sexual abuse that are identified within seventy-two hours of the report being made, an urgent examination will be conducted. It is possible to identify sexually transmitted fluids up until this point. If the abuse has occurred earlier, it is not possible to do so. The specific management and the course of action taken in investigations of sexual abuse and physical abuse are illustrated in Figures 9.1 and 9.2, respectively, and these intervention strategies are discussed in more detail below.

Repeated history taking and physical examination of a child victim can traumatize the child further. This is especially true in cases of sexual abuse. In our experience, the children may be less open to questioning the second time around. Physical examination of a child who has been sexually abused is often severely resisted by the child, and the child may need sedation. This resistance may be worse if a repeat examination is needed. Thus, doctors are given instructions to record their findings systematically and comprehensively so that these records can be referred without the need for further history taking or examination. Videotaping of the interview and examination has also been used on occasions in a Syariah (Islamic) court but not in a civil court.

Figure 9.1
Guideline in Management of Sexual Child Abuse

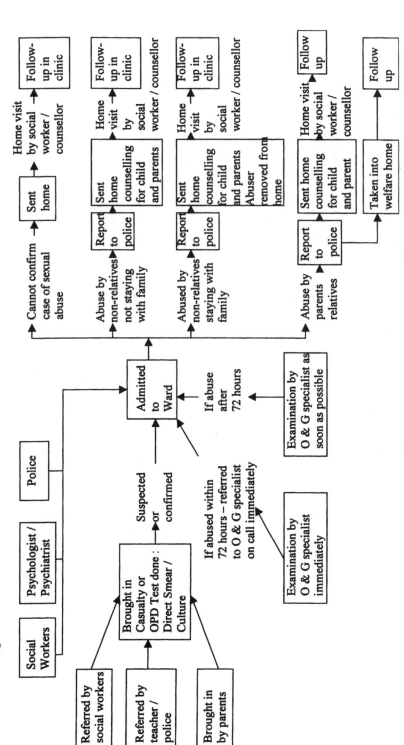

Notes: OPD = Out Patient Department; O & G = Obstetrics and Gynecology

Figure 9.2
Guideline in Management of Child Abuse and Neglect Cases

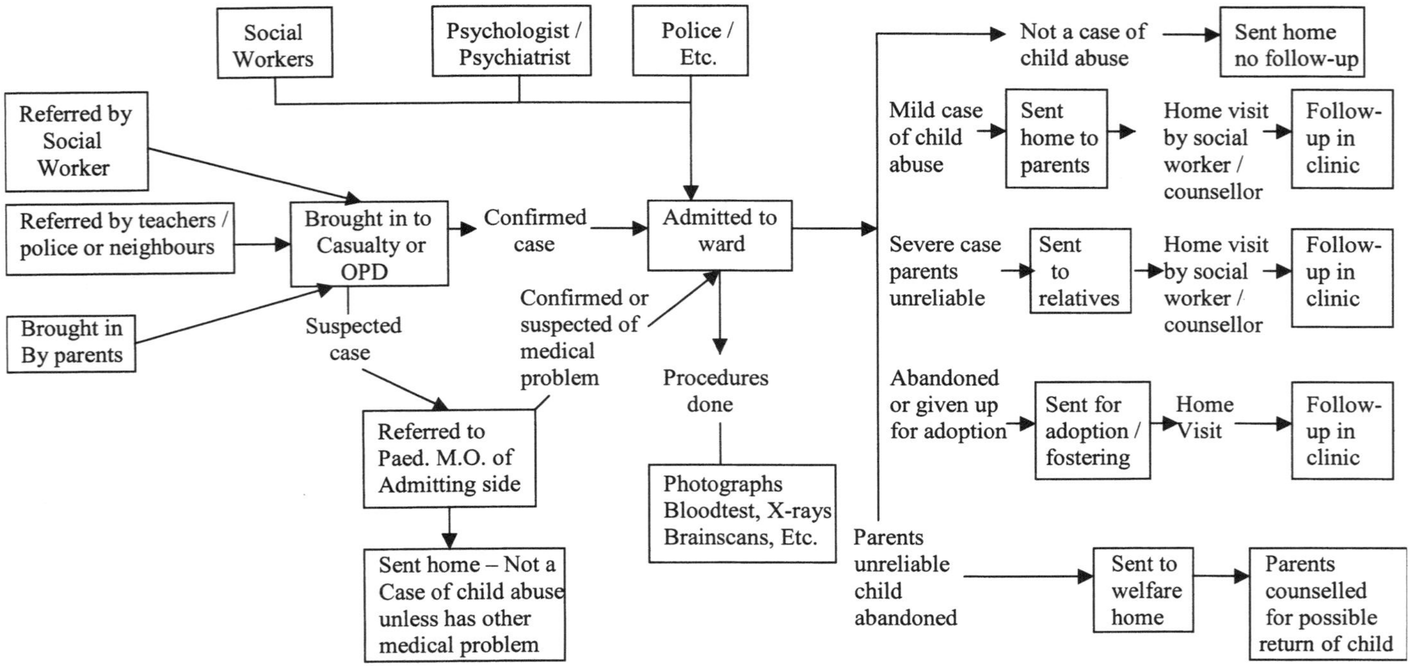

Notes: OPD = Out Patient Department; Paed. M.O. = Pediatric Medical Officer

CHILD PROTECTION

There are several lines of defense to protect children from child abuse. First, a member of the public, on justifiable suspicion that a child is abused or neglected, may report the case either directly to a social worker or through a hot line. This may be done without having to disclose the informant's identity. By allowing people to make anonymous abuse reports, it is hoped that as many children as possible will be protected.

Identified children can then be admitted to a place of safety, which may be a hospital, a children's welfare home run by the social welfare department, or any other place considered safe by the child protection officer. If the child's home is considered safe or if the home environment is modified such that safety is assured, then the child is sent home.

To ensure that abuse is not repeated, home visits are made by the social welfare officer, with the frequency of these visits dependent on the determined risk of repeat abuse to the child. At present, these visits are conducted by the social welfare officer. Due to overloaded schedules, however, it is proposed that a Child Protection Team member from the local community, after suitable training in counseling, do the home visiting.

Intervention Strategies of the Protective Services

At present, most abuse cases are identified by a doctor when the children are brought in for suspected physical or sexual abuse or because of injuries sustained by the child (Kasim, Shafie, & Cheah, 1994; Nathan & Woon, 1981). A small number are abandoned by their parents at birth in front of public buildings, often due to social problems or because of abnormalities or handicaps in the child (Kasim et al., 1989). Another means of detection is through the hot line established by the Department of Social Welfare Services. However, the department has found the effectiveness of the hot line to be unsatisfactory because less than 5 percent of the cases could be confirmed as abuse by the social welfare officers investigating these cases (Social Welfare Department, 1993).

Internationally, 30–40 percent of confirmed cases of abuse have been quoted in hot lines similarly established. Possibly, due to the shortage of social workers, there is a delay in home visits, resulting in most of the physical signs, such as bruises, abrasions, welts, and superficial lacerations having healed, and leaving minimal telltale signs by the time of the social welfare officer's visit.

It is the stated policy of the Department of Social Welfare Services that an abused or neglected child should remain with his/her family or be returned home as quickly as possible. In 1996, 118 out of 184 children (64 percent) were returned home after discharge from the hospital, and 19 out of the 184 children (10 percent) were sent to live with their relatives. Children are only separated from their immediate family members when the safety of the child cannot be assured. In Malaysia, there is currently no system to remove an abusing parent from the family home so that a child can return, although this has been proposed to the authorities.

If it is thought that a child's life or safety is at stake, and the parents cannot be relied on to assure the child's well-being, he/she will be brought into a juvenile court where a proper place of safety is determined. At present, a few alternatives are available. Some children are sent to stay with relatives, often grandparents, uncles and aunts, older siblings, or other close family members. In 1996, 10 percent were sent to live with their relatives, while another 20 percent found their way to welfare homes, most staying there briefly until taken in by a relative or sent back home when their safety had been assured.

Some children are sent to group homes, where four to six children, all of whom have similar problems, are taken in by a married couple who act as foster parents. Fostering of children by individual prospective parents has not yet been accepted in Malaysia, particularly because many of those looking for foster children have the ultimate objective of adopting them, presumably making them unsuitable for temporary custody.

A decision about whether to prosecute a case is usually made after discussion between the pediatrician and the social worker in charge of the case. In cases of physical abuse, a police report is made and prosecution is decided on depending on the severity of abuse and whether it has occurred on many previous occasions. The majority of sexual abuse cases brought to the hospital are reported to the police. However, some parents bring children into the emergency department of the local hospital wanting to be assured that there is no evidence of physical trauma and that the hymen is intact. Once assured, a police report is not usually made.

LEGAL INNOVATIONS

As mentioned above, the abused child is brought before a juvenile court to ensure his or her safety, sometimes by placing the child elsewhere if the parents or guardians are found to be unsuitable or unreliable. However, the suspected abuser usually appears in a civil court to hear the charges against him/her.

Child Witnesses

Malaysian laws were inherited from the British legal system and colonial laws. Based on these laws, a child less than fourteen years of age is not allowed to be sworn into court as a witness on the assumption that the child does not have the capacity to understand how to tell the truth. It is felt that the child might go into "flights of fancy and invent stories" (Munir, 1991).

Thus, many Malaysian courts require corroborative evidence from independent sources before a child's testimony is taken into account (Munir, 1993b). Corroborative evidence means different things in different courts. In some, it means that evidence has to be supported by another person, usually an adult, who has seen the act being perpetrated. In other cases, however, it can include a doctor's report. At the present time, there are still judges and lawyers who question the reliability of a child as a witness, quoting the old English law that children are prone to fantasy and cannot differentiate facts from fiction (Munir, 1992).

The child is also required to appear in court to testify in the presence of the accused. This can be very intimidating, particularly in cases of sexual abuse. Thus, if the accused chooses to fight the case in court, the case often gets thrown out, as the child either recants his or her disclosure or makes conflicting statements when cross-examined by the defense attorney. In most cases, to obtain a conviction, the accused needs to admit guilt at the start of the trial, there needs to be an adult witness to the offense, or there needs to be uncontroversial corroborating evidence regarding the offenses.

For example, a judge in a Syariah (Islamic) court had accepted videotaped evidence into court (Munir, 1991). In the four cases where this was allowed, a conviction was achieved because the accused admitted guilt upon viewing the videotape. However, no other Syariah court and not a single civil court have followed this judge's lead. In a civil court case, another judge interposed himself between the child and the abuser such that face-to-face contact between the abuser and abused was avoided. It was recommended to this judge that a screen be placed between the accused and the abused. This was not common practice in the Malaysian court system. However, he took it on himself to act as the screen and protect the child from having to face the alleged perpetrator. It has been our experience that convictions in Malaysia have been obtained only when evidence is overwhelming or when the accused has admitted guilt. In cases where there is no corroborating evidence or no adults witnessing the events, the accused is often found not guilty.

Penalties Imposed on Conviction for Child Abuse and Neglect

According to the Child Protection Act of 1991, any person can be found guilty of an offense if he/she abuses, neglects, or abandons a child or exposes the child to abuse and neglect. Upon conviction of such a crime, the individual shall be liable to a jail sentence not exceeding five years, or to a fine of not more than RM 10,000 (U.S. $3,800), or both.

Additionally, in lieu of a jail sentence, the court can allow the convicted person to be free on probation for good behavior while they undergo counseling and psychotherapy. If the convicted person fails to comply with any of the conditions imposed, he/she will be liable to the penalties previously discussed (Laws of Malaysia, 1991).

If the abuse is severe, ends in death, or is a case of sexual abuse, however, the charge can be transferred to the Penal Code. For the charge of sexual abuse to be transferred to the Penal Code, there must be sexual intercourse. The decision to do so is usually made by the prosecuting officer. Once convicted, the punishment according to the Penal Code (1950) is imprisonment of five to twenty years and/or whipping (Penal Code Act 574, 1950 Section 376).

A few measures have been instituted to decrease the incidence of child abuse and neglect in Malaysia. In all the major religions of the country, which include Islam, Buddhism, Hinduism, and Christianity, a couple has to attend a course in parenting before the marriage is sanctioned by the appointed clergy of the faith. It is hoped that this course will prepare the couple to be better parents in the future. To ensure better care for the children, especially in the first four years of life, creches or day-care centers, which are subsidized and affordable to low-income families, are built at places of work and close to the home.

To help those who are below the poverty level, the government gives a small stipend monthly per family. In addition, for every child who is underweight, a food basket containing nutritious food is given monthly. It is hoped that these two measures will help prevent severe malnutrition among these children.

Public Awareness

Malaysian society has been made aware of child abuse because of extensive coverage by the media. There is seldom a day when a case of child abuse is not reported on the local television or in the papers. No research studies have been conducted, however, to assess the impact this coverage has had on the understanding and prevention of child abuse. In addition to wide coverage by the media, the passage of the Child Protection Act in 1991 has also helped to make the public more aware of the conditions that constitute abuse and of the punishments that can be meted out to perpetrators.

CONCLUSION

It can be seen that child abuse and neglect constitute a severe social problem in Malaysia. The data collected by the Department of Social Welfare Services have shown that it occurs throughout the country, although the problem is more acute in the major urban centers. The report from the SCAN Team, Hospital Kuala Lumpur shows that all forms of child abuse are found, with the pattern reflecting that of Western countries.

However, there are still many weaknesses in the way in which the problem and each individual case are being handled. The Department of Social Welfare Services, the agency assigned the responsibility of designing an effective abuse prevention program, is given too few resources, and this has affected deployment and training of staff. Most cases of child abuse have not been properly investigated and documented, and this has made prosecution difficult. Court proceedings tend not to be child friendly. That is, children younger than fourteen years of age are not allowed to make sworn statements, and their evidence has to be corroborated, making it difficult for the prosecution to prove such cases. It is hoped that the problems highlighted here will be overcome so that children will get the protection they so desperately need.

REFERENCES

Amar, H., Woan, W., Hjh, Y., & Nurani, N. K. (1996). Prevalence of childhood sexual abuse among Malaysian para medical students. *Child Abuse and Neglect: The International Journal, 20,* 487–492.

Annual report of the Suspected Child Abuse and Neglect (SCAN) Team, Hospital Kuala Lumpur. (1996).

Chandran, V., Kasim, M. S., & Shafie, H. M. (1994). Social-culture factors leading to physical child abuse and neglect—A case-control study of 35 families admitted to the paediatric wards, Hospital Kuala Lumpur. *Malaysian Journal of Child Health, 6,* 22–31.

Cheah, I., Kasim, M. S., & Shafie, H. M. (1994). Intracranial hemorrhage and child abuse. *Annals of Tropical Paediatrics, 14,* 325–328.

Child Protection Division, Department of Welfare Services, Malaysia. Department of Social Welfare Services Report (1997).

Kasim, M. S. (1989). Impact of child abuse and neglect on professionals in developing countries. *Journal Perubatan UKM, 11,* 65–71.

Kasim, M. S. (1991). Multi-disciplinary approach in the management of child abuse and neglect. *Malaysian Journal of Child Health, Supplementary Issue,* 1–120.

Kasim, M. S. (1993). Epidemiology and clinical aspects of child abuse in Malaysia. *Journal of Malaysian Society of Health, 11,* 35–39.

Kasim, M., Cheah, I., & Sameon, H. (1995). Osteogenesis imperfect and non-accidental injury: Problems in diagnosis and management. *Medical Journal of Malaysia, 50,* 170–175.

Kasim, M. S., Cheah, I., & Shafie, H. M. (1995). Childhood death from physical abuse. *Child Abuse and Neglect: The International Journal, 19,* 847–854.

Kasim, M. S., George, R., Kassim, K., Mumtaj Begum, M. S., Cherian, M. P., Tajuddin, A. K., Chandran, V., Anan, A., Reddy, R., Singh, J., & Heyworth, B. (1989). Child abuse and neglect as seen in General Hospital, Kuala Lumpur: A two-year study. *Medical Journal of Malaysia, 44,* 111–112.

Kasim, M. S., Shafie, H., & Cheah, I. (1994). Social factors in relation to physical abuse in Kuala Lumpur, Malaysia. *Child Abuse and Neglect: The International Journal, 18,* 401–407.

Kasim, M. S., Shafie, H., Kassim, K., & Selvarajah, T. (1991). Child abuse and neglect (SCAN) team at General Hospital, Kuala Lumpur. *Malaysian Journal of Child Health, Supplementary Issue, 1*, 126–132.

Kasmini K., Cheah, Y. C., Zasmani, S., Mohd, A. S., & Rosdinom, R. (1994). Child abuse of schizophrenic parents: A controlled study. *Malaysian Journal of Psychiatry, 2*, 32–46.

Kasmini, K., & Kasim, M. S. (1995). Child sexual abuse—Psychosexual aspects of 101 cases seen in an urban Malaysian setting. *Child Abuse and Neglect: The International Journal, 19*, 793–799.

Kassim, K. (1993). Incest. *Journal of the Malaysian Society of Health, 2*, 45–48.

Kempe, C. H., Silverman, F. N., Steele, B. F., Droegmeuller, W., & Silver, H. K. (1962). The battered child syndrome. *Journal of the American Medical Association, 181*, 17–24.

Laws of Malaysia, Act 468 (1991). Child Protection Act 1991.

Malayan Union Ordinance. (1947). Children and Young Persons Ordinance, No. 33, pp. 231–252.

Munir, A. B. (1991). Video-taped evidence of children in Malaysia. *Current Law Journal, 3*, xciv–xciii.

Munir, A. B. (1992, March). Child abuse and the law of evidence. *Malaysian Law Journal, 1*, lxv–lxxii.

Munir, A. B. (1993a). Child protection: Principle and application. *Child Abuse Review, 2*, 119–126.

Munir, A. B. (1993b). The exception to the hearsay rules in child abuse cases. *Current Law Journal, 1*, xix–xxi.

Munir, A. B., & Yasin, S.H.M (1993). Child abuse: Facing the inadequacies of protection afforded by the law. *Malaysian Law Journal, 1*, xix–xxi.

Nathan, L., & Woon, T. H. (1981). Child abuse in an urban center in Malaysia. *Child Abuse and Neglect, 9*, 241–248.

Norhamidah, M. S., & Mohd, A. (1995). Physical and sexual abuse amongst teenage runaways. *Malaysian Journal of Child Health, 7*, 133–140.

Penal Code (1950), Act 574, Section 376, p. 136.

Reddy, R. (1991). Malaysian law and child abuse. *Malaysian Journal of Child Health, Supplementary Issue, 1*, 105–118.

Social Welfare Department, Malaysia. (1993 Press release).

Woon, T. H., Chin, C., & Lam, K. L. (1974). Battered child syndrome in a Malaysian hospital. *Medical Journal of Malaysia, 28*, 239–243.

10

MEXICO

Antonio Estrada

PROFILE OF MEXICO

The United Mexican States, located south of the United States in North America, has an area of 2 million square kilometers. The capital is Mexico City and the population of 95 million consists of Indian-Spanish (60 percent), Indian (30 percent), Caucasian (9 percent), and other ethnic groups (1 percent). The national language is Spanish. The religious faiths vary; 89 percent of the people are Roman Catholic, 6 percent are Protestant, and 5 percent are of other religions. The infant mortality rate is 30 per 1,000 and the life expectancy is seventy years for males and seventy-six years for females. The literacy rate is 89 percent, and education is mandatory from the ages of six to eighteen. The government is a federal republic with universal suffrage at age eighteen. In 1998 the gross national product per capita was $3,970 (U.S.).

A CASE STUDY

Adolfo, a nine-year-old boy who was abandoned by his parents, now works on the streets of Mexico City. In the morning he sells candy, and in the afternoon he works at his other "job." He paints his face and becomes a clown, ready to work on the dangerous avenues of Mexico City, where he juggles four oranges in an effort to earn some coins. At the end of the day, he may have earned three to four dollars, enough money to survive in the city for another day. At night, he goes to his "home," one of the town's sewers. He is a new "worker" on the Mexican avenues. Soon, he will probably be like the older workers, and will smoke cigars, marijuana, or other illicit drugs. Adolfo is the newest of 15,000 children living and working in the streets of Mexico.

HISTORY

Historically, the world has often ignored the mistreatment of children because the idea that children were suffering at the hands of their parents was unthinkable. Thus, the government and society denied the scope and seriousness of child abuse. We now know that the extent of past violence against children has been underestimated. As Besharov (1990) pointed out, "child abuse and neglect remained largely a hidden problem" (p. 7). Since Kempe and his colleagues coined the term "battered child syndrome" (Ciccheti & Carlson, 1991), however, we now think differently.

Child abuse in industrialized countries is considered a twentieth century phenomenon (Fontana & Moolman, 1992). Although it was only "recently discovered" (Steinmetz, 1987, p. 728), child abuse is not new. It is rooted in the early history of humanity and cuts across time, national boundaries, and all sectors of society (Ciccheti & Carlson, 1991). No country is immune to child abuse.

Before the Conquest

Even though battered child syndrome is a newly coined term, it is not difficult to find evidence of child abuse even in ancient Mexican tribes. For example, ancient records reveal that child abuse was practiced by Indian parents. Thompson (1970/1975) states that "children that were chosen to be sacrificed to the deity were tied up to a pole and lashed on the chest with a thorny branch till the child died" (p. 222). Gimpera (1975) tells us that Aztec children were forced to accompany their parents in war. This was done to teach them the art of war so they could defend themselves when they were older. However, the experience of war, the danger of being captured as a hostage and sacrificed to deities of the enemy, and the experience of witnessing violence and cruelty, including witnessing one's own father's death, might be traumatic events for a young child.

Aztec children and adolescents were also sacrificed to various gods in ancient times. "Many children were sacrificed or thrown down the well" in order to appease the gods Tlaloc or Huitzilopochtli. This was done so the gods would "maintain the sun in its course and the world in its existence, to ensure the success of the corn harvest, or to implore to the God of rain" (Thompson, 1970/1975, p. 27). If the sacrifice was offered to the god of fire, the children were burned. If it was offered to the god of water, they were drowned. If it was offered to the god of hunting, they were riddled with arrows.

The Mayans in the southeastern part of Mexico also practiced child sacrifice and often kidnapped and sold children for such sacrifices (Morley, 1946/1947). Additionally, they practiced several social forms of child maltreatment. Specifically, orphans were generally sold to work in the landlord's home, where they were forced to do work too strenuous for their age.

The ancient Mayans also practiced the deforming of their children's skulls, which they considered a symbol of beauty. According to Peterson (1959/1966), this practice fulfilled a social function (a nobility symbol) and had aesthetic value. Five days after birth, boards were placed behind a child's head and in front of the forehead and left there for several days for the purpose of disfiguring the front and back of the head. Landa, a Spanish missionary, wrote that this practice endangered many children's lives (Peterson, 1959/1966). According to Riva Palacio (1953a), "many of these children died in the operation" (p. 231). Because crossed eyes were also considered beautiful, many parents placed a ball of resin between newborns' eyebrows to encourage their eyes to cross. Additionally, children's ears, lips, and noses were pierced and their teeth were mutilated in order to put in adornments of gold and jade.

Adolescents were not exempt from maltreatment by their parents. According to Morley (1946/1947), in the patriarchal society, women were taught to show respect to men. When young ladies gave water to their fathers or older brothers, they were forbidden to look into their eyes. If a mother found her daughter looking into a man's eyes, she punished the girl by putting chile or pepper in her eyes. Chile was also smeared on a girl's genitals if she lost her virginity before marriage.

Among the Nahuatls, abusive rites of initiation were practiced to introduce boys into manhood. One of them was the *prohijacion* (adoption) ceremony (similar to the "cavalry custom"). According to Riva Palacio (1953a), this investiture was executed in the following manner: The godfather of the boy passed a tiger's claw over his nude body until he began to bleed. If he could not withstand the pain, he did not pass the test, was not considered an adult, and could not receive an adult's privileges and responsibilities. But the ultimate challenge for a boy was to stay awake all night in the cold without going near a fire. In order to play the well-known game patoli (similar to cards or dice), the boy had to pass an initiation rite that involved introducing a stick in his mouth as far as the throat. If he was able to bear the pain, he acquired the right to play. These ceremonies were practiced in order to establish a demarcation between childhood and adulthood. Men needed to learn to be strong, brave, and capable of enduring any pain and suffering.

To discourage robbery, drunkenness, and gambling (considered the worst behavior in youth), parents punished their children at home. According to Soutelle (1956/1974), "the punishment was severe on lazy children. The parents beat them with a cactus and forced them to smell smoke from burning chile" (p. 173). This punishment was quite inhumane because the child victim experienced a sensation of choking and severe nose, eye, and throat irritation.

Aztec children, however, received the most severe discipline. If a child misbehaved, he or she was "purified" with cold water, stones, sticks, or with a nettle (an irritable herb). Others were locked for a short time in a dark and humid room to teach them obedience to their parents (Reed, 1966/ 1972).

All of these disciplinary methods were intended to help children develop into respectable adults. Yet, in modern times, we can clearly see that they were abusive and reveal the existence of child maltreatment even in ancient Mexico.

After the Conquest

Child abuse did not disappear when the Spaniards conquered the Indians in 1521 (Collin, 1997). With the arrival of the Europeans, new forms of child abuse emerged. According to Malvido (n.d.), the most common forms were infanticide and exploitative child work.

Indians who were exploited by the Spaniards lived permanently in debt to their masters. One way to lessen their financial burdens was to abandon their children. Many parents hoped that some landowner would find their children and provide them with food. Known as "children with unknown fathers," "children of the church," or *expósitos* (abandoned children) (Malvido, n.d., p. 124), children were collected by landowners and sent to work on their ranches. Additionally, when a single Indian woman became pregnant as a result of being raped by a Spanish soldier or because of adultery or prostitution, she often abandoned her child or threw it in the streets to die.

During the following 300 years of Mexico's colonial period, many impoverished native families were unable to care for their children. Consequently, the number of *expósitos* increased dramatically. Abandoned children soon became a social problem, as is evidenced by a letter from the king of Spain dated October 3, 1533: "I have been informed that in the land there are a number of Spanish sons that have been born of Indians (half-breed children of Spanish and Indian descent). Many of them are lost, dead, and others have been sacrificed" (Riva Palacio, 1987, p. 21). The *Diario de Mexico* (Mexican Daily) reported in 1805 that "every day children's bodies appeared on the streets of the city, thrown from the roofs" (Malvido, n.d., p. 124).

Child abuse did not cease with the end of the Spanish conquest in 1821 (Collin, 1997). The *hacendados* (large state landowners) became the new masters. Native people and *mestizos* (half-breed children of Spaniards and Indians) continued living in a hopeless situation. Due to illicit liaisons between female Indians and *hacendados*, the population of *expósitos* increased.

Those illegitimate, unwanted, and abandoned children had a hapless fate—
to be thrown from the roofs to die or to be taken in and used as a cheap
source of labor (Blanco, n.d.).

In Modern Society

Child abuse is also a reality in modern Mexico. Before the end of the
1970s, child abuse was not viewed as a social problem because it was believed that parents had the right to punish their children and nobody had
the right to interfere. The problem of child abuse was not suspected by
physicians, lawyers, psychologists, scholars, or politicians. Society as a whole
was not concerned with the problem, and only a few people acknowledged
this disturbing situation.

The first known case of child abuse in Mexico was reported in 1965 at
the Pediatric Hospital of Mexico City (Foncerrada, 1982). But it was not
until 1968 that awareness of child abuse was raised in the medical community (Loredo et al., 1984). Specifically, Usbaldo Riojas and Carlos Manzano (1968) published an influential article in the *Jornadas Pediatricas del
IMSS* (Pediatric Journal of the Mexican Institute of Social Security).
Through X-ray diagnosis, they noted that there were subdural hematomas
evident in children's long bones. They concluded that these children had
not suffered the accidents that had been reported to their physicians. Rather,
they had been severely beaten by their parents or guardians (Loredo, et al.,
1984).

This study alerted medical professionals to a new area of study and contributed to the organization of a national congress that helped to awaken
other professionals and the general public to the problem of child abuse.
According to Osorio (1985), a series of meetings was held in the 1970s to
address physical child abuse issues. In 1971, the Mexican Institute of Social
Security organized a congress on child abuse with an emphasis on the psychiatric, medical, and legal aspects of the problem. In 1977, the Mexican
Society of Pediatrics organized a symposium on child abuse. In 1979, to
commemorate the International Year of the Child, the International Symposium on Child Abuse was organized in Mexico City. The result of these
meetings included publication of essays, the organization of local committees to work on behalf of abused children, a commitment to request federal
authorities to legislate reforms that would prevent any form of child abuse,
and the recognition of a dearth of studies on child abuse, leading to a commitment to do more research.

As a result of this meeting, Jaime Markovich published an influential book
in 1981 entitled *Tengo Derecho a la Vida: Prevencion e Identificacion del
Niño Maltratado* (I Have a Right to Live: The Prevention and Treatment
of Child Abuse). This book was pivotal in triggering increased social awareness of child abuse (Ayala & Cruz, 1983; Loredo et al., 1984).

The symposium also made an impression at the federal level. On January 10, 1977, Family Integral Development (DIF) was created in order to work on behalf of the family (Martinez, 1982). On December 20, 1982, the federal government decreed that DIF would work to protect abused children (DIF, 1983). This federal agency was assigned responsibility to investigate the extent of the problem and its causes, to develop methods of prevention and treatment, and to offer medical, legal, and psychological support to abused children (Ruiz, 1985).

These meetings also made an impression on researchers. Some of them began to inquire about child abuse issues. As a contribution to this new field, Loredo et al. (1984) reviewed cases of suspected child abuse identified by the National Institute of Pediatrics over the previous fourteen years (1971–1984). The main purpose of this study was to identify characteristics of abused children and their perpetrators, factors that triggered abuse, specific data that led to the diagnosis of abuse, and the responses that were made by physicians. In summary, Loredo et al. found that the mean age of abused children was three years, nine months. There was no gender difference on likelihood of being an abuse victim. The mother was the main perpetrator in most cases, and her mean age was twenty-seven years, four months. Most parents came from low socioeconomic classes. Aggression against the child was mainly triggered by severe family dysfunction and alcoholism (Loredo, et al., 1984; 1986).

In 1985, Ariza et al. published the first case of Munchausen syndrome by proxy. (According to Zumwalt and Hirsch "Munchausen syndrome by proxy occurs when a parent or guardian falsifies a child's medical history . . . including untruthful descriptions of symptoms, alteration of body fluids before laboratory testing, or by actually causing an illness or injury by poisoning or injuring the child" [1987, p. 276]). In the middle of the 1980s, physicians, nurses, social workers, and other professionals were made aware of the problem. This time, they were in agreement that child abuse "is a growing reality in México" (Loredo, 1994, p. 7).

DEFINITION OF ABUSE

When the reality of child abuse was made known and more professionals became involved in identifying and treating abuse, it became necessary to define the term "child abuse." Because the majority of professionals who pioneered this field were physicians, child abuse was viewed as any physical injury caused by parents or a guardian. Other professionals had a wider point of view. They included the neglectful behavior of parents, emotional and sexual abuse, child exploitation, and any other behavior that hindered the healthy development of the child (Loredo, 1994; Osorio, 1985). Despite disagreement on definitions, most professionals considered abuse to occur "when a child suffers occasional or habitual physical or emotional violence, or both, by omission or action, but always intentionally, nonaccidentally, by parents, guardians or other responsible persons" (DIF, 1986, p. 12).

This awakening of medical professionals was not an awakening of society as a whole, politicians, or people in academia. As an issue of academic study, child abuse was essentially ignored. Presently, there are no required or elective classes on family violence in the curriculum of any university in Mexico, nor are there any professional journals dealing with this issue. Mexico lacks reliable national statistics on abuse, and there are only a few Spanish books dealing with the issue of child abuse in Mexico.

Awareness of child abuse has increased to the point that newspapers and the media have begun to report frequently on the problem. Some universities now include topics on family violence in classes, and some are conducting research on the problem. For example, at the University of Montemorelos, Estrada (1995) conducted research looking at gender differences in child abuse. Obeso (1995) completed research on adolescent abuse and the age and educational level of parents. In 1998, Perez published research on domestic abuse. As of 1999, Estrada was conducting research on religion and abuse.

Results of such research have furthered our understanding of the dynamics of abuse. Specifically, violence committed by mothers appears more common than that by fathers. The tendency for mothers to be more abusive than fathers is intensified when the target of abuse is a daughter. Additionally, unemployed fathers seem to be more abusive than employed fathers. Further, it appears that the younger the age of the parent and the lower the educational level of the mother, the higher the frequency of severe abuse (Obeso, 1995). Research also reveals harmful effects of abuse for children even when they are not the direct target of the abuse. Specifically, when the mother experiences abuse by her husband, the adolescent child is less likely to succeed scholastically.

CHILD PROTECTION AND LEGAL INNOVATIONS

Child Protective Services

As we have seen, child abuse is a growing reality in Mexico. Fortunately, public and political awareness of the problem is growing. Government agencies and nongovernmental organizations (NGOs) have been created to deal with the issue of child abuse.

Mexican Legislation (Protecting Child Victims)

Work on behalf of children is not something new in Mexico. In fact, the first law to protect abandoned and neglected children dates from 1533. Due to the seriousness of the problem of abandoned children, the king of Spain ordered that these children be taken care of and nourished in special lodgings in Christian Spanish towns (Riva Palacio, 1987). In 1683, the College of Belem was founded to take care of poor Creole girls (Vazques, n.d.). In 1763, King Charles III of Spain contributed to the construction of a shelter for *expósitos* and orphaned children (DIF, 1983).

Prevention

In recent Mexican history, the federal office of Integral Family Development (DIF) was reorganized in 1982 to work on behalf of abused children. Its general objectives were to (a) assess the social situation of the family and its environment, (b) promote the healthy growth of children, and (c) take immediate action to detect and prevent all cases of child abuse (DIF, 1986).

The specific objectives of DIF are to (a) protect the abused child by giving social, legal, and medical assistance; (b) teach parents disciplinary skills and assist them in changing their dysfunctional patterns; (c) facilitate family integration; (d) promote systematic research conducive to discovering the causes and consequences of child abuse; (e) promote children's rights; and (f) expose the problem of abuse in order to eliminate it and promote the well-being of the family at the local, regional, and national level (DIF, 1986; Manterola, 1983).

This was an advancement in the 1980s, but it was not enough. There was still a need for specific and powerful laws. For example, a 1986 law that protected children contained only five articles. Fortunately, this law was revised in 1992 and now contains nineteen articles. Under this law, children must be cared for and protected by the state. Article 25 of the General Law states that all institutions belonging to the National System of Health must offer their services to those who need them, especially to vulnerable people (e.g., children who are abused or neglected). All children have the right to receive the following basic services: vaccination (free and obligatory), medical attention, and nourishment (Casamadrid, 1994).

Unfortunately, this revision still contained some anachronistic articles. For example, Article 423 in the Civil Law gave parents or guardians the right to punish their children with "moderation." Article 347 in the Criminal Law made reference to the nonguilty parents or guardians who have beaten their children with the "intention of reprimand" (Manterola, 1983). Fortunately, these gaps have been eliminated by the latest reforms. Now, children are protected against all forms of abuse. The anachronistic Article 423 has been modified to say that "those who have the custody [of children] have the right to correct their children without abuse. . . . Judges have the authority to make any decision necessary to prevent further abuse by those who have parental authority" (DIF, 1998, p. 2). Article 444 affirms that parents can lose their parental rights when they abuse their children, and Article 447 allows judges to request psychological treatment for abusive parents. Article 180 says that if a child is in danger at home, judges have the authority to send the child to a foster home or to a public institution (DIF, 1998).

Mexico signed the Universal Declaration of the Rights of the Child promoted by the United Nations that was approved by the General Assembly on November 20, 1989. Its fifty-four articles establish that children shall be protected by both family and state. For example, Article 6 affirms that each child has the right to live. Article 19 affirms that "each state must take legislative, administrative, social, and educational measures to protect children from all forms of physical or emotional violence. Children must be protected against any form of sexual or labor exploitation" (DIF, n.d., pp. 3–6).

This legislation is better than previous laws, but legal experts believe there are still gaps. For example, the exact definition of child abuse is not clear. Further, judges do not know whether all types of corporal punishment are classified as child abuse.

Others suggest that the law needs to be more specific regarding the sentencing of guilty parents. Medellin (1996) says, "It is necessary that new reforms be made to the Civil and Criminal Laws in order to typify and sanction more severely the abusers of the young" (p. 10). Interviews with lawyers and social workers reveal a lack of political commitment to address issues of child abuse and neglect. Even though the laws have been reformed at the federal level, there is still a gap at the state level. Currently, there are some states where an Office of the Protection of Minors does not even exist.

Investigation and Remedial Services

In its policies, DIF encourages people to report (anonymously) any suspected cases of child abuse. Hot lines are available to receive calls at all times. These reports can be made by phone, in writing, or by a personal visit to the Office of the Protection of Minors. In all cases, the informer's anonymity and confidentiality are guaranteed. The report is reviewed by an interdisciplinary team whose objective is to provide the best treatment for the child, the perpetrator, and the family. When a child is in danger, he or she is sent to a foster home or *casa hogar* (dorm). The DIF coordinates twelve public and thirty-nine private boarding facilities for children from birth to age 3 and from ages 3 to 11 (Colin, 1994). The perpetrator is not allowed to visit or communicate with the child.

TREATMENT

Generally, treatment for the child begins with medical attention and is followed by psychiatric or psychological intervention. The family is sent to family therapy and is given training in educational skills. If treatment is successful, the child is reintegrated into the family. A social worker then visits the family periodically to verify that the abuse has ceased (Barrera, 1998).

Treatment for the child and his or her family takes between three and four months, after which the child can be reintegrated into the family. The aim of this therapeutic intervention is to help reduce the child's anxiety, to help the child with depression, to improve his or her self-esteem, and to help the child cope with shame and guilt. For parents, the aim is to help them learn the stages of child development, to help the perpetrator control his or her impulsive behavior, to reduce parental guilt, and to help parents learn how to deal with frustration in a nonabusive manner (Corona, 1983).

If the family resists or does not cooperate with treatment, and if the child continues to be abused, a legal process against the abusive parent begins. If the judge considers it necessary, abusive parents can lose their parental rights. The child can even be given up for adoption. If the child is not adopted by a relative, the authorities send him or her to a foster home until he or she is adopted or comes of age (Barrera, 1998).

PREVENTION

Hopes, Dreams, and Challenges

Although there have been some advances, Mexico has not exhibited a strong cultural commitment against child abuse. At a conference on child abuse, Ayala and Cruz (1983) stated, "In our country, it is practically impossible to know the extent of the problem due to a lack of national statistics" (p. 38). Three years later the situation remained the same: "In Mexico there is no specific data on abused children" (DIF, 1986, p. 10). Unfortunately, even eight years later, Gonzalez, Associate Dean of the Law School in Metropolitan University, stated, "In Mexico the statistics are unknown" (quoted in Calderón, 1994, p. 3).

In recent years, however, there has been much publicity in the mass media aimed at preventing child abuse. Television and newspapers have contributed to an increased public awareness of the problem. Some television shows teach children how to guard themselves against sexual abuse. Newspapers have also frequently published articles on child abuse issues.

NGOs and the government have also been working to prevent child abuse and neglect. Through the news, commentaries, panel discussions, and reporting they are promoting public awareness of the importance of protecting children and recognizing children's rights.

The effectiveness of social and legal policies in increasing public awareness of child abuse appears to be confirmed by the number of hot line calls. According to DIF (1986), between 1983 and 1986 their central office received 3,378 calls reporting abuse, of which 34 percent were substantiated.

According to Gamboa, Chief of the Department of Social Services of the Legal Advisor of Integral Family Development, from the time the program began in 1982 until 1994, 14,012 reports were received at a national level, and 5,124 were confirmed (Colin, 1994).

The increasing number of reports does not necessarily mean that child abuse is becoming more prevalent in Mexico. Rather, public awareness of child abuse seems to be increasing, as is the commitment of personnel dedicated to promoting a safe environment for children.

CONCLUSION

Although there have been important advances in recent years, given the pervasiveness of the problem, Mexico is still lagging behind what other countries are doing to help children. Steinmetz (1987) affirms that there are five stages in preventing child abuse: "acceptance of the status quo, public awareness, the onset of systematic research, all states having mandatory child-abuse reporting, and the elimination of domestic violence" (p. 725). Mexico appears to be only in the second stage. A study done by Loredo, Sánchez, Castilla, Solís, López, and Trejo (1997) reveals that "only 59.9% of those surveyed considered child abuse to be a social problem. Eighty percent of the parents affirm that they do not know of any child abuse cases" (p. 6).

Professionals who work to prevent child abuse and neglect have dreams, hopes, and challenges. We hope that Mexico will be able to enact federal legislation that more effectively prevents any form of abuse. In addition, there should be a national organization where all information about child abuse and neglect can be reliably compiled to explore the extent of the problem. There is also a need for more work to prevent social problems that foster child abuse and neglect, such as poverty, unemployment, malnutrition, child exploitation, and overpopulated living situations.

At the state level, lawmakers should legislate mandatory child abuse reporting and have formal and informal mechanisms to help abused children. The general opinion is that politicians favor a culture that prevents child abuse if it benefits their political parties. If they do not see a benefit, they do not pay attention to the matter. Instead of looking to their own benefit, they should strive to protect children. The welfare of children should be placed above political ambition. Child abuse should be considered a matter of health, not of political interest.

At the professional level, coordinated work should be done to prevent child abuse. Presently, there are few organizations in Mexico City that work to prevent and eliminate child abuse, and those that do exist work in an uncoordinated manner.

Books about child abuse and neglect in Mexico can be counted on one's fingers. Professional journals in the field are virtually unknown. The few that do exist are published irregularly, only for a short time, and are poorly circulated.

Through mass media influence, we need to consolidate the first and second of Steinmetz's five stages for preventing child abuse, by placing posters in schools, hospitals, and bus and train stations, and through TV and radio advertising. At the same time, we need to advance to additional stages. Professionals need to be more aggressive and committed to conducting research, writing books, and editing professional journals. Research needs to be undertaken that will permit us to better understand the problem of abuse in our country. There is an urgent need to establish a network of professionals working on behalf of children. We also need to create a national organization that can coordinate and support professionals working on this matter. More Mexican professionals should be involved in international networking. Presently, no more than ten Mexicans appear on the directory of the International Society for the Prevention of Child Abuse and Neglect (IPSCAN), and no more than four attended IPSCAN's last three biennial congresses in Ireland and New Zealand. No more than ten have attended the San Diego Conference on Responding to Child Maltreatment, and no more than two have presented any research.

At a social level, it is imperative that we create better public awareness of the maltreatment of children. In Mexico, child abuse is not seen as a social problem but as a family issue. The public's lack of interest in reporting cases of abuse and neglect, and the difficulty of getting relatives to cooperate, are among the major obstacles that confront social workers when they try to help children who are in trouble.

In a country of underdeveloped economic resources, it is difficult to work systematically to prevent child abuse. Therefore, the challenge that Mexico faces is to take better advantage of available resources and to develop multidisciplinary coordination that will more effectively prevent all forms of abuse.

More coordination is needed between authorities and society to prevent and eliminate the maltreatment of children. Intensive campaigns to disseminate public information are required so that authorities, parents, and society can be more sensitive to the needs of children.

Our dream and hope is to see a greater number of politicians, professionals, and parents supporting and working on behalf of children. Dreams, hopes, and efforts will be centered in reducing, and, if possible, eliminating child abuse and neglect, and securing each child's future. We want our children to live in an environment of harmony, where they can develop to their full potential.

REFERENCES

Ariza, R., Frati, A., Monge, L., & Ruiz, L. (1985). Sindrome de Munchausen [Munchausen syndrome]. *Revista Médica del IMSS, 23*, 413–417.

Ayala, R., & Cruz, D. (1983). *Sindrome del niño maltratado* [Child abuse syndrome]. Mexico City: Mexican Government Printing Office.

Barrera, A. (1998). [Personal interview by the author]. Unpublished raw data, DIF, Nuevo León, Mexico.

Besharov, D. (1990). *Recognizing child abuse.* New York: The Free Press.

Blanco, I. (n.d.). El sexo y su condicionamiento cultural en el mundo prehispanico [Sex and its cultural conditioning of a pre-Hispanic world]. In A. R. Del Castillo (Ed.), *Between borders: Essays on Mexicana/Chicana history* (pp. 361–374). Floricanto Press.

Calderón, J. (1994, November 25). 500 mil casos de niños maltratados al año [Five hundred thousand cases of child abuse each year]. *El Universal.* p. D3.

Casamadrid, O. (1994). Intervención jurídica de las instituciones públicas de Mexico [Legal intervention of Mexican public institutions]. In A. Loredo (Ed.), *Maltrato al menor* [Child abuse] (pp. 127–132). Mexico City: Interamericana.

Ciccheti, D., & Carlson, V. (Eds.). (1991). *Child maltreatment: Theory and research on the causes and consequences of child abuse and neglect.* New York: Cambridge University Press.

Colin, A. (1994, September 4). Maltrato infantil laberinto con salida [Child abuse maze with an exit]. *El Dia,* p. A12.

Collin, C. History of Mexico. (1997). *Encarta Encyclopedia 98* [CD-ROM].

Corona, M. (1983). Manejo actual del niño maltratado en la Secretaría de Salubridad y Asistencia [Care of child abuse in the Secretary of Health]. *Congress of Present Attention to Child Abuse* (pp. 33–36). México: DIF.

DIF (Integral Family Development). (1983, 1984, 1985a, 1986). *Análisis sistemático de los datos registrados de menores maltratados en el programa DIF-PREMAN* [A systemic analysis of child abuse data]. México City: Mexican Government Printing Office.

DIF (Integral Family Development). (1985b). *Informe anual del Consejo Consultivo para las acciones en beneficio del menor maltratado en Mexico* [Annual report of Advisory Council on Behalf of Abused Children in Mexico]. Mexico City: Mexican Government Printing Office.

DIF [Integral Family Development]. (1998). *Data analysis of child abuse.* (No. 039/DIF/LGZ/98). Monterrey: Nuevo León

DIF [Integral Family Development]. (n.d.). *Those are your rights* [Brochure].

Estrada, A. (1995). *Gender differences in physical child abuse: A Mexican perspective.* Unpublished doctoral dissertation, Fuller Theological Seminary, Pasadena, California.

Foncerrada, M. (1982). El niño víctima de maltrato físico [The child victim of maltreatment]. *Revista Médica IMSS, 20,* 457–469.

Fontana, V., & Moolman, V. (1992). *Save the family, save the child.* New York: Mentor Books.

Gimpera, B. (1975). *La America pre-hispanica* [Pre-Hispanic America]. Barcelona: Editorial Ariel.

Joyner, A. (1994, April 19). Hay prostitución infantil [There is prostitution among children]. *Reform,* p. A1.

Joyner, A. (1996, June 1). Invade droga a niños de la calle [The drugs invade children of the street]. *Reform,* p. C1.

Loredo, A. (1994). Introducción [Introduction]. In A. Loredo (Ed.), *Maltrato al menor* [Child maltreatment] (pp. 1–8). Mexico City: Interamericana.

Loredo, A., Reynés, M., Carvajal, R., Vidales, B., & Bolaños, R. (1984). El niño maltratado: Una realidad actual en México [Child abuse: A present reality in Mexico]. *Acta Pediatrica de Mexico*, 5, 28–37.

Loredo, A., Reynés-Manzur, J., Martinez, C., Carbajal, L., Vidales, C., & Villaseñor, J. (1986). El maltrato al menor: Una realidad creciente en Mexico [Child abuse: A growing reality in México]. *Boletín Médico del Hospital Infantil de México*, 43, 425–433.

Loredo, A., Sánchez, V. A., Castle, S. L., Solís, A., López, D.J.M., & Trejo, H. J. (1997, October). *Encuesta de opinión sobre el tema "maltrato al menor"* [Public opinion poll about "child abuse"]. Paper presented at the meeting of I Taller Iberoamericano sobre el maltrato al menor [First Iberoamerican Workshop on Child Abuse], Villahermosa, Tabasco, México.

Malvido, E. (n.d.). El uso del cuerpo femenino en la epoca colonial Mexicana a través de los estudios de demografia [The use of the female body in the time of the Mexican colony through demographic history]. In A. R. Del Castillo (Ed.), *Between borders: Essays on Mexicana/Chicana history* (pp. 113–130). Floricanto Press.

Manterola, A. (1983). Manejo actual del niño maltratado [Present attention to maltreated children on Integral Family Development program]. *Congress of Present Attention to Child Abuse* (pp. 67–73). Mexico City: DIF.

Martinez, S. (1982). El Desarrollo Integral de la Familia [Integral Family Development]. *Revista del Menor y la Familia*, 2, 65–74.

Medellín, M. L. (1996, March 20). Piden reformas para proteger a los menores maltratados [Requested reforms to civil law in order to prevent child abuse]. *El Norte*, p. D10.

Morley, G. S. (1947). *The ancient Mayan* (A. Recino, Trans.). Mexico City: Fondo de Cultura Económica. (Original work published 1946)

Obeso, J. (1995). *Maltrato físico a los adolescentes y su relación con la edad y el nivel educativo de los padres* [Physical adolescent abuse related to age and educational level of the parents]. Unpublished master's thesis, University of Montemorelos, Montemorelos, Nuevo León, Mexico.

Osorio, C. (1985). *El niño maltratado* [The abused child]. Mexico City: Trillas.

Pérez, R. A. (1998). *La mujer maltratada* [Wife abuse]. Unpublished master's thesis, University of Montemorelos, Montemorelos, Nuevo León, Mexico.

Peterson, A. F. (1966). *Ancient Mexico* (S. Cruz, Trans.). Mexico City: Editorial Herreo. (Original work published 1959)

Reed, A. (1972). *The ancient past of Mexico* (M. Pérez, Trans.). New York: Crown. (Original work published 1966)

Riojas, U., & Manzano, C. (1968). Aspectos radiológicos en el síndrome del niño maltratado [Radiological aspects of child abuse syndrome]. *Jornada Pediátrica IMSS (Pediatric Journal Mexican Institute of Social Security)* 69, 79–73.

Riva Palacio, V. (1953). *México a través de los Siglos* [Mexico through the ages] (Vols. 1–6). Mexico: Editorial Cumbre.

Ruiz, L. (1985). DIF (Integral Family Development). Informe anual del Consejo Consultivo para las acciones en beneficio del menor maltratado en Mexico [Annual report of Advisory Council on behalf of abused children in México]. Mexico City: Mexican Government Printing Office.

Soutelle, J. (1974). *La vida cotidiana de los Aztecas en visperas de la conquista* [The daily life of the Aztecs the day before the conquest]. Mexico City: Fondo de Cultura Económica. (Original work published 1956)

Steinmetz, S. K. (1987). Family violence. In M. B. Sussman & S. K. Steinmetz (Eds.), *Handbook of marriage and the family* (pp. 725–765). New York: Plenum Press.

Thompson, E. (1975). *Maya history and religion* (F. Blanco, Trans.). Oklahoma: Oklahoma University Press. (Original work published 1970)

Vasques, Z. (n.d.) Educación y papel de la mujer en Mexico [Role and education of women in México]. In A. Del Castillo (Ed.), *Between borders: Essays on Mexicana/Chicana History* (pp. 377–397). Floricanto Press.

Zumwalt, R., & Hirscht, S. Ch. (1987). Pathology of fatal child abuse and neglect. In R. Helfer & R. S. Kempe (Eds.), *The battered child* (pp. 247–285). Chicago: University of Chicago Press.

11

NORWAY

Kari Killén

PROFILE OF NORWAY

The kingdom of Norway, located in northern Europe, has an area of 385,364 square kilometers. The capital is Oslo and the population of 4.4 million is comprised of Norwegians, Lapps, and foreign nationals from Nordic and other countries. The official language is Norwegian and the state church is the Evangelical Lutheran Church (94 percent). The infant mortality rate is 4 per 1,000 and the life expectancy is seventy-five years for men and eighty-one years for women. Education is free through the university level, and required from the ages of seven to sixteen. The literacy rate is near 100 percent, and the gross national product per capita in 1998 was $34,330 (U.S.). The government is a hereditary constitutional monarchy in which the right to vote is universal over the age of eighteen.

HISTORY

In Norway, as in other countries, there have always been children who have been abused and neglected both by their parents and society. The forerunner of our modern Child Welfare Service, Vergeraadet (the Guardian Council), was established in 1896 with the responsibility of helping neglected children. The focus of society at that time was mainly on poverty and extreme physical neglect. The modern Child Protection Service was established in 1953 by the Child Protection Law (Ministry of Child and Family Affairs, 1953). According to this law, each local authority was responsible for establishing a Child Protection Committee. Social workers were appointed within the local social service system to work with child abuse and neglect cases to prepare them for the Child Protection Committee, which made decisions concerning child abuse and neglect. The committees consisted of representatives from the different political parties and different professions, such as priests, teachers, and medical doctors.

Cases that were dealt with within this system were defined widely by the Child Protection Law. "Child protection might intervene when a child is treated in such a way or lives under such conditions that its health (physical and emotional) or development is exposed to damage or serious danger" (Ministry of Child and Family Affairs, 1953, p. 6). Parents could be ordered by the Child Protection Committee to accept assistance or supervision in the home by a social worker or a volunteer, or the child could be taken into care and placed in a foster home or institution. The latter could be done either with the consent of the parents or by order of the committee. The act required that any decision to take a child into care needed to be based on an evaluation of both the child's present circumstances and the likely future situation. A child taken into care could only be adopted when the parents were unable to create satisfactory conditions for the child at home. In such cases, a judge was required to chair the decision-making process. Until recently, child abuse and neglect were dealt with exclusively by the Child Protection Committee and the Child Protection Service. Child abuse and neglect were hardly ever a police matter until sexual abuse made its appearance in the middle of the 1980s (E. R. Normann & Michalsen, 1988). There was, however, some cooperation between the police and the Child Protection Service. This cooperation consisted mainly of the police notifying the Child Protection Service of cases in which children were exposed to alcohol, drug abusing parents, and/or marital violence, or when young people were involved in criminal activities. Child abuse as a focus of professional attention, however, is more recent. The responsibility for detection of abuse by medical professionals was introduced in Scandinavia, as in so many other countries, by the American pediatrician Henry Kempe in the early 1960s (Harlem, 1967). Many years passed, however, before Norway used the knowledge about physical abuse in a more systematic manner.

Despite a number of publications on child abuse in the United States and England (e.g., Elmer, 1967; Kempe, Silverman, Steel, Draegemueller, & Silver, 1962), the issue was given very little attention in Norwegian professional literature. Slowly the topic began to receive some recognition when the first professional contribution, a case description, was published by a pediatrician in the *Norwegian Journal of Medicine* (Gjerdrum, 1964). Three years later the Ministry of Health published a brochure that included an article on child abuse that was based on American and British literature (Harlem, 1967). These publications, however, did not receive much attention among professionals or in society at large.

In the 1970s, a growing recognition of the problem was finally observed. An interpellation (a question to the Minister of Justice) in the House of Parliament in 1971 resulted in the abolition of the law that permitted parents to physically discipline their children. The abolition of this law did not cause much discussion outside of the House of Parliament, probably because its abolition was consistent with the opinion of the majority of the population.

A few additional articles in professional journals (Gjertsen & Lühr, 1972; Piene, 1973) and sensationalistic presentations of abuse cases in daily newspapers prompted another interpellation in the House of Parliament, this time directed to the Minister of Social Affairs in 1973.

A national survey of the extent of child abuse was proposed at that time, but has never been carried out. Thus, there are still no prevalence statistics for physical abuse or neglect in Norway. Only after Henry Kempe's visit to Oslo in 1974, during which he lectured about child abuse, did abuse begin to receive more attention from professionals. Inspired by his visit, the Norwegian Pediatric Society and the Ministry of Health organized a meeting with wide participation of professionals from the health and social services. The focus was on how to develop cooperation between these services and families (Mental Barnehjelp, 1976). The nongovernmental organization Mental Barnehjelp (Mental Health for Children), now called Voksne for Barn (Adults for Children), played an important role at that time, as did a small number of pediatricians who contributed to the *Norwegian Journal of Medicine* and tried to raise public awareness about child abuse (Hagå, 1975; Hjermann & Sommer, 1977). Additionally, professionals such as Skjaelaaen (1978) and Tangen (1975) published books on child abuse, increasing lay people's awareness of the problem of child abuse in Scandinavia.

Voksne for Barn continues to play an important role today, providing active advocates for children. Currently, they are conducting countrywide interprofessional training concerning the needs of children of psychiatrically ill parents. They are creating self-help programs in which young people help other young people and parents help parents. They also train district nurses in prevention of child abuse and neglect.

TREATMENT

The First Child Abuse Team

In 1978, the first team to work specifically with child abuse and neglect cases was established in Oslo, the capital of the country, in the pediatric department of one of the university hospitals (Killén Heap, 1981). The team consisted of four permanent members: a professor who was head of the department (because of his special interest in abuse), a child psychiatrist, a senior staff member of Child Protection, and a social worker that led the team and did most of the assessment and crisis work. A pediatrician and a pediatric nurse, who were responsible for treating and caring for children while they were in the hospital, collaborated with the team during the children's hospital stays. Professionals who were involved with the family from outside the hospital (e.g., Child Protection Service and mental health professionals) were also invited to contribute to the assessment and the planning of a child's treatment (Killén Heap, 1981a, 1981b).

Although the team consulted with the police, the police supported the team's philosophy that child abuse and neglect were not a police matter. Treatment was based on understanding family dynamics and the processes underlying abuse, and not on investigation and evidence. Only if abuse resulted in a child's death, or if there was a danger of a repeated pattern of serious abuse, were the police notified. Anonymous consultation with the police was encouraged and used. This policy distinguished Norway from the United States and Great Britain, where the police had a more active role in cases of child abuse and neglect.

This team functioned well during the three years it was established and developed effective ways to cooperate with each other and with families. Consequently, an interactional-multifactorial model for clinical assessment and intervention was established (Killén, 1984, 1991, 1994, in press), based on a psychodynamic tradition of child guidance and a social work tradition of intervening to protect both children and their parents. The model suggested that abuse and neglect result from an interaction between political, cultural, socioeconomic, network, marital, and personality factors in parents as well as in children. Little attention was given to proving whether abuse occurred, and focus was placed on understanding the processes underlying abuse.

The Organization of Services for Abused and Neglected Children

A principal decision was made in 1985, based on the recommendation of a governmental committee, that special services for abused and neglected children and their families would not be provided. The Child Protection Service was to be developed further, and closer cooperation between the Child Protection Service, school psychology services, and the health services was to be encouraged.

This decision had considerable limitations. Specifically, after this decision was made, there was increasing passivity within pediatric departments in responding to abuse, as they were not given the additional resources needed to deal with the "new" challenge of abuse. Pediatric departments, child guidance clinics, school psychology offices, and health clinics for mothers and babies did not take on the responsibilities delegated to them. An insufficient number of social workers were trained within the Child Protection

Service, and interagency cooperation was difficult to establish. Due in part to the withdrawal of the medical professions, few serious physical abuse cases were identified. First-line workers, health visitors, and the Social Service (of which the Child Protection Service is a part) identified cases of neglect and emotional abuse related to alcohol abuse and violent marriages. However, although Norway had increased its knowledge of abuse, there was no similar increase in identification of abuse. Resources were made available to research why physical abuse went underidentified.

Challenges Confronting Professionals

A number of studies have been carried out to assess the services provided to combat child abuse. The studies have shown results that have given grounds for serious concern (Killén Heap, 1984; Killén, 1991, 1996). Specifically, a number of studies in Norway and other countries have shown that despite great investments in improving parental functioning, there has consistently been a fairly high percentage of cases (35–60 percent) where no improvement or only limited improvement has been observed (e.g., Cohn & Daro, 1987; Killén Heap, 1981; Morse, Sahler, & Friedman, 1970; Rothe, 1983).

These follow-up studies have evaluated families and professionals and the processes they have gone through. Multi-method approaches have been used, including in-depth interviews with workers, observations of workers in case discussions, analyses of workers' case records and decisions, and interviews with parents and teachers. These studies have shown with great clarity that it has been more important for the professionals to protect themselves than to protect the children and the parents. These studies revealed that dealing with the emotional challenge of abuse and neglect is a pressing, but neglected, international issue. Specifically, the distress and pressure of working with neglectful and abusive families create problems against which professionals need to defend.

To evaluate, to have an opinion, and to take responsibility in ways that might have decisive consequences for both children and parents evoke anxiety and inner conflict in professionals. To be part of a process where one may need to remove a child from home also evokes strong feelings. The emotional challenge of facing these realities is tremendous.

The studies showed that professionals develop survival strategies, mechanisms that make it possible for them to function and do their jobs. Consequently, they choose to ignore or minimize the aspects of parents' personalities that place great burdens on the children. The parents are seen as having more resources than they do. This leads to treatment plans and goals that may not be consistent with the parents' potential or the children's needs.

The severity of abuse and neglect, their toll on children, and long-term consequences are minimized. A distorted picture of children is developed: They are seen as healthier and stronger than they are, in order that professionals may feel better. This makes it difficult to help parents and children with those very aspects of life with which they need the most help. Professionals play into the parents' denial of the problems that need to be solved in order to make the children's home situation adequate. Consequently, progress and development are hampered.

Closely related to this process is the mechanism of emotional withdrawal from both the child and the parents. For example, home visits are postponed, there is a sigh of relief when nobody opens the door, or professional appointments are canceled. Professionals collude with the parents in not facing the reality of abuse.

Another mechanism that allows professionals to fail to acknowledge is what has been called "problem-displacement." When the chaos and problems in families are overwhelming, the professionals focus on one specific aspect of neglect and abuse and not on the process of neglect and abuse itself. For instance, they focus on the developmental lags of the child. Although such deficiencies are important, trying to alleviate developmental lags does not stop neglect and abuse. Lack of a common theoretical frame for observing, analyzing, assessing, and treating abusive and neglectful families also prevents professionals from adequately addressing abuse.

These and other mechanisms prevent professionals from seeing how detrimental neglect and abuse are to children's development and how resistant to treatment serious neglect and abuse often are. Surprisingly, this aspect of professional work and suggestions for dealing with it have not received much attention in either the clinical or research literature. The attention received has mostly been related to professionals' failure to report suspected abuse (Morrison & Clasen, 1989; Nightingale & Walker, 1989; Sanders, 1972).

CHILD PROTECTION SERVICE TODAY

In the early 1980s, the government initiated a plan of action to strengthen the Child Protection Service. Considerable resources have been invested to increase the number of child protection workers and improve training facilities. There is stronger awareness of abuse among professionals, and the media have become slightly more balanced in their presentation of abuse cases.

A new Child Protection Act, called the Child Welfare Service Act, was passed in 1992. The most radical departure from the old act is the introduction of County Social Welfare Boards (Grinde, 1993). These boards were created to neutralize the local authority's role of enforcer. Other aims were to strengthen parents' civil rights and facilitate uniformity in the handling of abuse and neglect cases. The preparation of cases, however, is still the responsibility of the local authority and its social workers.

INVESTIGATION

Building up a system of County Social Welfare Boards has been a major task. The new act contains various provisions to ensure that the Child Welfare Service is brought in at an earlier stage in the investigation and intervention process than was previously done. To bring the Child Welfare Service in early, however, requires not only that the need for intervention be identified, but also that the abuse be reported to the Child Welfare Service. The act mandates a disclosure obligation for professionals who are otherwise subject to a confidentiality obligation. In other words, all professionals who work in the social and health field are required to report suspected abuse and neglect. The act also established time limits (i.e., six weeks) for examining reports, making investigations, and implementing measures.

One of the features of the new act involves consideration of the future, whereas legal decisions in general primarily deal with the past. Consideration of the future allows professionals to focus on understanding and documenting the processes of abuse and neglect. Theoretical knowledge about child development, parent-child interactions, attachment, and parents' personality and functioning is used extensively in analyzing the facts of a child abuse case.

Several questions are considered: Can conditions in the child's home be made "good enough" by providing services to the family? What will be the effects on the child of staying with the parents versus being placed in a foster home? As in the old act, parents may be ordered to accept assistance in the form of kindergarten or other suitable day-care facilities. Parents may also be ordered to accept home supervision. Under the new act, only the County Social Welfare Board is empowered to order such measures.

According to the new act, when it is clear that the child is being abused or is suffering from other serious deficits of care, it is not necessary to prove that the child may suffer long-term harm. In addition, even under circumstances where the child's current situation is satisfactory, a decision to take the child into care may be made when it seems likely that the child will suffer future harm as a result of the parents' inability to look after the child properly. In other words, it is permissible to consider a child's potential of being harmed and respond accordingly. This portion of the act is primarily applied in cases when parents lack the competence needed to look after their child. Sometimes this is due to the parents' own mental or emotional disability.

A decision to take a child into care should only be made when it is not possible to create satisfactory conditions for the child by providing assistance to the family. Usually, before a child is removed, there has been extensive investment in improving the situation at home and in facilitating parental functioning.

A child's removal may be compulsory (i.e., by the decision of the county board) or voluntary (i.e., by a parent's consent). Cooperation with the parents has been increasingly emphasized in the new act, leading to reduced compulsory decisions. The best interest of the child has also been emphasized, and families now accept more interference in their privacy, as is often the case with drug abuse and serious neglect of newborns or very young children.

A decision to place a child into care may be reevaluated if parents later become able to look after the child properly. Even if this precondition is satisfied, however, children cannot be returned home if they have developed close ties to foster parents and their new home such that they may suffer serious problems upon being removed.

In extreme cases, the Child Welfare Act permits the termination of parental rights, thus freeing the child for adoption. Adoption against the parents' wishes may also occur. Adoption requires the consent of the County Social Welfare Board and is only granted when the transfer of parental responsibility will be permanent.

Most children who are taken into protective care are placed in institutions. Over the last ten years, new parent-child institutions have been established. These institutions function as care institutions for mothers and children (very few fathers move in) where they can receive help and support. There has been an increasing focus on early mother-child interactions; thus, mothers are being taught to understand and respond appropriately to their young children's needs. These institutions often also have assessment responsibility for the local Child Welfare Service.

The new act permits the local authorities to choose untraditional ways of organizing themselves. This has given rise to some innovative approaches, such as "open kindergarten" for parents and children and support groups for parents. Because the health services have a tradition of working collaboratively, the Child Welfare Service often uses formal authority to investigate against parents' will. Closer cooperation between the Child Welfare Service and the health services has historically been difficult. Fortunately, the new act has also stimulated more interprofessional cooperation.

SEXUAL ABUSE

The "appearance" of child sexual abuse in the middle of the 1980s has temporarily shifted the focus away from physical abuse and neglect. Unlike other types of abuse, the police have taken an active role in addressing sexual abuse. This has presented new challenges to professionals, including learning how to cooperate with the police and how to accommodate legal investigations and clinical assessments.

Prevalence

The first study of sexual abuse in Norway was published by Saetre, Holter, and Jebsen (1986) and documented a 16 percent prevalence rate of abuse.

The study was based on two representative samples of the population who answered self-administered forms with questions about their experiences of sexual abuse prior to the age of eighteen. (In this survey, victims self-defined whether they considered what they had experienced to be abusive.) Although their prevalence rates are consistent with international studies (Finkelhor, 1994), other studies have revealed different findings of 5 percent (e.g., Normann, Tambs, & Magnus, 1992).

In 1993, the House of Parliament decided to establish a National Resource Center for Sexually Abused Children (NRSB) (Stortingsmelding nr. 53, 1992–1993). The center has a staff of seven individuals who represent child protection, pediatrics, and clinical psychology. A primary focus of the center is to increase its competence, as it builds professional networks and develops routines for handling cases within child protection, child and adult psychiatry, and pediatrics.

The National Resource Center has been linked to the Social Medical Section for Children and Youth within the pediatric department in one of the university hospitals in Oslo. This has allowed the center to contribute clinically to assessments and collection of data there. Additionally, county consulting teams from the center have been established in eleven counties to provide consultation to professionals. The National Resource Center has had less formalized cooperation, however, with the police and legal authorities (Norman, 1998).

It has become increasingly clear that not enough has been invested in increasing the competence of the police and the legal authorities (Texmo & Aarvik, 1998). Texmo and Aarvik examined the legal rights of sexually abused women and children and how their cases were followed up. The questions raised were, "Who is responsible for reporting such cases to the police?" and "In what ways are victims being followed up with after the criminal process?"

Over a five-year period, 497 sexual abuse cases were reported. The decision as to whether to report to the police was made by each individual child welfare worker. In some districts, almost all notifications to the police came from the Child Welfare Service, while in other districts few came from the Child Welfare Service.

The 497 cases consisted of 226 rape cases, 206 cases of sexual abuse of children under fourteen years of age, and 65 cases of repeated serious sexual abuse of children under ten years of age. Of the rape cases that were reported, 77 percent were dismissed, 5 percent were acquitted, and 17 percent were convicted. Disturbingly, as many as 80 percent of the most serious repeated sexual abuse cases perpetrated against children under ten years of age were dismissed. The report concluded that such cases had a very low priority.

During the early 1990s, professionals have begun to document sexual abuse in Norway with a focus on abusive acts that can be proven. This has not taken advantage of the Child Welfare Service Act that involves consideration of the future. It has also not helped in developing prevention and treatment programs. Several cases of suspected sexual abuse in a kindergarten which were badly handled and widely publicized have led professionals to be careful about notifying the Child Welfare Service (Haugsgjerd, 1994).

Proving sexual abuse is difficult and rarely helps the child and the family. Thus, Norway is slowly realizing that in order to help, we need to increase our understanding of the problem. First, sexual abuse often co-occurs with other types of abuse. Second, treatment should not be based on proof about who perpetrated the abuse and how it occurred. Treatment must be based on understanding the abusive processes and the parent-child interaction.

Projects are now being established independent of the police (Tjersland, Gulbrandsen, Jensen, Reichelt, & Mossige, 1998). Parents and children can consult with professionals without having their case reported to the police. While child guidance clinics in several parts of the country treat victims of sexual abuse, there are unfortunately few treatment facilities for abusers. In one county in the south of Norway, the County Child Protection Service, along with county child psychiatric clinics, adult psychiatric clinics, and family counseling services, are working closely to provide family treatment for sexual abuse cases.

PREVENTION

Society's increasing concern about the lack of good treatment facilities for psychiatrically ill persons has led to increased awareness of the suffering of children. The above-mentioned organization, Voksne for Barn (Adults for Children) is building a network for these children, and the Ministry of Health is financing nationwide, multiprofessional training for practitioners in the field. Similarly, programs are now focusing on children whose parents abuse alcohol and drugs. Professionals who treat parents with alcohol and drug abuse problems have started to cooperate with the Child Welfare Service.

Over the last few years, alcohol and drug abuse during pregnancy has received increased attention (Lindeman, 1996, 1997). A law has been passed that makes it possible to keep pregnant women in treatment institutions to prevent alcohol and drug abuse of the fetus. So far, the law has only been implemented a few times, but many mothers seem willing to accept such treatment voluntarily as they are aware of the possibility of being forced to accept such conditions.

Norway is slowly acknowledging the complexity of child abuse and the difficulties of treatment. Early intervention is necessary and prevention is required. Prevention is slowly gaining higher priority.

Norway has a well-developed system of health clinics for parents and small children. These are attended by close to 100 percent of the population (Heian, 1996). Mothers (and, to a slowly increasing extent, fathers) and babies are attending from pregnancy onward. Originally these clinics mainly saw to the physical health of children. Today, with the development of knowledge about early parent-child interaction and child attachment, we are seeing a change of focus. The health clinics have become centers for building social networks and for supporting families. In fact, families who are not considered at risk and families that are at risk are helped within the same system. Different types of groups are offered, including parent-child interaction groups, fathers' groups, and discussion groups. Some groups are problem focused (e.g., on sleep problems or limit setting) and some are more general (e.g., about raising children). Groups of parents with special needs, for instance young parents and deprived parents, are also being established. However, the quality and quantity of these preventive measures vary from one part of the country to another and even from one part of a city to another. In some areas, there is close cooperation between these health clinics and the local Child Welfare Service, and in other areas there is hardly any.

CONCLUSION

The continual and interwoven challenges that Norway is confronting in dealing with the emotional challenge of child abuse and neglect and in increasing its knowledge and competence in the field will most likely be an ever-evolving process. It seems that there is considerably more knowledge available than is being integrated and used in practice.

REFERENCES

Cohn, A. H., & Daro, D. (1987). Is treatment too late? What ten years of evaluative research tell us. *Child Abuse & Neglect, 11*, 422–433.

Elmer, E. (1967). *Children in jeopardy. A study of abused minors and their families.* Pittsburgh: University of Pittsburgh Press.

Finkelhor, D. (1994). The international epidemiology of child sexual abuse. *Child Abuse & Neglect, 18*, 409–417.

Gjerdrum, K. (1964). Vanrøktsyndromet [The syndrome of neglect]. *T. norske laegeforening* [Norwegian Journal of Medicine], *84*, 1609–1612.

Gjertsen, J. C., & Lühr, J. (1972). Barnemishandling. Meddelse om et dødelig tilfelle [Child abuse: Communication about a case ending in death]. *T. norske laegeforen, 92*, 2251–2253.

Grinde, T. V. (1993). *Child care perspectives—English and Norwegian views: Report 2.* Oslo: Norwegian Institute of Child Welfare Research.

Hagå, P. (1975). Barnemishandling: The battered child syndrome. *T. norske laegeforen, 95.* 752–755.

Harlem, O. K. (1967). *Det skamslåtte barn* [The battered child]. Oslo: Ministry of Health.

Haugsgjerd, H. (Ed.). (1994). *Hva skal vi tro etter Bjugnsaken?* Oslo: Aschehough.

Heian, F. (1996). *Early interaction*. Oslo: Child and Family Ministry.

Hjermann, V., & Sommer, F. (1977). Child abuse. *T. norske laegeforen, 97*, 784–787.

Kempe, H. C., Silverman, F. N., Steele, B. F., Droegemueller, W., & Silver, H. K. (1962). The battered child syndrome. *Journal of the American Medical Association, 181*, 17–24.

Killén, K. (1994). *Sveket: Omsorgssvikt er alles ansvar* [Understanding and dealing with abuse and neglect]. Oslo: Kommuneforlaget.

Killén, K. (1996). How far have we come in dealing with the emotional challenge of abuse? *Child Abuse & Neglect, 20*, 791–795.

Killén, K. (in press). *Interactions understanding and dealing with child maltreatment*. St. Louis: G. W. Medical Publishing.

Killén Heap, K. (1981a). *Child abuse*. Oslo: Tano.

Killén Heap, K. (1981b). *Child abuse II*. Oslo: Sinnets Helse.

Killén Heap, K. (1984). Families with abused children: A follow-up study of post-crisis support. *Child Abuse & Neglect, 8*, 467–472.

Killén Heap, K. (1991). A predictive and follow-up study of abusive and neglectful families by case-analyses. *Child Abuse & Neglect, 15*, 261–273.

Lindemann, R. (1991). Congenital renal tubular dysfunction associated with maternal sniffing of organic solvents. *Acta pediatrica Scandinavia, 80*, 882–888.

Lindemann, R. (1995). Neuroleptica og gravide. *Tidsskr. Nor Laegerforening, 115*, 2440–2539.

Lindemann, R. (1997). Children born of drug and alcohol abusing mothers. *Stoffmisbruk, 4*, 12–15.

Mental Barnehjelp [Mental health for children]. (1976). Child abuse Sinnets Helse. *Mental Health Journal*. Published by Mental Health for Children.

Ministry of Child and Family Affairs. (1953). *Child protection law*.

Morse, C. W., Sahler, O.J.Z., & Friedman, S. B. (1970). A three-year follow-up study of abused and neglected children. *American Journal of Disabled Children, 120*, 439–446.

Normann, E. K., Tambs, K., & Magnus, P. (1992). Seksuelle overgrep mot barn—et Folkehelseproblem? *Nordisk Medicin, 107*, 326–330.

Normann, E. R., & Michalsen, H. (1988). Seksuelle overgrep mot barn. *Tidskrift Norwegian Laegeforening, 108*, 1891–1894.

NOU, Norwegian Governmental report (1982). Child abuse and neglect. *Ministry of Social Affairs*, no. 26.

NOU, Norwegian Governmental report (1991). Sexual abuse of children—Punishment and compensation. *Ministry of Justice*, no. 13.

Piene, F. (1973). Filicide and the battered child syndrome, with special references to the psychological implications. *T. Norske Psyk, 10*, 23–28.

Saetre, Holter, H., & Jebsen, E. (1986). Tvang til seksualitet act [Forced to sexuality]. Oslo: Cappelen.

Skjaelaaen, P. (1978). *Diagnose barnemishandling* [Diagnosis: Child abuse]. Oslo: Tiden.

State Department of Health. (1998). Veileder for helsestasjons og skolehelsetjenesten [Advisor for Health Service for parent-child and school health], no. 2.

Tangen, O. (1975). *Barnemishandling* [Child abuse]. Oslo: Author.

Texmo, A., & Aarvik, L. (1998). *Seksuelle overgrep mot kvinner og barn* [Sexual abuse against women and children]. Fornærmedes rettsstilling i praksis. Utredningsprosjekt i Nordland, Troms og Finnmark. Kvinneuniversitetet Nord-Norge, p. 46.

Tjersland, O. A., Gulbrandsen, W., Jensen, T., Reichelt, S., & Mossige, S. (1998). *A model for interventions in families with child sexual abuse—control or conversations?* Paper presented at the Twelfth International Congress on Child Abuse and Neglect, Auckland, New Zealand, September 6–9, 1998.

12

ROMANIA

Ana Muntean and Maria Roth

PROFILE OF ROMANIA

Romania, with a population of approximately 22.7 million, lies on the lower basin of the Danube River system and the middle Danube basin, covering 237,499 square kilometers. The majority of the population is Romanian, but also includes Hungarians, Germans, Ukrainians, Serbs, Croats, Russians, Turks, and Gypsies. The people of Romania speak Romanian, Hungarian, and German. The majority's religious affiliation is Orthodox, with a minority who are Roman Catholic, Reformed Protestant, Baptist, and Pentacostal, and an even smaller number who are Greek Catholic or Jewish. The infant mortality rate is 20 per 1,000, and the life expectancy is 68.1 years for men and 74.8 years for women. The Republic government includes an executive, legislative, and judicial branch, with universal suffrage at age eighteen. Education in Romania is compulsory until age ten, and the literacy rate is 98 percent. In 1998, the gross national product per capita was $1,390 (U.S.).

A CASE STUDY

Christi, a twelve-year-old boy, was caught stealing a car with a group of teenagers. Christi's mother was called to the police station and required to pay damages. While there, a policeman remarked, "It happened because you did not beat him enough." At home, the mother took a belt and beat Christi, leaving visible traces on his back. Subsequently, Christi went to the swimming pool and a social worker saw the marks. She took him to the child protection office and Christi told the workers how he had received the marks. His mother was called in and severely blamed by the Commission of Child Protection. Christi's mother became confused and started to cry when the commission accused her of being a "bad mother." Nonetheless, Christi was placed in an institution. As a consequence of the intervention by the Commission of Child Protection, Christi is now one of thousands of children placed in Romanian institutions. From there, he sends desperate messages to his mother asking for necessities, such as food and clothes. Christi plans to run away from the institution. Christi's mother questions her capacity as a mother: "I do not understand what happened. I love my children." Christi's brother is frightened by Christi's experiences, thinking, "Christi is not such a bad boy. Maybe this can happen to me too."

INTRODUCTION

Romania has been greatly harmed by the communist period. Communism seriously affected family values by encouraging the submission of individuals' needs to those of the community. The centralization of all decision making on child welfare matters also hurt Romania's families and children. During the communist period, which ended in 1989, child abuse and neglect were not discussed in Romania. But such abuse was part of daily life, one of the pieces in the overall image of an unhappy society. Child abuse and neglect happened so frequently during this period that it could have been described as normal. Fortunately, we are now passing through a transition period during which abuse is beginning to be acknowledged. The government is beginning to pay attention to this problem, while nongovernmental agencies are implementing programs to help the society learn how to deal with child abuse and neglect. Yet this transition period is an uncertain time: it gives us the feeling that the door behind has been almost closed, while the door in front of us is only slightly open.

HISTORY

Prior to 1990, the Romanian child protection system was focused primarily on income and productivity issues. Because of the state's industrialization policy, women were encouraged to leave the home to work, usually for low wages. The state in turn subsidized food, clothing, school materials, and other goods for children. Large state-run nurseries and kindergartens were created to care for children too young to attend school. As a result of the industrialization and systematization policies, rural peasants were attracted, or even forced, to move into small apartments in urban blocks of flats. As a result, many families were separated from their natural ties and culture.

Central to the ideology of the national communist state and of its main ideologist, Nicolae Ceausescu, the communist dictator between 1967 and

1989, was a pro-natal policy to increase Romania's population from 23 to 30 million. During this period, birth control methods were banned, sexual education was ignored, and abortion was outlawed (Baban & David, 1994; Johnson, Edwards, & Puwak, 1992). Women younger than forty-five were expected, as a patriotic duty, to have four children. To encourage this child quota, women were periodically checked for pregnancy, and guaranteed allowances and pensions as rewards for bearing children. A woman was valued primarily for her reproductive function. Unfortunately, children born to families as a result of this policy were often perceived as an unbearable and undesirable burden by their families. The residual effects of Ceausescu's pronatal population policies were tens of thousands of temporarily or permanently abandoned and institutionalized children, for whom their parents were not able to care. Estimates of their number vary between 90,000–100,000 (Roth, 1995) and 200,000 children, or 4 percent of the total child population (Hines, Kessler, & Landers, 1991, p. 13).

Social History

Although Romania experienced a short period of restorative reforms and a temporary increase in the quality of life after the end of the communist state, since 1992 the country has experienced a process of "pauperization" (Zamfir, 1994). In 1993, the average income of a Romanian citizen was only 66 percent of the average income in 1989. Moreover, the portion of the average income attributable to child allowances decreased from 2.9 percent in 1989 to only 0.8 percent in 1993. The country also experienced an increase in unemployment, primarily among people with low qualifications.

The pauperization process hit families with numerous children especially hard. Parental contributions to day-care creche and kindergarten have increased, and, as a result, many parents, mostly those with many children, cannot afford to send their children to preschool institutions. In addition, the additional allowance provided to mothers with many children, which had a low value even before 1990, has lost its value completely in recent years. In addition, state subsidies for basic food, clothing, shoes, and school supplies have ceased.

Before 1990, mothers were provided with other benefits. On the birth of a second child, and after the birth of each child thereafter, the mother received an additional allowance. The spouses of young men in military service who had an income of less than the minimum national wage were entitled to a monthly allowance if they were pregnant, handicapped, or had children less than seven years of age. These two benefits almost completely lost their value after 1990, but in 1995 there was a slight increase. In addition, in 1995, a social benefit was introduced for families and persons who had no, or extremely small, incomes. This benefit provides a real help for families with numerous children. In addition to monetary allowances, persons in especially difficult situations may receive, free of charge or at a discount rate, two meals a day in a social canteen.

However, the realities of the Romanian economy make life a general fight for survival for most families, and, in this struggle, the "minority pattern of raising children" becomes more common. This pattern, developed during the communist time, is characterized by indifference toward children (Zamfir, 1997).

Stages of Change, 1990–1991

Immediately after the 1990 change in the political system, the Romanian child welfare system recognized some of its problems and introduced "reparative" regulations (Zamfir, 1995). First, the laws prohibiting abortion were repealed. The staffing in child institutions was increased, and the amount of money spent for children in rural areas was brought to levels equivalent to that spent in urban areas. Much of this change was accomplished through child protection professionals who took the opportunity to introduce new models of child protection and services. Numerous foreign organizations, mostly from the West, provided funding for these programs and professionals. In September 1990, the president of Romania signed the UN Convention on the Rights of the Child (hereafter the Convention) in New York, and Parliament ratified the Convention one year later.

After two years of rapid positive changes, new problems specific to Romania's transition to a market economy emerged. The mass media presented a variety of new topics, including sex, gangs, the problem of AIDS, and the appearance of drug dealers. These presentations contributed to rapid changes in the values of both adults and young people and increased the burdens placed on the Romanian child protection system. However, the lack of services and trained professionals made facing these issues almost an impossible task. The government partially acknowledged these difficulties in a report on the current status of child protection written for the Committee on Children's Rights (1993).

As a consequence of ratifying the Convention, the Romanian government created the National Committee for Child Protection in 1993 and charged it with the task of unifying all of Romania's varied ministry regulations concerning child protection. In addition, this agency organized the acceptance and implementation of aid offers from Western organizations such as UNICEF, PHARE, and other nongovernmental organizations (NGOs).

At the same time, hundreds of NGOs continued or started to work in Romanian orphanages. These NGOs focused on preventing abandonment, teaching about children's rights, and educating the handicapped. A 1994 government publication mentioned 400 NGOs acting in the domain of child protection, and this number has since increased.[1] The *Directory for*

Central and Eastern Europe, Commonwealth of Independent States and the Baltic States[2] lists 222 NGOs maintaining projects for children, and 85 of these are acting in Romania. Some of these programs are still directed by foreign organizations that came to Romania in 1990 or 1991, but most are newly formed Romanian NGOs that collect the majority of their funds from the Western world.

There have been many other important positive changes in the post-communist period. Tens of new university departments have been created in the social sciences. In particular, several new schools of psychology and social work were formed in the last six years, and many of their graduates are already working. In addition, Parliament has enacted new laws to help avoid the institutionalization of children and to keep families together by giving salaries to family members who take care of handicapped persons and allowances to persons who have no or minimal income, depending on the number of persons in the family.

LEGAL INNOVATIONS

Unfortunately, until June 1997, the only child protection laws in effect were those enacted in 1970. The 1970 laws proposed some regulations for protecting children, but did not provide for methods of investigating or reporting child abuse, and suffered from a variety of other inadequacies. Under the old law, there was no systematic way for a child, or anyone else, to report abuse. There was no definition of "emergency" cases and no guidance on how to act in such cases. The old law did not regulate foster care, adoption, or the agencies that deal with child victims.

Investigation

When a claim of abuse did make it to the authorities, decision making was given to the Commission for Minors, which was composed of representatives of the Health, Police, and Education districts, as well as other official authorities. This group met once a month to make decisions regarding the institutionalization of abused or neglected children. Social workers were not asked to participate in any phase of this process, and determinations of whether a child was abused were based on parents' declarations and, possibly, a report based on a single home visit.

During the next period of Romanian history (from 1992 to 1996), the state protected children with material support in the form of a universal child allowance. This allowance was paid to the parents until the child was fourteen, at which time the child could collect the check him- or herself. Parents were not entitled to collect a child's check unless they had identity cards for themselves and a birth certificate for the child. The child allowance was an important aspect of Ceausescu's pro-natal policy. The allowance for handicapped children was double the normal allowance rate (Pasti, 1997), and before 1990, the allowance constituted 10.5 percent of the average salary and was an important form of family support. However, between 1989 and 1996, the size of the allowance was decreased, and it has dropped in value to approximately 4 percent of the average salary.

Legal System

The post-communist period from 1991 to 1996 represents a second stage of development in the child protection system in Romania. Since 1989, the Romanian legal system has, step by step, adopted the basic international regulations governing child welfare. The Romanian Parliament approved the UN Convention on the Rights of the Child in 1991 (Law 26). It approved the Hague Convention on Child-kidnapping (Law 100/1992) and the European Convention on the Legal Status of Children Born out of Marriage (Law 101/1992) in 1992. In 1993, Parliament approved the European Convention on Adoptions (Law 15/1993) and the Hague Convention on Child Protection and Cooperation in the Area of Adoption (Law 84/1994). However, official communications between representatives of the Romanian government and the Committee on Children's Rights during this second stage of development provide grounds for questioning the willingness of Romanian authorities actually to implement the changes required by these international agreements (Roth-Szamoskozi, 1999).

One communication is particularly revealing. In 1994, the Committee on Children's Rights asked the Romanian government to provide a report on the status of child protection and children's rights in Romania. The government's official answer provides a representative overview of the conflict between the government's official pronouncements and the actual state of affairs in Romania.

For example, the committee asked the government how the Convention on the Rights of the Child was broadcast to children and the way in which children were introduced to the Convention in school curricula. The Romanian government answered these questions by pretending that everything that could be done had already been done. The official communications claimed that children's rights were broadcast widely and that children learned about their rights in school during fourth and seventh grade. The government also stated that several organizations distributed the Convention directly to school children, and that the mass media were doing their best to present cases of abuse or neglect of children's rights. Unfortunately, none of these representations were completely true.

The 1994 report also reflects governmental satisfaction with the manner in which the best interests of children were understood and considered by the Romanian legal system. The government emphasized that, under then-existing law, a child who had reached the age of fourteen was entitled to express his or her opinion on such matters as vocational training, housing, maintaining a relationship with divorced parents, and maintaining or changing citizenship, and to have his or her opinion on these issues be considered and respected. In addition, the official communications state that children older than ten are listened to on issues of divorce and consent to adoption, and observe that the law requires the legal system to listen to a child's complaints regarding the manner in which he or she is treated. The communications also mention an important principle in the Code of the Family (taught to students in law schools), which provides that a child older than ten has the right to be heard by a jury. The government's official answers to the committee's inquiries conclude that these provisions give sufficient guarantees that all decisions respecting children are made in the best interest of the child. However, the official communications do not mention anything about the existence of special judges to hear a child's complaints or special procedures designed to ensure that a child's complaints and opinions are actually heard.

With respect to abuse, the 1994 report notes that each child has a legal right to complain to the office of the mayor about mistreatment. However, the report does not discuss how the child is supposed to know about this right. As mentioned previously, the 1970 laws governing child welfare and protection do not provide for the recognition, investigation, or treatment of emergency cases. As a result, even when children were in danger, institutions were not obliged to board children unless they had official certificates, which usually took several days to obtain. The 1994 report did not discuss this problem.

The 1994 report also ignored the importance of substance abuse and its relationship to child maltreatment, probably because Romania was not considered, at that time, to be a market for drug dealers. Instead, police and doctors were supposed to handle substance abuse issues. Another two years had to pass before the mass media began to consider this issue and for the police to recognize that Romania has a real and large problem with drugs. The 1994 report also ignored the dangerous practice of juvenile prostitution, probably because, at that time, the government provided no services for its prevention. In sum, the second stage of the development of Romania's child protection system was characterized by important changes in policy and law, coupled with official complacency and denial.

Current Developments in Romania's Child Protection System: The Third Phase

Until June 1997, judicial regulations did not require the implementation of the international conventions mentioned above. Although Parliament had approved the Convention on the Rights of the Child and other international agreements protecting children's rights, no procedures or laws were created for enforcing children's rights or penalizing those who violated them. This lack of official procedures was particularly telling, since the Convention makes the state responsible for offering assistance to children with difficulties. Professionals and those active in the voluntary sector of Romanian child welfare were left on their own to apply and implement the requirements of the international agreements. Meanwhile, terrifying images of the Romanian institutions responsible for protecting abandoned children began to reach the Western world.

However, 1997 saw a major change in the legal reform of Romania's child protection system: the abolition of Law 3/1970 and the adoption of two new child welfare laws, Law 192/1998 (Government Order 26) and Law 139/1998 (Government Order 25). Although these new laws provided significant advances in the protection of children, the history of their passage still reflected official complacency and denial. The original 1997 draft of Law 192/1998 did not focus on "abused" children or "abuse." Instead, it focused on the "child with difficulties." This phrase, "child with difficulties," referred to children who are endangered physically or with respect to their moral development or integrity. The original draft did not even use the word "abuse," even though the issues addressed by the law clearly encompass the kind of dangers usually associated with the term. Professionals perceived the law's avoidance of the term "abuse" as a sign of resistance by people working at the highest levels of decision making, who, it was believed, had difficulty admitting the existence of child abuse in Romania. This situation was partially corrected in the final form of the law (108 and 192), which was enacted in June 1998 and finally stated the obligation of the state to protect abused, abandoned, neglected, or exploited children.

TREATMENT AND THE HEALTH SYSTEM

In Romania, child abuse and neglect mean acting against or ignoring the needs that guarantee the normal development of the child. In practice, this definition has produced an emphasis on the physical needs of children, although in theory, and in actuality, the negative consequences of abuse and neglect are not limited to the physical. Because child abuse and neglect phenomena in Romania are related primarily to the child's physical needs, the quality of the health system must be discussed.

Under Romanian law, health care is provided free of charge to children. However, the Romanian health care system is marked by a lack of financial resources, due mostly to a lack of proper organization, as health care units are generally run by medical staff and physicians who are not trained in management. In many health care units, lack of training also produces poor and unresponsive client handling practices. The treatment provided in health care units also suffers because regulations and legislation protecting the interests of the clients vis-à-vis the medical staff and health care system are quite weak.

The persistent lack of financial resources produces other adverse consequences. There is a general lack of medicines, including vaccines. The food in the hospitals is very poor, as are the hygienic conditions within many health care units. The country's health care units also suffer from a lack of paramedical staff (e.g. psychologists, social workers, educators), a lack of technical equipment and medical tests, and low salaries for the medical staff. In addition, there is a shortage of toys and leisure time activities for children within the health care units.

Generally, the staff of the health care units is concerned only with the physiological condition of the clients. Little attention is given to understanding the children's social and psychological condition. Discussions of child abuse and neglect phenomena are almost unknown, even in the situation where the child needs medical care as a consequence of familial or institutional abuse or neglect. The staff does not pay any attention to the causes that brought the child to the hospital; they do not investigate the general situation and do not generate reports about the child's condition. Their focus is almost exclusively on treating the children's physical conditions (Enachescu & Vladescu, 1995, pp. 244–255).

PREVALENCE

We do not have any national statistics concerning child abuse and neglect phenomena within Romanian families. Romania does not yet gather any official statistics concerning child abuse and neglect. What data there are usually come from the social work departments of universities such as those in Cluj, Bucharest, and Timisoara. These statistics, however, cover only very specific geographic areas, periods, and types of abuse.

However, as a result of the recent debates and new laws regarding children in difficult situations, the Direction of Children's Rights conducted a detailed review of twelve child maltreatment cases handled during 1997 and 1998. Four of these twelve cases involved sexual abuse. In seven of the twelve, the parents were declared unable to accomplish their parental duties, and their parental rights were withdrawn.

The review provides an indication that there has been real progress in Romania with respect to the investigation of child abuse reports since 1996. According to the review, all the social workers who dealt with the cases were seriously involved and tried to do their best under the circumstances. But the review also reveals that we are still a long way from truly protecting children. Investigations are slow, and protection is not offered to victims who are not physically injured. Children at risk in the presented cases were not visited regularly enough, and cooperation between institutions and services was often absent. For example, in the case studies presented in the review, the Direction of Children's Rights did not receive notification of children's reintegration. Supportive parents were not offered enough help to resist abusers, and in the cases where children were placed in institutional children's homes, there was no significant long-term planning for the children's future welfare. Moreover, in some cases, children were not included in therapy programs, even though they exhibited specific symptoms of post-traumatic stress disorder. These unpleasant realities must be corrected in the future.

CHILD ABUSE AND NEGLECT WITHIN THE SOCIAL SYSTEM

After the first years of confrontation with the Western world, which revealed the sad picture of institutionalized children, Romania is beginning to face its own child protection problems, in all of their complexity. Zamfir (1997), in one of the best analyses of the traditional Romanian child protection system, discusses the following main characteristics of the system: overcentralization in administration, decision making, and distribution of funds; undue emphasis on the institutionalization of children; lack of, and unfair distribution of, resources; and lack of future planning. These characteristics may in part be related to the medical model that is the essential feature of the traditional Romanian child welfare system (Tobis & Vitillo, 1994). Within this model, the child is viewed only in relation to his or her biophysiological needs. There is no concern for the child's psychological or social development.

The use of the medical model has hindered the discussion and understanding of many child protection problems in Romania. For example, the causes of child neglect, abandonment, and abuse were not considered, and the symptoms of these problems were willingly hidden. Moreover, the solutions adopted to deal with child welfare, such as institutionalization, were more punitive then remedial—a common characteristic of Romania's traditional child welfare system. Instead of focusing on helping the parents deal with the root causes of abuse and neglect, families were separated and children were institutionalized. As if this situation were not sad enough, many homes (especially those of children under the age of three and those of severely handicapped children) denied their children the right to be loved and stimulated, to play and develop. In sum, the traditional Romanian child welfare system did not protect children's needs and rights.

CHILD ABUSE AND NEGLECT WITHIN THE FAMILY

Child abandonment is a major problem in Romania, and is due largely to poverty, lack of education, and lack of services to assist families. The family is the place where every child's needs should be fulfilled. However, given the conditions of family life mentioned above, many Romanian families become the setting for all kinds of child abuse and neglect. Emotional, physical, and even sexual abuse is quite frequent within the Romanian family system, as well as neglect. In addition, according to Budiu and Pop (1997), 3,262 children were abandoned in hospitals in 1997.

In 1996, End Physical Punishment of Children Worldwide (EPOCH Worldwide) conducted a study of the Romanian population (EPOCH & Barnen, 1996). EPOCH found that 96 percent of Romanians do not feel that beating a child would be humiliating for the child or impact the child's development and character. EPOCH also found that 84 percent of Romanians admitted beating their children. We found similar results in a study conducted during 1997 on violent child-rearing practices within the Romanian families in Timis County (Muntean, 1998a). This study found an interesting dynamic of practice and beliefs through three generations of traditional Romanian families. Eighty-seven percent of grandparents declared that they were hit in their childhood by their parents, and 84.37 percent of these grandparents consider beating a child a necessary child-rearing method. Interestingly, of the middle generation (the grandparents' children), only 78.12 percent declared that they were hit by their parents during childhood, and only 18.75 percent considered beating a child to be an efficient method of child rearing. Finally, only 68.75 percent of the third generation (the grandchildren of the first participants) declared that they were hit by their parents (the second generation), and only 18.75 percent of the parents (the second generation) considered beating an efficient method of child rearing. These data suggest that people are becoming increasingly aware that beating is not the right method to use in disciplining children, even if they still keep using this method.

Child Abuse and Neglect Within Social Care Units (Institutions of Child Protection)

Until the new legislation of 1997, child welfare institutions were divided among three governmental agencies: the Ministry of Health, which directed homes for children from birth to three years of age (called Leagan); the Ministry of Education, which managed preschool and school-age children (both normal and special, for children with different handicaps); and the Ministry of Labor and Social Protection, which directed the institutional homes for severely handicapped children (and adults).

The weaknesses in Romania's child protection system are clear in a number of places. First, the institutional space available for children has decreased at a time when the need for more beds has been growing (UNICEF & Department of Child Protection, 1997). In 1997 the secretary of state for the Department of Child Protection made several declarations in the press (Budiu & Pop, 1997) and on television about the existence of 100,000 children in institutions, a number considered to be a serious problem for the country. Furthermore, approximately 3,262 children are abandoned annually in hospitals (Budiu & Pop, 1997). These homeless children should have been institutionalized (and counted as such), but they were refused due to the absence of identity papers or because of conditions in the specific county where they were abandoned. Moreover, there are 5,469 children reared in institutional children's homes over the age of eighteen for whom there are no housing and employment possibilities (Budiu & Pop, 1997).

The Ceausescu government suggested that child institutionalization was not a problem because it only affected 1–2 percent of the country's children (Roth-Szamoskozi, 1999). Unfortunately, the exact number of children in state care has always been difficult to assess due to poor methods of statistical data collection and uncertain criteria for the term "institutionalization." Sometimes, official statistics include children living in special day-care schools for those with handicaps and learning disabilities; sometimes they do not. Thus, official statistics are only a starting point to understanding the actual levels of abuse in Romania.

The number of children admitted into institutions actually decreased in 1990 and 1991 (UNICEF & Department of Child Protection, 1997). However, since 1996, this downward trend has reversed, and the number of children admitted to institutions has been growing by approximately 10 percent per year (Sellick, 1998; Tobis & Vitillo, 1994; Popescu & Roth, 1995). This increase in institutionalization is especially prominent in Cluj County, known as the "children's cradle." Cluj County had 215 institutionalized children during the summer of 1997; by August 1998, their number had increased to 244 (Olteanu, 1998).

Although it is a common assertion that institutionalized children suffer all kinds of abuse (emotional, physical, and sexual), there are no studies concerning the frequency of abuse and neglect within the institutions. However, researchers assessing child development have found developmental differences between children who live with their families and children of the same ages who live in institutions. Muntean (1998b) evaluated the complex language and cognitive abilities of thirty children between four and five years of age. She found that the cognitive development of children living in institutions was only 36.8 percent of that of their peers living with their families. This difference may be indicative of abuse or neglect within the institutions.

LEGAL ISSUES

An Analysis of the Legal Frame of Child Welfare

This section describes the characteristics of the current Romanian child protection system, comparing and contrasting Romanian laws with international practices (Hill & Aldgate, 1996; Thorpe, 1994). To make this comparison, we trained a team to examine how Romanian law (both statutes and governmental orders implementing those statues) differed from the policies of the June 1998 International Convention on Children's Rights on ten key issues. In particular, we wished to assess the current state of law (i.e., changes already introduced by the Euro-Atlantic way of thinking) as well as the contradictions between the official statements about change in the child protection system and the real state of the Romanian child protection system.

The raters concluded that current Romanian law is consistent with a few of the principles of the International Convention on Children's Rights. For example, the raters found that Romanian law (numbers 108 and 192) addresses the goal that child protection should always be based on the best interest of the child (articles 3 and 7). In particular, the raters felt that the Romanian system did a good job of considering the child's right to have a family and of considering the role of the natural parents, even after the child has been removed from the home (article 13). In addition, Romanian law states that natural parents have a right to have contact with a child who has been removed from the home (article 11). Furthermore, the law is clear that the child welfare departments have a duty to help families in preventing abandonment (articles 20.c, 25.b) and in returning the child to his or her own family as soon as possible (article 20.d). Unfortunately, the law does not offer clues about the nature of the help needed to prevent abandonment or abuse—the law just mentions the necessity of help, without further regulations.

The raters also note important changes consistent with the spirit of the International Convention in the area of protecting children from abuse. The old law (3/1970) rarely mentioned the protection of the abused child, while the new law (article 14) states that the child protection service can intervene in exceptional situations to protect children from parents who endanger their security, development, or moral integrity. The new law also requires those who know about abuse cases to report the abuse to the Commission on Children's Rights. However, it is not clear if this mandatory reporting refers to all citizens or only to professionals, and there is not currently any other legal statement explaining the conditions under which child abuse must be reported. A second positive change is the new law's explicit statement that the state is obligated to be the "guaranty of protecting children from all forms of violence, including sexual violence, physical or psychological abuse, abandonment or neglect" (Law 108). It is unfortunate that the government has still omitted the word "abuse" from the governmental orders that actually implement the new laws.

The raters found that one of the worst represented principles of child protection is long-term planning for children separated from their families (International Convention 2.16). This principle affects about 100,000 children in residential homes. Although the new law provides that family placement and adoption should be favored over institutional placement when decisions are made with respect to these children, the new laws do not grant the Commission on Children's Rights the authority to make long-term plans for these children, beyond the time during which the "difficult situation" is ascertained and acted upon. The main progress in this area is the requirement stated in Law 108 that decisions of the commission should be periodically revised (articles 9.2, 21.1.a).

The raters were also critical of the responsibilities undertaken by the state (article 2.25) on behalf of the local communities because the new law does not define these responsibilities or identify the resources to be used in meeting them. In the final version of the law, the responsibilities of the state are also declared (articles 2.12 and especially 3.2), but the new law does not provide for how local communities will gain the resources needed to help children in difficult situations. Furthermore, the law does not mention the use of professional social workers (or other child welfare professionals), even though the law introduced a new profession called the "maternal worker ('assistant')," which seems to refer to the person who provides foster care to children living within the care provider's home. In sum, although there have been many positive changes in the legal framework of the Romanian child welfare system, there are many international principles of child protection that remain incomplete.

CHILD PROTECTION IN THE PRESS

The press has been instrumental in raising public awareness about abused and neglected children. Since 1990, the press has repeatedly reported on child victims, both in and out of institutions. Some journals like *22—Journal for Social Dialog* and *Medical Life* do a good job reporting the legitimate issues and problems. *22—Journal for Social Dialog* published a series of articles on adoption in 1996 (volumes 8 and 9), as well as a supplement on child protection issues which offered UNICEF representatives a forum to present their opinions (Maye Ayoub van Kohl, 1997). *Medical Life* published a scientific series on child maltreatment, which provided a unique presentation of the domain of abuse very helpful to professionals working with children (January 1998, March 1998).

However, the mainstream publications tend to report only the more sensational stories. The newspaper *Adevarul*, published in Bucharest, periodically covers results of the Sociological Institute of Quality of Life and interviews with personalities in the social services field. The newspaper uses striking titles focused on perils of society, such as "Children—First Victims of Transition in Romania" (1997); "Directors of Orphanages Are Guilty Because 100,000 Children Do Not Have a Family" (1997); "In Four Years the System Will Be Normalized" (1997); and "The Most Endangered Are Lonely Women" (July, 1997). Often the stories exaggerate reality, as in the case of a story that bore the headline "A Quarter of Romania's Children

Live in Institutions" (1997). Many local newspapers and TV stations publicize cases of sexual abuse, but they rarely go beyond reporting the fact of the abuse to discuss the underlying causes and potential interventions.

On the positive side, media coverage often helps the general public understand the various aspects of abuse, and the involvement of professionals in the media helps people understand the human aspects of abuse. Increased awareness of the fact of abuse has also reduced the shame associated with being a victim. For example, after articles concerning the sexual exploitation of children, prostitution, and sexual abuse were published during the Belgian pedophilia scandal in 1996, speaking about pedophilia became less taboo, and victims came forward for help.

CONCLUSION

Romanian society is currently in a transitional period with respect to child abuse and neglect. The Ceausescu government's pro-natal policies continue to have a residual effect on Romanian society, reflected in the general low level of economic activity, tens of thousands of temporarily or permanently abandoned and institutionalized children, and a large number of families living on the edge of poverty. These conditions continue to exacerbate the problem of child abuse and neglect within Romanian society.

Although new legislation has brought significant reform to the Romanian child protection system, such legislation is still quite tentative and unnecessarily vague about the existence of abuse and about the procedures and methods for investigating, treating, and preventing abuse. Instead, the new laws continue to emphasize the traditional approach of punishing perpetrators. Despite the numerous seminars, round tables, and conferences taking place under NGO initiatives, and the very frequent broadcasts and newspaper articles on the subject, child abuse and neglect is still not well understood by Romanian pediatricians, psychologists, social workers, and other professionals who interact with abused children.

The initial resistance to adapting modern Euro-Atlantic standards with respect to child abuse and neglect (1992–1996) was due, in large part, to the absence of legislation that could provide a proper framework for implementing those standards. In 1997–1998, the laws regulating child welfare were significantly amended to provide a new framework for understanding and approaching child abuse and neglect.

However, these legal reforms have not solved the problems inherent in Romania's child welfare system. Although the new laws represent significant reforms, it is clear that the official regulations implementing those laws must be based on a better understanding of child abuse and neglect. Similarly, although the legal reforms have been well received by professionals and staff working in social services for children, these reforms have not produced uniform changes in actual practice. One reason for the poor implementation of the laws is that many individuals currently within the system are resistant to change. Additionally, many of the staff are poorly trained.

Finally, we must acknowledge that the child welfare system needs more improvement in the area of evaluation. The current methods of gathering social statistics are defective, and workers need feedback concerning the results of their work to evaluate the effectiveness of their efforts.

We believe that four important tasks must be performed in order for the Romanian system to develop in the future. First, the agencies and organizations working in the child welfare domain must learn to cooperate with one another. Child welfare agencies and their qualified staff must be more cooperative with other professionals and with representatives of mass media to create a stronger impact on public awareness in the interest of children. These agencies and professionals should network at the community, county, national, and international levels.

Second, the country must improve its training and education with respect to child abuse and neglect prevention. Training programs should be available to professionals and workers all over the country at a variety of levels. In addition, parents should be more informed about child development and the consequences of abuse and neglect. Third, new structures and services with multidisciplinary teams specializing in child abuse and neglect should be created and implemented on the community, county, and national level.

Finally, information regarding child abuse and neglect should be gathered, translated, and disseminated. Research in the field should be organized and published, and statistics should be properly kept. Databases related to abuse and neglect should be created and made available. In addition, information in the field is not readily accessible in the Romanian language. Currently only one newsletter, *Today's Children Are Tomorrow's Parents*, directly addresses the issues of abuse and neglect. There is therefore a great and constant need for translations.

We remain hopeful that the future will bring better times for the next generations of children. These hopes are captured in the words of Octavia Graur (1995): "I can imagine a film about Romania and East European countries. It would be a black and white film, just like life in communism was. At the end of it, a little child in a colored coat, a child born under a luckier star, would take his parents' hands leading them to a better world, the world of a happy childhood, a world his parents never experienced."

NOTES

1. Conventia O.N.U. cu privire la drepturile copilului—stadiul aplicarii in Romania. (1994). Guvernul Romaniei, Comitetul National pentru Protectia copilului. Bucharest, Buletin nr. 4(18).

2. NGO projects for children, 1995, *Directory for Central and Eastern Europe, Commonwealth of Independent States and the Baltic States*, comp. NGLS for the

NGO/UNICEF Coordinating Committee on Activities for Children in Central and Eastern Europe, Commonwealth of Independent States and the Baltic States, NGLS, Geneva.

REFERENCES

Anghel, I., 1997. Situatia copiilor din Romania s-a deteriorat continuu [The situation of children in Romania continuously worsened]. *22—Journal for Social Dialog, 29*, 12.

Baban, A., & David, H. P. (1994). *Voci ale femeilor*. Bucharest: UNICEF.

Berridge, D., & Brodie, I. (1998). *Children's homes revisited*. London: Jessica Kingley.

Berry, M., & Cash, S. (1998, January-February). Creating community through psychoeducational groups in family preservation work. *Families in Society: The Journal of Contemporary Human Services*, 15–24.

Budiu, L., & Pop, D. (1997, July 21). In 4 ani, sistemul de ocrotire a copilului se va normaliza [In four years the system will be normalized]. *Adevarul*.

Coffey, A., & Atkinson, P. (1996). *Making sense of qualitative data*. London: Sage Publications.

Csokai, L., Domszki, A., & Tn, M. (Eds.). (1994). A gyermekvedelem nemzetkozi gyakorlata [The international practice of child protection]. Budapest: Pont.

Directia judeteana de statistica Cluj. (1998). *Statistical data for Cluj county, 1990–1997*. Cluj: Directia judeteana de statistica.

Enachescu, D., & Vladescu, C. (1995). Social policy and health systems. In E. Zamfir & C. Zamfir (Eds.). *Politici sociale*. Bucharest: Alternative.

EPOCH, & Barnen, R. (1996). *Hitting people is wrong—and children are people, too*. London: Expression Printers.

European Convention on Adoptions. (1993). In *Monitorul Oficial, 63*, March 31, Bucharest.

European Convention on the legal status of children born out of marriage. (1993). Mentioned in the *Raportul dezvoltarii umane. Departamentul Informatiilor Publice, Buletin nr. 4(18), Bucuresti*.

Filipescu, I. (Ed.). (1997). *Adoptia si protectia copilului*. Bucharest: All Educational S.A.

Graur, O. (1995). Consequences of an abusive system and possibilities to break the cycle. Personal communication, ISPCAN Congress, Oslo.

Guvernul, Romaniei, Comitetul National pentru Protectia Drepturilor Copilului. (1994). Coventia ONU cu privire la drepturile copilului—stadiul aplicarii in Romania. Bucharest, Buletin nr. 4(18).

Hague Convention on Child-kidnapping. (1995). Mentioned in the *Raportul dezvoltarii umane, Departamentul Informatiilor Publice, Buletin nr. 4(18), Bucuresti*.

Hague Convention on Child Protection and Cooperation in the Field of Adoption. (1994, October 21). Published in *Monitorul official, 298*, Bucharest.

Heifner, C. J. (1994). *A model for managing change*. Paper presented at the 26th International Conference of the International Council of Social Welfare, Tampere, Finland.

Herczog, M. (1997). *A gyermekvedelem dilemai* [The dilemmas of child protection]. Budapest: Pont.

Hill, M., & Aldgate, J. (1996). The Children Act 1989 and recent developments in research in England and Wales. In M. Hill & J. Aldgate (Eds.), *Child welfare services*. London: Jessica Kingley.

Hill, M., Hawthorne, Kirk R., & Part, D. (1995). *Supporting families*. Edinburgh: HMSO.

Hines, J. R., Kessler, S., & Landers, C. (1991). *Children in institutions in central and eastern Europe and a first look at alternative approaches*. Florence: UNICEF, International Child Development Centre.

Ilut, P. (1997). Abordarea calitativa a socioumanului. Iasi: Polirom.

Johnson, A., Edwards, R., & Puwak, H. (1992). *Foster care and adoption issues*. Bucharest: Country Office, UNICEF.

Kendrick, A. (1995a). The integration of child care services in Scotland. *Children and Youth Services Review, 17(5/6)*, 619–635.

Kendrick, A. (1995b). *Residential child care in the integration of child care services*. Glasgow: Scottish Office Central Research Unit.

Kendrick, A. (1996, March). A better kind of home. *Practice Paper, 3*. Glasgow.

Muntean, A. (1998a). *Limbajul si dezvoltarea structurilor temporo—spatiale, studiu comparativ: Normal/patologic*. Unpublished doctoral thesis, Universitatea Babes-Bolyai, Cluj-Napoca.

Muntean, A. (1998b). *Violent child rearing practices: Dynamics and effects*. Paper presented at Conference on Child and Family, Athens.

National Commission for Statistics. (1996). *Statistical yearbook of Romania*. Bucharest: HMSO.

Olteanu, T. Director of Protection of Children's Rights. (1998, August). Interview.

Parker, R., Ward, H., Jackson, S., Aldgate, J., & Wedge, P. (Eds.). (1991). *Assessing outcomes in child care*. London: Crown.

Pasti, S. (1997). Principii de baza ale protectiei copilului si ale serviciilor de asistenta sociala pentru copiii si familiile aflate in situatii deosebit de dificile [Principles of child protection and social services for children and families in difficult situations]. In R. Vitillo & D. Tobis (Eds.), *Programul de consolidare a serviciilor pentru copii si familii aflate in situatii deosebit de dificile*. Bucharest: Departmentul pentru protectia copilului si UNICEF.

PHARE presentation booklet 1993. Bucharest: PHARE.

Popescu, L., & Roth, M. (Coord.). (1995). *Asistenta Sociala ca activitate de mediere in societate*. Cluj-Napoca: Presa Universitara Clujeana.

Roth, M. (1992). *Child welfare and socio-economic status*. Paper presented at Social Work Conference, Debrecen, Hungary.

———. (1995). Az allami gondozas Romaniaban [Residential child protection in Romania]. *Csalad, Gyermek, Ifjusag, 1* (Budapest).

———. (1998). *Intersection of modernization and tradition in child protection structures*. [Manuscript]. Research sponsored by Research Support Scheme and Open Society Institute.

Roth-Szamoskozi, M. (1999). *Protectia copilului, Dileme, Conceptii si metode*. Cluj-Napoca: Editura Preas Universitara Clujeana.

Sellick, C. (1998). Developing professional social work practice in Romania. *Social Work in Europe, 4(2)*, 49–52.

Social Services Inspectorate. (1994, 1995). *Inspecting for quality: Standards for residential child care services.* London: HMSO.

Thorpe, D. (1994). *Evaluating child protection.* Buckingham: Open University Press.

Tobis, D., & Vitillo, R. (1994). *Analiz privind comisiile pentru protecia minorilor si autoritile tutelare in Romania* [Analysis concerning Commission of Minors and the tutorial activity in Romania]. Bucharest: UNICEF.

Trielitis, J., Borland, M., Hill, M., & Lambert, L. (1995). *Teenagers and the social work services.* London: HMSO.

UNICEF and Department of Child Protection. (1997). *Situatia copilului si a familiei in Romania* [Report on the situation of child protection and family in Romania]. Bucharest: UNICEF.

Ward, H. (Ed.). (1995). *Looking after children: Research into practice.* London: HMSO.

Zamfir, C. (1997). *For a society centered on the child.* Bucharest: Department of Child Protection, UNICEF, European Commission, European Council, USAID, World Bank.

Zamfir, E. (1994). *Situatia familiei si a copilului in Romania.* Bucharest: Country Office, UNICEF.

———. (1995). Politica de protectie a copilului in Romania. In E. Zamfir & C. Zamfir, (Eds.). *Politici sociale.* Bucharest: Alternative.

13

RUSSIA

Frederick B. Berrien, Tamara Yakovlevna Safonova, and Evgeny Iosifivich Tsimbal

PROFILE OF RUSSIA

Russia, located in Eastern Europe and Asia, has an area of approximately 17 million square kilometers, spanning eleven time zones and two continents. Moscow is its capital. The population of 14.7 million is comprised of primarily Russians, but also includes Tatars and Ukrainians. Religious affiliations include Russian Orthodox, Islam, Judaism, Roman Catholicism, Protestant, and Buddhist. The Federation government gained its independence in 1991 and consists of an executive, judicial, and legislative branch. The gross national product per capita in 1998 was $2,300 (U.S.). The official language is Russian; however, there are more than 140 other languages and dialects. The infant mortality rate is 17 per 1,000 and the life expectancy is fifty-eight years for males and seventy-two years for females. The literacy rate is 98 percent, and suffrage is universal at age eighteen.

A CASE STUDY

Four-month-old Dimka was admitted to the hospital for head injuries after his parents called an ambulance to take him to the trauma department at the Children's Hospital. Dimka's parents reported that he had fallen from his crib and began vomiting. Dimka was very fussy, refused to nurse, and experienced a seizure. An X-ray revealed that he had a skull fracture, and a scan of Dimka's brain revealed a subdural hematoma near this fracture. Doctors and nurses spoke with his mother and father and received two different accounts of how Dimka had fallen to the floor. During his hospital stay, Dimka's parents always visited him together, and during these visits his mother spoke very little and his father constantly demanded that Dimka be discharged home. The medical staff suspected that someone had injured the boy; however, when the parents were asked about this, they insisted that he had fallen from his crib. Unfortunately, the hospital staff did not know how to pursue an investigation, thus no further inquiry was undertaken. After one month in the hospital, Dimka was still not exhibiting developmentally appropriate behaviors, such as reaching for objects or showing interest in his environment. Nonetheless, Dimka was discharged from the hospital into his parents' care.

HISTORY

Child abuse has only recently been recognized as a problem in Russia, although throughout the twentieth century Russians have been aware that society has an obligation to care for children in need. Following the Civil War of 1918–1920 and World War II, hundreds of thousands of children were orphaned, and the state made it a priority to provide basic necessities for them (Harwin, 1997). Russians were aware of homeless or street children (*bezprionye*), but no term existed to describe abused children. Communist ideology during the Soviet period (1922–1991) encompassed a paternalism toward children, including numerous institutions of social management that provided and enforced moral standards (Bronfrenbrenner, 1972; Harwin, 1997). Parents were expected to provide food, shelter, and clothing. Children were morally protected by the state, and if parents died or were unable to provide basic necessities, the state would place children in an orphanage (*detski dom*) or boarding school (*internat*) where food, shelter, and clothing were provided. There was a shared responsibility for raising children between state and family, creating an illusion of stable child rearing. As such, the state could not acknowledge that this system might fail or that child abuse might occur.

In the 1960s, it was recognized that some parents who were not physically or mentally impaired were failing to carry out their responsibilities to their children. The state identified these children as neglected and referred to them as "social orphans" or "orphans with living parents." It was legislated that the state would take full responsibility for these children and provide for them just as if their parents had died.

DEFINITIONS

Child abuse is now legally recognized in Russia and includes neglect, physical abuse, emotional abuse, and sexual abuse. Marriage and family law first identified the problem in 1968, but definitions were not clearly artic-

Table 13.1
Number of Children Separated from Parents

Status	1992	1996
Abandoned	67,286	113,243
Denial of parental rights	10,677	34,865
Separated with parental rights	3,401	6,724

Source: "The status of children in the Russian Federation: Annual report to the government of
Russia." Moscow: Ministry of Labor and Social Development of the Russian Federation,
1993 and 1996.

ulated. The 1997 criminal law in Russia identified sexual misconduct, emotional abuse, excessive physical punishment, and neglect as crimes. In 1998,
the Supreme Court of the Russian Federation (Supreme Court N10, 5/27/
98) broadened the concept of abuse to include systematic beatings, psychological abuse, and use of unacceptable measures of discipline when inflicted
by parents, trustees, teachers, or institutional caregivers.

PREVALENCE

There is no centralized registry for child abuse and neglect in Russia in
spite of mandatory reporting. The 1997 annual report prepared by the Ministry of Labor and Social Development, *The Status of Children in the Russian
Federation*, reported 17,000 crimes annually against children, including
2,000 murders, 6,000 sexual crimes, and 1,313 cases of physical abuse or
neglect. These crime statistics vastly underestimate the actual number of
cases due to underreporting and reluctance to investigate crimes against
children.

Tsimbal (1997) estimated that there are at least 26,000 sexual crimes
against children each year. This figure was based on (a) the 6,000 registered
crimes, (b) an estimate of 8,000 pregnancies in girls as a result of intercourse
with older men, and (c) extrapolation of boarding school data that identify
an additional 12,000 victims.

The 1996 *Status of Children in the Russian Federation* identifies 113,243
children who were abandoned, 34,865 children whose parents were denied
their parental rights, and another 6,724 children who were separated from
their parents without termination of parental rights (see Table 13.1). Based
on a Russian child population of 147,987,101 (*World Almanac*, 1997), 0.6
percent of children are not living with their parents. Harwin (1997) notes
that recently more children are entering state care due to inadequate par-

enting; however, it is not specified if this is due to abuse, neglect, or other issues.

Russia had a long-standing problem throughout the Soviet period with child abandonment, particularly with newborn children. A study by Lvoff, Lvoff, and Klaus (2000) of abandoned newborns in St. Petersburg hospitals showed rates of 50–60 abandonments per 1,000 births in 1995, an increase of 32 percent since 1990. These data demonstrate that the rate of abandonment and neglect is not only high, but increasing.

Physical abuse has been the subject of a small number of surveys of adolescents and children. Berrien, Aprelkov, Ivanova, Zhmurov, and Buzhicheeva (1995) found in a self-report survey of 375 public school children in Siberia (ages eleven–sixteen years), that 29 percent had experienced inflicted abusive physical trauma by adults at some point in their lives. In addition, 17 percent of these children reported observing abuse of other children. In another group of 339 children (ages thirteen–fifteen years), Berrien and Aprelkov (1996) found that 6 percent of children had medically significant injuries including punches, burns, fractures, and injuries caused by instruments. Lvoff and Lvoff (1998) surveyed 723 nursing students and found that 12 percent of male students and 5 percent of female students experienced medically significant injuries during their lives. However, despite the fairly high rates reported by children, only 3 percent of 2,060 adults surveyed from various regions of Russia acknowledged severely beating their children within the past year (Achildieva, 1997).

Similar to physical abuse, sexual abuse has been minimally studied in Russia. Lvoff and Lvoff (1998) surveyed nursing students to determine the incidence of abusive childhood sexual contact. Twenty-seven percent of female students acknowledged experiencing attempted intercourse, and 24 percent reported touching of their sexual parts by an adult when they were a child. For males, 9 percent reported attempted intercourse, while 11 percent reported touching of their sexual parts by an adult. Tsimbal (1997) surveyed youth from unstable families in a Moscow shelter for children and found that 21 percent of the children had experienced sexual abuse and that two-thirds of the sexual abuse was intrafamilial.

A report by Loseva (1997) on childhood sexually transmitted diseases (STDs) at a Moscow facility identified thirteen children ranging in age from one to twelve years who were treated for syphilis. Prostitution was the source of the STDs in three of the boys and six of the girls. In a survey of 263 Moscow school personnel by Safonova, Tsimbal, Sautkina, Fetisova, and Michailov (1998), 448 children were identified as victims of abuse or neglect. According to this survey, 50 percent were psychologically abused, 30 percent were physically abused, 13 percent were sexually abused, and 7 percent suffered from neglect. Parents and other adults responsible for children were frequently identified as the perpetrators (see Table 13.2). However,

Table 13.2
Percent of Abuse by Perpetrator Type

	Parents	Peers	Other Adults	Education Workers
Physical abuse	29.5	53.8	14.4	2.3
Sexual abuse	56.7	8.3	18.3	16.7
Psychological abuse	39.1	28.9	16.9	15.1
Neglect	35.5	32.2	32.3	0
Combined	38.4	33.7	17.4	10.5

Source: "Incidence of child abuse and neglect: Data of sociological interview," in T. Y. Safonova, E. I. Tsimbal, T. I. Sautkina, N. N. Fetisova, & A. Michailov (1998), *Psychological, social, and medical centers and complexes for social help to children and adolescents: Information guide* (pp. 126–127). Moscow: Moscow Education Committee.

Safonova et al. (1998) additionally identified educational workers to be responsible for various forms of abuse in a significant percentage of cases.

The studies performed to date indicate that child abuse occurs as frequently in Russia as in other developed countries. As noted above, the estimates of physical abuse are based on very limited data and vary from 5 percent to 29 percent, while sexual abuse prevalence is estimated at 10 percent for males and 27 percent for females. It is acknowledged that prevalence rates are highly variable from country to country depending on the definitions and methodology used in surveys (Gilbert, 1997; International Society for Prevention of Child Abuse and Neglect, 1996). For comparative purposes, Gelles and Straus (1987) estimated the incidence rate of physical abuse in the United States to be 110 per 1,000 children in 1985, while the prevalence rate of sexual abuse in the United States was conservatively estimated at 20 percent for females and 5–10 percent for males (Finkelhor, 1994). The preliminary data in Russia appear to be comparable to these U.S. rates.

The statistical rise in abandonment, increasing denial of parental rights, and an increase in infanticide (from 121 cases in 1993 to 178 in 1997) (Ministry of Labor and Social Development of the Russian Federation, 1998) suggest that the child abuse and neglect problem in Russia is increasing. It is not clear from current data whether there has been an actual increase or if the statistics reflect an increasing awareness of the problem. It remains to be seen if the actual incidence of child abuse and neglect is greater than that of other countries and whether differing political, economic, and social factors influence incidence rates of abuse.

SOCIAL FACTORS

Unfortunately, factors believed to cause child abuse and neglect have not been extensively studied in Russia. Concern exists that the high incidence of alcoholism in Russia, conservatively estimated to affect 3 million individuals, has an adverse effect on the care of children. Anecdotal experience indicates that alcoholism is related to abandonment of children. However, Berrien and Aprelkov (1996) failed to demonstrate a specific correlation between child abuse and family alcoholism in their child self-report study. This public school study did find a correlation between child abuse and families in "constant conflict" as reported by the children surveyed.

A second undocumented view is that unstable socioeconomic conditions have increased family stress, thus contributing to the incidence of child abuse. The decade-long transformation of Russia's social, economic, and political systems has disrupted much of the social network that supported families and children in the Soviet era. The financial security guaranteed to families has disappeared and has been replaced by soaring inflation and the constant threat of unemployment (Harwin, 1997). Economic resources for health and education have been eroded, leaving families with fewer government services, thereby shifting the financial burdens to the family. Since the USSR never established family-oriented mental health services or child guidance services, families have always turned to relatives or informal personal contacts to obtain support and advice concerning psychological, emotional, and social problems (Harwin, 1997). The change to a more competitive economy, the loss of personal economic stability, and the spread of poverty have created an environment that is less conducive to this informal support network (International Society for Prevention of Child Abuse and Neglect, 1998).

LEGAL ISSUES

The Russian legal system distinguishes family law dealing with parents' rights and responsibilities from criminal law dealing with prosecution of criminal acts against children. A family law code, passed in 1968 under the Soviet system, identified abuse as a reason for revoking parental rights. Following Russia's ratification of the United Nations Convention on the Rights of the Child in 1996, the Russian Federation further delineated the rights of children and the state's responsibility to adjudicate abuse and neglect cases as stated in articles 19, 20, and 21 of the Convention. These articles included the denial of parental rights and provisions for adoption in cases of abuse and neglect. A 1998 ruling by the Supreme Court of the Russian Federation (Ruling N10, May 27, 1998) expanded abuse to include physical abuse, sexual abuse, psychological abuse, and exploitation of children. Legislative and judicial action has not provided functional definitions of the various forms of abuse. However, the child advocacy professionals in Russia have adopted working definitions based on English and American standards.

Under the family law code, all citizens and institutions are mandated to report child abuse to the Local Guardianship Organization. This municipal organization has inspectors who examine the complaints and make a decision within three days, while providing temporary shelter for the child, if deemed necessary. Decisions regarding the status of parental rights are made by a judge based on testimony provided by the Local Guardianship Organization, the prosecutor, the parents, and the child, if over nine years old.

The family law code permits the full revocation of parental rights when physical, emotional, or sexual abuse has occurred. Substance abuse and violent threat to a child's life are also grounds for revocation of parental rights. Despite the revocation of parental rights, parents maintain financial responsibility for their child. However, this financial obligation is often not fulfilled. If parents are suffering from psychological or chronic physical illnesses that interfere with their care of the child, there may be limited revocation of parental rights. In this case, the parents may visit the child, but they do not have specific responsibility for raising the child.

The enforcement of the family law code has been difficult because of the small number of inspectors in the Local Guardianship Organization. It is estimated that there is approximately one inspector for every 30,000 children (Harwin, 1997). These inspectors have many responsibilities regarding children and often lack specific training or knowledge of child abuse and neglect issues. Their major responsibility has been to provide basic needs for children who are orphaned.

Definitions

Criminal law regarding child abuse passed by the parliament in January 1997 recognizes physical abuse, neglect, sexual abuse, and emotional abuse as crimes. Physical abuse is considered a crime when a mark is left by the physical contact. Criminal neglect occurs when it is severe enough to endanger the life of the child or could lead to child abuse, and this applies to parents, surrogate parents, teachers, and tutors. Sexual abuse includes penetration of any child under fourteen years and any sexual contact that is imposed by force or by preying on the dependent status of the child. Unfortunately, these definitions lack both inclusiveness and specificity for practical implementation of the criminal code.

Legal Penalties for Offenders

Perpetrators of crimes who are over the age of fourteen years are prosecuted as adult criminals. Infanticide is punishable with five years imprisonment, and other child murders are punishable with eight to twenty years imprisonment. Convictions of sexual abuse carry a sentence of four to fifteen years, depending on the age of the victim. Child pornography is prosecuted under general pornography laws and carries a two-year jail sentence. No effort is made to rehabilitate perpetrators of crimes against children.

Similar to the family law code, the criminal law code for child abuse has not been strongly enforced due to problems throughout the law enforcement and judicial systems. Federal laws fail to provide specific definitions of abuse that can be effectively applied for prosecution. The relatively rapid passage of new statutes has created seemingly conflicting laws. As a result, only the Supreme Court can resolve these conflicts, and this requires time. Because of these complex judicial issues, police are reluctant to become involved in child abuse cases. Furthermore, legal precedents have not generally been established, therefore adjudication has been difficult. These factors contribute to a low level of criminal prosecution and are reflected in the low incidence rates of crimes against children recorded in official reports.

Court procedures for child abuse have not been adapted to permit children to participate effectively. At the present time, there are limited private services available to assist children and families with legal and court proceedings. The lack of child-oriented legal services discourages families from pursuing legal and court action against perpetrators of abuse.

Although child abandonment and the increasing number of children entering state care are recognized issues, child abuse and neglect are not yet considered widespread social issues in Russia. The mass media accentuate the criminal aspects of abuse and neglect, creating the impression that child abuse is the result of mental pathology, amoral parents, or extremely difficult family circumstances. It is not generally recognized that child maltreatment occurs in many forms, nor is there awareness that this problem can affect children across all socioeconomic and ethnic groups. The identification of child maltreatment within families that have extremely aberrant problems or circumstances conflicts with the reality that all children are potential victims because of their dependent and vulnerable position in all societies. The resulting maladaptive and criminal behaviors are not recognized, nor is the intergenerational nature of the problem appreciated.

CHILD PROTECTION

As a result, little has been done to deal actively with the problems of abuse and neglect. Social work was first created in Russia in 1991 (Harwin, 1997). Families can voluntarily engage with social work, but there is still no judicial or legislative mandate that forces or encourages families to work in this manner. Therefore, there is little opportunity to work effectively with problem families to influence the behavior of parents and improve family dynamics. Organized services for abused children and their families are not generally available. Assistance to families and children is provided through professionals who work in a general human service capacity and develop individual interest in abuse issues. One unique facility created in Moscow to provide assistance to families dealing with abuse is the Psychological, Medical, Social Center for Abused and Neglected Children (OZON). From 1996 to 1998, the center received 276 referrals in a twenty-two-month period. Twenty-three percent of these referrals involved sexual abuse, 11 percent psychological abuse, 7 percent physical abuse, 1 percent neglect, 2 percent suicide, and 55 percent problems related to mental health, behavioral, and social adjustment needs. Approximately 80 percent of these children were referred to the center by family, friends, or self-referral. OZON is supported by the Moscow Central District Committee of Education and the Child Abuse Protection Foundation. It provides psychological and social work support for families as they deal with legal and court procedures. A children's trust line at the center provides telephone advice. In the initial ten months of operation, there were 2,158 calls, primarily from family members and children regarding sexual abuse, children's rights, crisis situations, suicide, and abandonment. The OZON center, in addition to its successful individual advocacy, has worked with legislators to advocate for a system which will be responsive to the needs of abused children and their families.

The primary management modality for victims of abuse and neglect has been placement in state care. When children are removed from their parents by a decision of the Local Guardianship Organization, they may be placed in temporary shelter for up to three months or placed permanently in orphanages or boarding schools. The 1996 Family Law created foster homes, but there were only 339 foster homes in 1997 (Ministry of Labor and Social Development of the Russian Federation, 1998). The orphanages and boarding schools, created for homeless children decades ago, provide basic housing, food, and education. They provide no therapy or special services for abused children and rarely have social workers or psychologists on their staff. Reunification with families is unusual, and contact with families is not usually promoted. At present, these 600 institutions are overcrowded, accommodating two to three times their intended capacity. Recent economic conditions in Russia have reduced financial support for these facilities. Some institutions have failed to provide basic necessities such as heat, food, clothing, and health care, while others have lost their professional staff due to delays in payment of salary. Accompanying these financial problems has been the emergence of reports of abuse perpetrated by staff on the children, including physical abuse, sexual abuse, and inappropriate child labor practices (Harwin, 1997).

The shortage of placement resources has resulted in some children being placed in temporary facilities for extended periods of time, including hospitals or centers intended for adolescents who have committed crimes. Approximately 6,000 of the children who ran away from boarding schools reentered the system through the juvenile prison system, with 1,500 remaining in the prison system for more than forty-five days (Ministry of Labor and Social Development of the Russian Federation, 1996). These deplorable conditions compound the problems faced by children who have been neglected and abused by their own families.

Therapeutic programs for perpetrators of crimes against children are generally not available. If mental illness accompanies a crime against children, the mental illness will be treated, but no specific therapeutic effort will be made to address issues related to the abuse. Therapeutic programs to assist individuals or families with interactional problems are also unavailable. Reunification of families is rare, and no specific programs exist to assist that process.

PREVENTION AND TREATMENT

Awareness of child abuse and neglect is growing in Russia, but few educators and child health professionals have the knowledge to understand the necessary interventions for prevention and treatment of these problems. The study conducted by Safonova et al. (1998) demonstrated that 39 percent of school personnel agreed with the use of physical punishment as a disciplinary measure, reflecting an attitude of acceptance of physical violence toward children. Sadly, only 53 of 263 respondents could identify a law or legitimate legal document related to child abuse or neglect. When given a scenario of a twelve-year-old girl who complained of sexual abuse, less than one-third of the respondents selected to report the abuse and support the child. In fact, 10 percent recommended ignoring the situation. In an informal oral survey of seventy-five teachers and physicians conducted by Berrien and Aprelkov (1996), there was clear acknowledgment of the problem but confusion regarding how abuse and neglect are supposed to be managed in Russia.

At a basic level, Kirillova (1996) contends that professionals have failed to acknowledge the importance of familial attachments in the etiology and treatment of abuse. Soviet ideology minimized the influence of the family, in comparison to the influence of the state, in raising children. When children were removed from their family and placed in institutional settings, attention was not given to the importance of maintaining relationships with the child's family of origin or to establishing new attachment relationships. This condition continues to persist today in orphanages and boarding schools, and Kirillova (1996) believes that this contributes to an intergenerational cycle of interpersonal problems and child abuse. She further states that family separation in maternity hospitals and mothers' early return to the workforce have interfered with early attachment between mother and child and may be contributing to child abuse.

Ironically, Russia had one of the most progressive child abuse primary prevention models during the Soviet period. Nurses (*patronazh*), often accompanied by physicians, regularly visited families in their homes, providing health care and parenting advice (Berrien & Kolesnikov, 1995). This model of home visiting, which is being rediscovered in many other countries (Olds et al., 1999), has become less available in Russia due to overall reductions in financial allocations for health care (Harwin, 1997). The health visits have become more focused on medical pathology with less attention to nurturing issues. Increasing dependence on private financing of health care in Russia has decreased the investment in this model of primary prevention. Although a few child abuse programs in Russia provide prevention programs targeted at parents, children, or professionals, general programs of primary and secondary prevention have not been established in Russia. There simply has not been a government initiative to promote prevention of child abuse and neglect.

CONCLUSION

Official reports and a limited number of research and anecdotal studies indicate that child abuse and neglect are significant problems in Russia. The increasingly large number of children who do not live with their parents reflects the magnitude of neglect. The frequency of child and parent reports of inflicted injuries and the pervasive use of corporal punishment indicate that physical abuse is a major problem. Collected data and clinical experience at shelters and specialized services show that sexual abuse is also a profound and serious problem in Russian society.

A code of family and criminal law is beginning to emerge, providing a legal framework for adjudicating this problem. The infrastructure for implementing the intent of the laws, however, has not been established to permit effective and efficient utilization of the legal system to protect children and prosecute offenders.

The management of child abuse and neglect is restricted to separation of the children from offending parents. Limited support and intervention services are provided in urban centers, but no standard system of therapy or care for victims or perpetrators has been established. The institutions where children are placed for protection have inadequate resources for basic necessities, fail to provide therapy for the children, and often exacerbate children's problems.

The information available to the public and professionals has stigmatized abuse and neglect as a problem of specific populations, failing to acknowledge the risk that exists for many other children. Unfortunately, education of professionals regarding the causes, detection, and management of child abuse and neglect in Russia is still in its infancy.

REFERENCES

Achildieva, Y. F. (1997). Atypical family: Research conventionality or objective reality? In Y. F. Achildieva (Ed.), *Atypical family: The standard of living and social status* (pp. 5–8). Moscow: Idz-vo "Stankin."

Berrien, F. B., & Aprelkov, G. N. (1996). *Prevalence and management of child abuse in Russia.* Dublin: Eleventh International Congress on Child Abuse and Neglect.

Berrien, F. B., Aprelkov, G. N., Ivanova, T., Zhmurov, V., & Buzhicheeva, V. (1995). Prevalence of child abuse in Russia: A preliminary report. *Child Abuse and Neglect, 19,* 261–264.

Berrien, F. B., & Kolesnikov, S. I. (1995). Russian pediatric health care: A role for professional collaboration. *International Child Health, 6,* 67–72.

Bronfrenbrenner, U. (1972). *Two worlds of childhood: US and USSR.* New York: Simon and Schuster.

Finkelhor, D. (1994). Current information on the scope and nature of child sexual abuse. *Future of Children, 4(2),* 31–53.

Gelles, R., & Straus, M. (1987). Is violence toward children increasing? *Journal of Interpersonal Violence, 2,* 212–222.

Gilbert, N. (1997). *Combatting child abuse: International perspectives and trends.* New York: Oxford University Press.

Harwin, J. (1997). *Children of the Russian state: 1917–95.* Bookfield, VT: Avebury.

International Society for Prevention of Child Abuse and Neglect. (1996). *World perspectives on child abuse: Second international resource book.* Chicago: International Society for Prevention of Child Abuse and Neglect.

International Society for Prevention of Child Abuse and Neglect. (1998). *World perspectives on child abuse: Third international resource book.* Denver: International Society for Prevention of Child Abuse and Neglect.

Kirillova, M. (1996). *A dramatic choice between child neglect in the family and psychological neglect in state child caring institutions in Russia.* Dublin: Eleventh International Congress on Child Abuse and Neglect.

Loseva, O. K. (1997). The influence of the parent family on the formation of stereotypes of children's deviant sexual behavior. In Y. F. Achildieva (Ed.), *Atypical family: The standard of living and social status* (pp. 130–139). Moscow: Izd-vo "Stankin."

Lvoff, N., & Lvoff, V. (1998). *Prevalence of child physical and sexual abuse in Russia.* Amsterdam: International Congress of Pediatrics.

Lvoff, N., Lvoff, V., & Klaus, M. (2000). Effect of the baby-friendly initiative on infant abandonment in a Russian hospital. *Archives of Pediatric and Adolescent Medicine, 154,* 474–477.

Ministry of Labor and Social Development of the Russian Federation. (1993, 1994, 1995, 1996, 1998). *The status of children in the Russian Federation: Annual report to the government of Russia.* Moscow.

Olds, D., Henderson, C., Kitzman, H., Eckenrode, J., Cole, R., & Tatelbaum, R. (1999). Prenatal and infancy home visitation by nurses: Recent findings. *The Future of Children, 9(1),* 27–43.

Safonova, T. Y., Tsimbal, E. I., Sautkina, T. I., Fetisova, N. N., & Michailov, A. (1998). Incidence of child abuse and neglect: Data of sociological interview.

Psychological, social, and medical centers and complexes for social help to children and adolescents: Information guide (pp. 126–127). Moscow: Moscow Education Committee.

Tsimbal, E. I. (1997). *Extrafamilial and intrafamilial sexual abuse in children.* Paper presented at the National Conference on Children of Russia: Violence and Defense, Moscow.

World Almanac and Book of Facts 1998. (1997). Mahwah, NJ: World Almanac.

14

SPAIN

Joaquín De Paúl and Olayo González

PROFILE OF SPAIN

Including the Balearic and Canary Islands, the Kingdom of Spain covers 504,750 square kilometers, with the capital city located in Madrid. The population is approximately 40 million, predominantly Roman Catholic, and comprised of a number of distinct ethnic groups including Basques, Catalans, and Gallegos. The official language is Spanish, with additional languages including Catalan-Valenciana, Galencian, and Basque. The government is a constitutional monarchy. The infant mortality rate is 5 per 1,000 and the life expectancy is seventy-eight years. Public education is free from the ages of six to fourteen and compulsory until the age of sixteen. Seventy percent of students attend public schools or universities, with the remainder attending private schools or universities operated primarily by the Catholic Church. The literacy rate is 97 percent and in 1998 the gross national product per capita was $14,080 (U.S.).

HISTORY

In Spain, it is not possible to speak of the existence of a child protection system in any real sense until the middle of the twentieth century. Until then, protection of neglected or abused children was carried out by charitable organizations, usually embodied by religious organizations (Ripol-Millet & Rubiol, 1990), and on occasion by the government.

On June 11, 1948, rules and regulations governing the proceedings of juvenile courts were published. The juvenile courts were entrusted with both the protection of maltreated children and the behavioral correction of young criminals. Under the 1948 regulations, however, the juvenile courts did not have the power to deprive parents of custody of their children (i.e., basic parental authority). Instead, the power of the juvenile courts was limited to the temporary suspension of parental rights. That is, the court could withhold parents' rights to live with their children, to take care of them, and to provide them with an education. The definitive deprivation of custody and/or any other limitations placed on the remaining powers of parental authority (e.g., children's representation or the administration of children's patrimony) became the exclusive competence of judgeships different than juvenile courts.

During this period, the juvenile courts' protective functions were only utilized when parents failed to fulfill their custodial and educational duties to their children. Parents were deemed to have failed in these duties when their children were maltreated, given corrupting orders or advice (e.g., allowed to participate in prostitution or delinquency), or provided with corrupting examples (e.g., alcohol or drug abuse). In addition, parents were deemed to have failed in their duties when children were abandoned, maltreated, or forced to work in immoral places.

The juvenile courts were empowered to restrain parental conduct or to order surveillance of the parents by court representatives to ensure that parents fulfilled their duties. If the situation was deemed serious enough to require the suspension of parental custody, the courts could entrust the children to substitute families (i.e., foster care) or governmental or religious foundations for the period of suspension. Unfortunately, there were several problems with such procedures. First, the procedures used to determine if these measures were needed were kept secret. Second, the procedures were not strictly governed by legal principles and were intended to minimize investigative activity. Finally, a decision about a particular case was not made in accordance with evaluation or advice from multidisciplinary teams. For these reasons, these procedures were declared unconstitutional by the Constitutional Court on February 14, 1991, and the 1948 regulations were replaced by a new act in 1992. The 1992 act will be discussed in greater detail later.

Unfortunately, the 1948 Spanish child protection system did not work. Instead of counting on highly qualified substitute families or representatives to take charge of children's foster care, Spain relied on large residential centers. These centers were run mostly by religious organizations that held economic agreements with the government. Under these agreements, the government paid the residences money and left the protection of children to the residence administrators. This was a problem because there was a lack of resources for prevention and for individualized treatment of children and families.

LEGAL INNOVATIONS

The Current Spanish Child Protection Legal System

The publication of the Spanish Constitution in December 1978 changed the Spanish child protection system. The Spanish Constitution explicitly incorporated the wealth of the entire international legal knowledge concerning human rights into the Spanish law system. By doing this, the Constitution acknowledged the importance of protecting children's rights and interests. In particular, the Constitution supported the view that it is essential to keep children in their natural environment, if possible, and if this is not possible, to provide them with an alternative family. In addition, the Constitution stressed that procedures used to place children in residential care must be legally regulated and that such placements must be used only as temporary measures. Finally, the Constitution states that the staff in charge of providing for children must be trained and qualified to do so.

Although the Spanish Constitution does not expressly recognize the child's right not to be maltreated, it does provide a sufficient base for inferring that right. Specifically, article 39.4 states that children will be provided with protection detailed by the United Nations Convention. The United Nations Convention on the Rights of the Child (article 19) states that the signatories will adopt all the necessary legislative, administrative, social, and educational measures needed to protect children from all forms of violence, prejudice, physical or mental abuse, negligent inattention or treatment, maltreatment, and exploitation, including sexual abuse. It would appear, therefore, that the Spanish Constitution adopts all the rights for children to be free from maltreatment expressed in the UN Convention.

When discussing the Spanish child protection system, it is necessary to discuss both the general nationwide system and the system in place within each autonomous region (since 1978, Spain is composed of seventeen regions that have autonomy for social services, education, and health). Each of these regions has (or is creating) its own child protection system. Because the Spanish Parliament has exclusive jurisdiction over penal, procedural, and civil law, these systems are mainly extensions of the Constitution's position.

The creation of the current child protection system began in 1987 with the publication of what is known as the 21 Act for Child Protection (Spanish Ministry of Justice, 1987), and achieved the current situation in 1996 with the passage of the Legal Protection of the Minor Act (Spanish Ministry of Justice, 1996). As Gullón-Ballesteros (1996) suggests, however, the 1996 act does not significantly alter the rules regulating the protection of children's rights. Instead, it simply repeats rights extracted from the Spanish Constitution or other legal texts. Furthermore, the modifications introduced by the 1996 act will not likely have any normative effect, given that the act provides no sanctions for failure to fulfill its provisions. The most important flaw in the act is that it does not establish an easy procedure by which children may obtain protection when their rights are violated. Although legislation to correct this flaw and provide juvenile penal law is currently being studied by the Parliament, the current child protection system in Spain rests on the 1987 and 1996 acts, the general features of which are discussed below.

DEFINITIONS AND FORMS OF ABUSE

Spanish Definitions of Child Maltreatment

Before 1987, there was no consensus in the way professionals classified cases of child maltreatment. Thus, there were no commonly used definitions of child abuse and neglect. As a result, it was impossible to determine the prevalence of child maltreatment or to compare detection rates from different child protection services. Since 1987, however, the publication of the 21 Act and several handbooks for professionals has improved the homogeneity of definitions of child maltreatment throughout Spain. The 21/87 Act promoted the utilization of the concept of *desamparo* to outline every situation of child maltreatment that should be the object of child protection intervention and to offer the most adequate classification of child maltreatment situations. The concept of *desamparo* was defined as any situation in which (a) parents or relatives are unable to fulfill the duties of protection, (b) parents or relatives fail to fulfill the duties of protection, or (c) parents or relatives inadequately or inappropriately fulfill the duties of protection. Parents are considered unable to fulfill duties of child protection when children do not receive necessary care and attention from their parents or caregivers and when it is completely impossible, either temporarily or definitively, to modify such a situation. This classification includes parental death, imprisonment, and incapacity due to serious physical or psychological illness. Accordingly, children in these situations are considered unprotected, and intervention by child protection services is required.

Nonfulfillment of protection duties occurs in all those situations in which there is a total absence of child protection. Situations typically covered by this classification are those instances in which (a) no adult will acknowledge parenthood of a child, (b) the child is abandoned and the parents are missing, or (c) parents are completely disengaged from the child.

Inadequate fulfillment of protection duties occurs when any type of child maltreatment is present. Definitions appearing in professional guidelines come from texts and handbooks that have been widely circulated among professionals (e.g., Arruabarrena & De Paúl, 1994; De Paúl & Arruabarrena, 1995; Martínez-Roig & De Paúl, 1993). The definitions of sexual abuse used by social services frequently accord with those in the Penal Code and are very similar to those used in most other European countries and in America.

Any non-accidental behavior by a parental or caretaker that provokes physical harm or illness or places the child at serious risk of suffering is considered physical abuse. In order to substantiate the occurrence of physical abuse, the presence of physical injuries is required. When physical injuries have not been clearly observed, there must be true knowledge that the child has suffered physical injuries as a result of parental or caretaker behavior or that parents or caretakers used excessive corporal punishment or beat the child (Junta de Castilla y León, 1995; SASI, 1994).

Physical neglect occurs when the main physical needs of the child (e.g., food, clothing, hygiene, protection and supervision in potentially dangerous situations, education, and medical care) are not well attended, either temporarily or permanently, by any member of the group living with the child (Junta de Castilla y León, 1995; SASI, 1994).

Emotional abuse occurs when there is chronic verbal hostility from any adult in the family, such as insults, scorn, criticism, threats of abandonment, and a constant blockage of a child's interaction with others (ranging from avoidance to reclusion or confinement) (Junta de Castilla y León, 1995; SASI, 1994).

Emotional neglect occurs when there is a persistent absence of response to signals (e.g., crying, smiling), emotional expressions, proximity behaviors, and child interactions by a stable and significant adult (Junta de Castilla y León, 1995; SASI, 1994). Emotional abuse and neglect are only indicated when the required behaviors occur in a chronic and continuous way, and their presence is clearly observable.

Any kind of sexual relationship between an adult and a child under eighteen years old is considered child sexual abuse. According to such definitions, for sexual abuse to occur, children can be used either for sexual activity or as a means of sexual stimulation. Four types of child sexual abuse are included in the Spanish definition. Incest is defined as sexual abuse with physical contact by a perpetrator who is a close relative of the child. Rape is defined as sexual abuse with physical contact by a perpetrator who is not a member of the victim's family. Sexual molestation involves an instance in which the perpetrator intentionally touches erotic areas of a child's body or the perpetrator demands that the child touch erotic areas of the perpetrator's body. Finally, sexual abuse without physical contact includes verbal abuse, exhibitionism, or sexual intercourse in the presence of a child (Arruabarrena & De Paúl, 1994).

CHILD PROTECTION

Principles and Characteristics of the Current Child Protection System in Spain

The main goal of the current child protection system in Spain is the preservation of the family unit or the reinsertion of the child into the original family when preservation is not an immediate option. The 1996 Legal Protection of the Minor Act (Spanish Ministry of Justice, 1996), which slightly modified article 172.4 of the Civil Code, states that, whenever it does not interfere with the child's interest, a child should remain in his/her own family. This provision, however, merely asserts that the child should be maintained in his/her own biological family, or reintegrated into his or her biological family after a temporary separation, whenever it is possible to do so without harming the child's interests. The provision is not intended to return a child to (or to keep a child in) a maltreating family. The act has, however, prompted the creation of new resources to help parents regain adequate functioning in their parental roles. Treatment programs for abusive and neglectful families were developed with two objectives: (1) to avoid separation of children from parents, and (2) to promote reunification of children with their parents. These objectives are carried out both by a home visitor, who is an individual who works with abusive or neglectful parents in the family's home, and by family therapy or parent training groups.

During the 1990s, despite these new resources, it has been difficult to achieve the act's legal requirements. Many problems have prevented the system from reaching its desired goals. First, the act demands that professionals solve problems the causes of which are unknown or multifaceted. Scientific knowledge about the multiple causes of family relation problems has not developed adequately enough to address the severe family situations that result in child abuse and neglect (Arruabarrena & De Paúl, in press). Second, many psychologists and social workers do not have confidence that rehabilitation can occur in maltreating families. These mental health providers are classically trained. From their perspective, problem awareness and motivation to change are basic requirements for therapeutic intervention to be effective. These characteristics are generally absent, however, in child abuse and neglect situations (Asociación Catalana per la Infancia Maltractada [ACIM], 1989).

Child Protection Measures Outside the Courts

In response to the requirements of the former juvenile courts (whose enforcement methods were essential to successfully impose child protection measures), the 21/87 Act clearly increased the role of the public administration by providing it with the power to protect children. This was accomplished by creation of different public entities controlled by the autonomous regions. Consequently, the courts' role in child protection has gradually decreased. Courts now supervise the role of the public entities (the governments of the autonomous regions), adjudicate custody disputes, establish or suspend foster care when the parents oppose it or do not consent, and establish adoption procedures. The power of the public entity is almost absolute in the child protection arena because the public entity is responsible for prevention and for a child's care as soon as a risky or menacing situation arises. Thus, the public entity is charged with primary responsibility for creating and implementing child protection measures (Junta de Castilla y León, 1995; Spanish Ministry of Justice, 1987, 1996).

These changes in the roles of courts and entities have had important implications for the daily handling of child abuse and neglect cases. Most abusive or neglectful parents, and most sexual abusers, are no longer confronted by representatives of the judicial system. Instead, these parents and abusers are far more likely to interact with public authority in the form of social service professionals (mostly social workers and psychologists). When a maltreating family is experiencing a stressful or crisis situation, social service interventions can prove more convenient, positive, and supportive than judicial interventions. The new structure of child protection in Spain, with its separation from the courts, offers important advantages for many child maltreatment cases.

On occasion, there are parents who do not accept the authority of the social services professional. In these cases, it is difficult to begin the necessary interventions, as the parents are uncooperative. Under such circumstances, protecting the child's rights may require the symbolic use of authority and the implementation of punitive mechanisms. These circumstances are difficult for social services professionals who are not trained to take such a role. Thus, the child protection system functions best when there is optimum coordination between social services and the judicial system (Barudy, 1991).

Decentralization of the Child Protection System

As discussed above, each of the Spanish autonomous regions has created its own protection system to the extent legally possible. This process of decentralization is meant to bring a greater degree of decision making to community services. Furthermore, assigning responsibility for prevention to municipalities and counties is meant to encourage greater citizen involvement. Decentralization should also allow the design and planning of child protection resources to approximate more closely the actual needs and characteristics of each region. Unfortunately, decentralization has produced heterogeneity of services and divergent interpretations of the 21/87 Act that are unacceptable. With this decentralization, some counties are allowed to give priority to residential care over foster care, while other counties can provide treatment programs for only certain types of families. It is unacceptable that resources and services devoted to child maltreatment are different in cities separated by less than a mile, simply because each city lies in a different county. Regardless of a family's geographical background, the children's needs and rights should be the same.

Individualization of the Intervention

Increased complexity is perhaps the most important characteristic of the new child protection system in Spain. Until 1987, the majority of detected cases of child abuse and neglect were handled by automatically placing children in residential centers that served more than 100 children. The system was not complex in its evaluation or decision making, such that most children, regardless of their needs, received the same intervention. Absence of individualization was therefore the rule.

However, the development of family treatment programs and temporary family foster care, and the fact that the child's return to her or his family was the primary goal, made individualization the main principle in the decision-making process. As a result, it became necessary to match particular services with the specific needs of each child. This process necessarily implies individualized decisions, making complete and exhaustive knowledge about the child and the family situation the main condition for high-quality decision making. This has resulted in the focusing of resources on the development of investigation and evaluation procedures (SASI, 1994).

During the last ten years, child protection services have been developed to put this process of individualized attention and improved evaluation into practice. From 1990 to 1996, the Spanish Social Affairs Ministry was assigned the task of training, researching, and coordinating Spain's child protection system. As a result of this, child abuse and neglect reports are now channeled to the County Department of Child Protection. The Ministry-trained child protection professionals have developed experimental intervention programs and elaborated guidelines and instruments to meet the goal of improving the quality of interventions. Protocols, forms, and guidelines for conducting investigations (to substantiate the report and determine a child's level of risk) have been developed (SASI, 1994). Professionals can use data collected in this process to form hypotheses regarding which factors in the family are related to success (or lack of success) in treatment. Thus, decision making in a particular case is based on information accumulated through investigation of the specific case, as well as on what professionals have learned about child protection in general (Sánchez, 1995).

Role of the Protected Children and/or Their Families

United Nations and Council of Europe resolutions explicitly discuss the importance of the role of both children and their families in the child protection system. The Spanish law system supports this principle.

Children up to twelve years old must give their acceptance for family foster care or for adoption. Children under the age of twelve have the right to be heard in family foster care or adoption decisions, but their opinions are not judicially decisive. Nonetheless, young children are entitled to execute the right to be heard themselves or to be represented by another person of their choice. However, the right to be heard can be rejected by a judicial resolution, but the rejection must be justified explicitly and notice of the rejection must be provided not only to those likely to execute a placement or adoption, but also to the Department of the Public Prosecutor. The Department of the Public Prosecutor can appeal this rejection, and the judge has to make a decision.

The family's role is not very important in the Spanish child protection system. Families involved in a judicial procedure about child abuse or neglect have several possibilities for intervention. Families may (a) consent to or reject the establishment of protective placement or request a suspension of protective placement, (b) accept or reject an adoption, (c) ask child protection services to take custody of a child due to justified parental illness or other serious circumstances, and (d) appeal the decisions of child protection services.

In child protection procedures, children's families must be heard, but their opinions are not judicially conclusive when suitable measures are imposed or suspended. Furthermore, the family can lose the right to be heard in a child protection procedure when parents are either deprived of their parental authority or involved in a parental authority deprival case (even though it has not been formally declared).

TREATMENT

Fortunately, over the last ten years, theoretical prejudices have softened and resources have provided many supportive intervention programs for maltreating families. There are several options for the treatment of abusive or neglectful families. Some families are receptive to family therapy or individual therapy. Other families choose to participate in self-help or support groups. Finally, some families choose to rely on a home visitor to provide emotional support and to teach parenting skills. Currently, professionals are working to improve the efficacy of treatment programs (Arruabarrena & De Paúl, in press; De Paúl, Múgica, & Alday, 1997).

At the time of the 21/87 Act, international law clearly prohibited the institutionalization of children (i.e., indefinite placement in residential foster care). The Spanish legislation obeyed international law by suggesting that placement of a child in an institution must be a temporary measure. Further, when a child was placed in out-of-home care, the child protection agency was required to review this decision every six months. It would have been helpful, however, if the act included residential placement as a valid alternative for cases in which all other measures have failed. It would also have been helpful if guidelines governing placement procedures were provided. Such guidelines might require a two-step procedure in which child protection agencies first attempt to keep the family together, but, if this is not possible, remove the child from the home. The first phase would be skipped, of course, in situations where leaving the child with the family jeopardizes the child's well-being (Junta de Castilla y León, 1995).

On the other hand, by suggesting that the institutionalization of children was unacceptable, the act promoted a number of reforms. First, children's basic needs can now be provided through family foster care while the biological family undergoes rehabilitation. Unfortunately, temporary family foster care is seldom used in Spain (Barjau, 1995), and in many cases, family foster care programs that were meant to be temporary have become long-term placements for children (Barjau, 1995; Ripol-Millet & Rubiol, 1990). Thus, revitalizing temporary family foster care is a priority for the Spanish child protection system.

The second major development of the act has been the modification and specialization of out-of-home services. Over the years, big residential centers for children have been replaced by smaller centers where individualized treatment and resources are matched with individual children's needs. It has become clear to child protection professionals that many children need, and will continue to need, residential services (Fernández del Valle, 1992; Fuertes & Fernandez Del Valle, 1995; Muñoz, Redondo, & Torres, 1998). In accordance with the act, Spanish child protection services have (a) diversified residential centers to meet the needs of children with different characteristics, (b) reduced the number of children living in residential centers, (c) increased and improved human resources, and (d) developed therapeutic services to aid in the rehabilitation of children and their families.

PREVALENCE

Data from Recent Studies

Since 1990, several studies about child maltreatment prevalence have been carried out in three different Spanish counties: Basque Country, Catalunya, and Andalucia (De Paúl, Arruabarrena, Torres, & Muñoz, 1995; Inglés, 1991; Moreno, Jiménez, Oliva, Palacios, & Saldaña, 1995). In these studies, information about child maltreatment cases was collected from teachers, pediatricians, and social workers. All practitioners received a definition of child maltreatment and information about the main indicators of abuse. These professionals were asked to report the number of maltreated children that they identified in their professional environment. The objective was to assess the prevalence of cases not detected or not referred to child protection services. In the Catalunya study, a rate of five maltreated children per thousand was found for the general population. This rate increased to fifteen per thousand for studies conducted in Andalucia and in the Basque Country. Methodological differences may explain differences in results. However, most of the data are consistent with the frequency of reported abuse and with rates from other countries (Palacios, 1995).

Additionally, there was a clear pattern of typologies across the three studies. Professionals most frequently reported cases of physical neglect (50 percent), followed by cases of emotional abuse and neglect (25 percent) and physical abuse (approximately 20 percent). There were very few cases of sexual abuse detected and reported by professionals (i.e., less than 2 percent) (Palacios, 1995). Data about gender and age were very similar in the three studies. Rates of abuse were similar for males and females, despite a slight predominance of males. Child physical abuse and child physical neglect cases typically involved children from three to ten years of age. Importantly, the studies found that the prevalence of abuse and neglect decreased for children older than fourteen years.

Very different results can be observed in a subset of substantiated cases of child maltreatment based on open files in a child protection services study (Saldaña, Jiménez, & Oliva, 1995). It must be assumed that in these cases, severity of maltreatment provoked reporting and subsequent intervention by child protection services. Results from this study showed interesting differences in the number of substantiated child abuse and neglect cases. In some counties (e.g., Basque Country, Canary Island, and Castilla y León) it was possible to observe more cases of child maltreatment than expected. However, in other counties (e.g., Madrid, Catalunya, and Valencia) fewer cases of child maltreatment were found than expected. It is difficult to know if these differences are due to a greater prevalence of child maltreatment in different counties or to improved detection by social services in certain counties.

Finally, physical neglect cases were most frequently observed, followed by physical abuse and emotional abuse. It is important to emphasize that in 1993 only 4.3 percent of substantiated cases from child protection services were sexually abused children. This low incidence may be due to limited training of professionals and limited capacity of detection with respect to child sexual abuse. These data contrast with the results of a general population retrospective survey about sexual abuse carried out in 1993 (López, Hernández, & Carpintero, 1994). López and colleagues examined the memories of childhood sexual abuse victims collected from 2,000 subjects randomly recruited within Spain. Results were similar to major data observed in surveys from other countries. Fifteen percent of males and 25 percent of females had memories of having experienced childhood sexual abuse (with or without physical contact) before age sixteen. Thus, it appears that many cases of sexual abuse go undetected by child protection services.

CONCLUSION

By the incorporation of the entire international legal wealth concerning human rights, the publication of the Spanish Constitution changed the Spanish child protection system. Until 1987, however, and the publication of the 21 Act for Child Protection, the current child protection system had no clear rules for the development of actual practices and resources.

Fortunately, child protection activities are currently based on (a) the preservation of the family unit and the reinsertion of the child into the family of origin, (b) temporary placement of children in small, specialized residential care centers, (c) prioritization of foster family placement whenever possible, and (d) development of family treatment and family prevention programs.

Two main characteristics of the Spanish child protection system must be highlighted. First, important child protection activities can be developed by social services without the active participation of juvenile or family courts. Social services have primary responsibility for creating and implementing child protection resources and measures. Second, child protection services can be decentralized, and developed and enacted in different ways in different counties or cities.

Since 1987, many important changes and improvements in child protection services have been developed, specifically in case detection and reporting, in procedures for investigation and evaluation of children and families, and in family treatment programs. However, the Spanish child protection system has very important challenges for the future, including the development of temporary family foster care, the specialization and improvement of children's residential care facilities, and the development of effective family preservation programs and secondary prevention programs for high-risk families.

REFERENCES

Arruabarrena, M. I., & De Paúl, J. (1994). *El maltrato a los niños en la familia.* Madrid: Pirámide.

Arruabarrena, M. I., & De Paúl, J. (in press). Evaluación de un programa de tratamiento para familias maltratantes/negligentes y familias alto-riesgo. *Intervención Psicosocial.*

Asociación Catalana per la Infancia Maltractada [ACIM]. (1989). *Actas del I Congreso Estatal sobre la Infancia Maltratada.* Barcelona: ACIM.

Barjau, C. (1995). El acogimiento familiar. In J. De Paúl & M. I. Arruabarrena (Eds.), *Manual de protección infantil* (pp. 359–392). Barcelona: Masson.

Barudy, J. (1991). La coordinación entre Justicia y Servicios Sociales. *II Congreso Estatal sobre Maltrato Infantil.* Vitoria/Gasteiz: AVAIM.

Calvo Cabello, J. L. (1985). Aspectos juridisccionales de la aplicación del Código Civil y de la Ley de Tribunales Tutelares de Menores en materia de adopción y guarda y custodia. In Ministerio de Justicia, *Aspectos juridicos de la protección a la infancia* (pp. 47–64). Madrid: Servico de Publicaciones del Ministerio de Justicia.

Cots i Moner, J. (1991). La Convención de las Naciones Unidas sobre los derechos del Niño. *II Congreso Estatal sobre Infancia Maltratada.* Vitoria/Gasteiz: Federacion de Asociaciones para la Prevencion del Maltrato Infantil.

De Paúl, J., & Arruabarrena, M. I. (Eds.). (1995). *Manual de protección infantil.* Barcelona: Masson.

De Paúl, J., Arruabarrena, M. I., Torres, B., & Muñoz, R. (1995). La prevalencia del maltrato infantil en la provincia de Guipúzcoa. *Infancia y Aprendizaje, 71,* 59–68.

De Paúl, J., Múgica, P., & Alday, N. (1997). *Evaluación del programa de apoyo a familias en situaciones de desprotección infantil en Castilla y León.* Valladolid: Servicio de Publicaciones de la Gerencia de Servicios Sociales de la Junta de Castilla y León.

Fernández del Valle, J. (1992). Evaluación de programas residenciales de servicios sociales para la infancia. *Psicothema, 4,* 531–542.

Fuertes, J., & Fernández del Valle, J. (1995). Recursos residenciales para menores. In J. De Paúl & M. I. Arruabarrena (Eds.), *Manual de protección infantil.* Barcelona: Masson.

Gullón-Ballesteros, A. (1996). Comments on the Act on Child Juridical Protection. *La Ley, Revista Juridica Española de Doctrina, Jurisprudencia y Bibliografia, 17,* 3970.

Inglés, A. (1991). *Els maltractments infantils a Catalunya. Estudi global i balanc de la seva situatió actual.* Barcelona: Departamento Bienestar Social.

Junta de Castilla y León. (1995). *Manual de intervención en situaciones de desamparo.* Valladolid: Servicio de Publicaciones de la Dirección General de Acción Social.

López, F., Hernández, A., & Carpintero, E. (1994). *Los abusos sexuales de menores: Lo que recuerdan los adultos.* Madrid: Servicio de Publicaciones del Ministerio de Asuntos Sociales.

Martínez-Roig, A., & De Paúl, J. (1993). *El maltrato infantil.* Barcelona: Martínez-Roca.

Moreno, M. C., Jiménez, J., Olivia, A., Palacios, J., & Saldaña, D. (1995). Deteccion y caracterización del maltrato infantil en la Comunidad Autonoma Andaluza. *Infancia y Aprendizaje, 71,* 33–47.

Muñoz, R., Redondo, E., & Torres, B. (1998). *El Acogimiento Residencial. Manual de la Buena Práctica.* Madrid: Federación de Asociaciones para la Prevención Infantil.

Palacios, J. (1995). El maltrato infantil en España: Un estudio a través de los expedientes de menores. *Infancia y Aprendizaje, 71,* 69–77.

Ripol-Millet, A., & Rubiol, G. (1990). *El acogimento famialiar.* Madrid: Servicio de Publicaciones Ministerio de Asuntos Sociales.

Saldaña, D., Jiménez, J., & Olivia, A. (1995). El maltrato infantil en España: Un estudio a través de los expedientes de menores. *Infancia y Aprendizaje, 71,* 59–68.

Sánchez, J. M. (1995). La toma de decisiones. In J. De Paúl & M. I. Arruabarrena (Eds.), *Manual de protección infantil.* Barcelona: Masson.

SASI. (1994). *El maltrato infantil. Detección, notificación, investigación y evaluación.* Madrid: Ministerio de Asuntos Sociales.

Spanish Ministry of Justice. (1978). Spanish Constitution. *Boletín Oficial del Estado, 311.1.*

Spanish Ministry of Justice. (1987). Ley de 11 de Noviembre por la que se modifican determinados artículos del Código Civil y de la Ley de Enjuiciamiento Civil en materia de adopción. *Boletín Oficial del Estado, 275.*

Spanish Ministry of Justice. (1996). Ley Orgánica de Protección Jurídica del Menor. *Boletín Oficial del Estado, 15.*

15

SRI LANKA

D. G. Harendra de Silva

PROFILE OF SRI LANKA

The Democratic Socialist Republic of Sri Lanka is an island in the Indian Ocean off the southeastern coast of India with an area of 65,610 square kilometers. The capital is Colombo and the country's population of 18.1 million consists of various ethnic groups such as Sinhalese (74 percent), Tamils (18 percent), Muslims (7 percent), and other groups (1 percent). Sinhala and Tamil are the official languages, but English is also spoken. The primary religious faiths are Buddhism, Hinduism, Islam, and Christianity. The infant mortality rate is 19 per 1,000 and the life expectancy is seventy-three years. Education is compulsory until the age of twelve. The rate of primary school attendance is 98 percent and the literacy rate is 88 percent. The government is a republic and suffrage is universal over the age of eighteen. In 1998, the gross national product per capita was $810 (U.S.).

A CASE STUDY

An alcoholic father is constantly fighting with his wife, resulting in her being beaten and their ten-year-old son being exposed to the violence. One day, after a heavy bout of drinking and an argument, the father commits suicide by ingesting insecticide. The mother, desperate to provide for her son, migrates to Colombo to work in a garment factory. Consequently, the son is kept at a distant relative's home in a suburb with the hope that this will enable him to continue his studies. Unfortunately, the boy is expected to complete too many domestic chores and attends school irregularly. Further, two neighbors, under the pretext of taking him to a restaurant for dinner, sexually abuse him in an abandoned hut. The boy discloses this to his caregiver, but he is ignored. Consequently, he runs away and is confronted by the police. The police slap him for not telling the truth and lock him up. The boy is handcuffed and presented before the magistrate. He is referred to as the "accused," and the "learned" judge finds him guilty of vagrancy. The boy is placed in a correctional school for two years. In this school, he is again referred to as the "accused," and in the local school as a "delinquent." The boy is again sexually abused, this time almost daily by the older boys.

HISTORY

Although child abuse is often denied in the Indian subcontinent, probably one of the oldest recorded histories of child abuse is a 2,500-old Buddhist story called "Sopaka." In the story, a jealous stepfather leaves a boy named Sopaka tied to a corpse in a cemetery to be eaten by wolves. Buddha comes to the boy's rescue and preaches to the child, perhaps one of the earliest recorded instances of counseling. The Buddhist scriptures also record the story of a boy named Mattakundali whose miserly father severely neglects him and deprives him of medical care. Although "Sopaka" and "Mattakundali" are based in ancient India, both stories still resonate today in the predominantly Buddhist Sri Lankan society.

Today, child abuse in Sri Lanka exists in a variety of forms, including physical abuse, sexual abuse, sexual exploitation, neglect, and child labor. In addition, recent times have seen the rise of a new form of child abuse, the conscription of children.

FORMS OF ABUSE

Physical Abuse

Like all countries, Sri Lanka went through a phase of denial, and "acceptance" of physical abuse of children as a norm. An eighteenth century verse (translated from Sinhala) entitled "Ganadevi hella" reads as follows:

> Canes, eckles [Thin sticks from the coconut leaf], gripped in hand,
>   used as whips
> My eyes are always filled with tears while in class
> Although I hear the soft and loving voices of my parents
> My body is full of red lumps and bumps.

This verse, as well as the collection from which it was taken, justifies severe corporal punishment for the sake of "discipline" and "education," an attitude that was widely accepted as the norm in the past.

This norm still has relevance today, as it is still not unusual for parents and teachers to feel they have a right to impose corporal punishment on children. Moreover, the Education Ordinance of 1939 of Ceylon (Regulations for the Instruction and Guidance of Teachers in Government Schools, 1939) is still in effect and permits caning a child, even though Sri Lanka is a signatory to the UN Convention on the Rights of the Child (CRC), which requires signatories to the convention "to take all measures to ensure that school discipline is administered in a manner consistent with the child's human dignity and in conformity with the provisions of the Convention" (United Nations Convention on the Rights of the Child, 1989, Article 28 [2]). Although the 1939 Education Ordinance allows a principal to give a child a maximum of four "cuts," this limitation is rarely observed in practice. Further, doctors often do not consider a child's injuries caused by parents or teachers to be child abuse. Until recently, the curriculum of undergraduate medical programs did not include information about battered children or children with non-accidental injuries. Such instruction was not considered necessary because medical teachers believed that Sri Lanka's extended family system would prevent physical battering.

The first published cases in Sri Lanka recognizing and describing physical abuse appeared in the latter half of the 1980s (Chandrasiri, Lamabadusuriya, & de Silva, 1988; Fernando, Soysa, & Nanayakkara, 1987). These reports were followed by a few other case reports in the 1990s (e.g., S. G. de Silva, 1993; Fernando & de Silva, 1996; Mahendrarajah, Rajagopalan, & Wickremasinghe, 1993). During this time period, however, doctors who recognized child abuse were faced with a management dilemma because no infrastructure or procedure existed to accommodate action in cases of child abuse (D.G.H. de Silva, 1995; 1996a).

Sexual Abuse of Children

The sexual abuse of boys by adults is common in Sri Lanka, although Sri Lankan society has been somewhat slow in acknowledging this fact. One early example of child sexual abuse was documented in the case of a tailor named L. L. Jayawardene (Alles, 1962), who was sentenced to death by hanging in 1949 for murdering a fourteen-year-old schoolboy. Jayawardene was a pedophile who lured boys into sex traps in his fitting room attracting the children with the promise of rides on his motorcycle. Jayawardene lured a fourteen-year-old boy into his web in this fashion, but the boy later rejected Jayawardene, and the tailor murdered him with an electrically detonated parcel bomb.

During the 1940s, "pedophilia" and "child abuse" were not recognized terms, and such conduct was instead considered "homosexuality." In this type of situation, the child was often considered a criminal participant rather than a victim. Although the use of young schoolboys by teachers, hostel masters, School Cadet Masters, sports coaches, and older boys was (and is) no secret in schools, it was not (and is not) discussed openly. Even today, there are those who "justify" sexual abuse and exploitation of boys by saying "boys do not get pregnant" or "ships don't leave tracks on water," without realizing (or not wanting to realize) the abuse's long-term emotional effects. These feelings are reflected in a newspaper article by a well-known journalist, reacting to a press statement by the author: "That's true and is old hat, because the truth is that the kind [of abuse] Dr. de Silva is talking about has taken place in schools and even among priests at Buddhist temples of all places" (Abeynayake, 1998).

The work of Carl Muller, a Sri Lankan author, provides an example of the ambivalent attitude within Sri Lankan culture toward the sexual abuse of boys. Muller has written a number of accounts that provide cultural descriptions of child abuse in Sri Lanka, particularly within Colombo. His novel *Colombo* (Muller, 1994) contains a chapter entitled "Colombo's Child" which, although quasi-fiction, nonetheless provides an accurate reflection of the abuse endured by children in Colombo society. Muller's fictional account is supplemented in his autobiography, where he highlights at least four instances of sexual abuse of boys during the 1930s and the 1940s in Colombo's "burgher" community, comprised predominantly of persons of European descent but often mixed with locals (Muller, 1993). Muller acknowledged the psychological effects of child abuse in a 1995 book entitled *Once upon a Tender Time*:

It was a peculiarity that in those times, sexual assaults on children left them besmirched more in mind than in body. One cannot say which is worse, of course, but one had little doubt that thousands of today's upright citizens could say—if they had a mind to, that is—that childhood sexual encounters were, at the worst, rather messy, quite shameful at the moment, but never physically hurtful. Mental degradation, oh yes, but physically unharmful. (pp. 69–70)

Yet, this acknowledgment is qualified when Muller characterizes childhood sexual assaults as "mutual acts of masturbation and the satisfaction of genital friction at the most, [which] although most deplorable, carried little aftermath" (pp. 69–70).

Sexual Exploitation of Children by Tourists

Although commercial sexual exploitation of boys (often referred to as "boy prostitution") was known to the sexually transmitted diseases control program in 1965, this exploitation catered to only a few local people (Arulanantham, 1992). However, the 1970s and 1980s brought an explosion in tourism, and foreigners came in increasing numbers to the tourist paradise for child sex. Early reports documenting the abuse were prepared by non-governmental organizations (NGOs) or sociologists and presented at professional meetings, but they were not well documented and there were no supporting reports in the medical literature.

International publications such as *The International Gay Guide*, produced in the Netherlands and Germany, achieved particular notoriety for promoting certain countries such as Sri Lanka, the Philippines, and Thailand for homosexual tourism, as they highlighted the availability of children at these destinations, (Gmünder, 1995–1996). Tour operators (including some airlines) openly promoted child sex tourism in Sri Lanka. Pedophiles flocked to these countries in response to the promotions.

In 1980, Tim Bond published a well-documented report that identified Sri Lanka as second only to the Philippines as a source for "cheap child sex." This report highlighted the demand for boys, starting as young as eight years of age, while citing poverty, being orphaned, and broken homes as factors contributing to the boys' exploitation. Bond estimated the number of commercially exploited boys in Sri Lanka in 1980 to be around 2,000. (Sri Lanka's total child population is around 4.2 million.)

Officials at that time considered "child prostitution" (as it was called then) to be a sensitive issue that could "harm tourism" (Seneviratne, 1997). However, due to pressure by many NGOs such as UNICEF, PEACE, Sarvodaya, and individuals, the government presented an act titled the Young Persons (Safeguarding from Exploitation for Immoral Purposes) Draft Act of 1987. The act was approved by the cabinet of ministers, but was not presented to Parliament in detail, as the minister in charge of state tourism at the time thought the act was not relevant to present times. He justified this decision by citing the decline in tourism due to insurgencies in the country. In response, many NGOs cited sometimes conflicting numbers of children commercially exploited for sex, with the quoted figures going as high as 30,000. In the early 1990s, Ratnapala (1999) found 926 child sex workers under sixteen years of age and 533 younger than eighteen years of age in the tourist areas of the country.

Neglect also occurs in Sri Lanka, although the extent of this form of abuse is difficult to evaluate because Sri Lankan society has been slow to recognize neglect as abuse. For example, Mirando (1965–1966), a Sri Lankan pediatrician working in Colombo in the 1960s, reported a case of severe neglect that was later attributed to "poverty" and "ignorance," and thus not recognized by the medical profession as a form of child abuse. This lack of recognition continues today.

Child Labor in Sri Lanka

Although not usually included in pediatric textbooks as abuse, child labor is increasingly recognized as a form of child abuse in Sri Lanka. Industrial exploitation of children is not as much of a problem in Sri Lanka as it is in other countries in the region. However, domestic employment of children is a major problem, and many Sri Lankans are guilty of having child servants. The recent trend of poor Sri Lankan women seeking employment in the Middle East as housemaids, the demand for high wages by service personnel, and the high cost of feeding an adult have made it difficult and expensive to recruit help for Sri Lankan households. These conditions probably have contributed to an increase in domestic employment of children. In part this is due to the fact that children, as compared to adults, are paid lower salaries (if any) and demand less of their employers in terms of food and basic human rights. The refugee situation of all communities in the zones affected by civil war, especially the East, also compounds this problem. In addition to being forced to perform hard physical labor, most of these children are physically abused. They are often sexually abused, and almost always emotionally abused through denigration. In addition, many of these children are deprived of schooling and nutrition.

How grave is this problem? A recent survey of almost 700 households in urban areas in the South indicated that one in twelve houses have a child servant, and one-third of the domestic labor force consists of children (D.G.H. de Silva, 1997). This is a bigger problem in the tea estate areas, where children comprise as much as 44 percent of the domestic labor force. Professionals, including doctors, businessmen, and landowners, are the main perpetrators. A follow-up study showed that most of these children are from tea estate laborer families who migrate from estate to estate, rather than from families on estates with proper facilities (D.G.H. de Silva, 1997). In order to solve this problem, the broader primary issues of economic problems must be addressed. Action is now being taken to change the women and children's employment act to strengthen the law in order to deter employers from hiring children.

Child Conscription in Armed Conflicts

The public and the media, both local and foreign, may not always interpret armed conflict as detrimental to a child's proper development and may even consider children to be heroes or martyrs (Hamann, 1991). Sri Lanka has faced a civil war for nearly two decades which has caused more than 60,000 deaths. Several media reports have described child conscripts among the militant groups (Hamann, 1991; Newsweek, Aug 7, 1995). The conditions under which these conscripts exist arguably constitute a form of child abuse.

In an effort to explore the manner in which child conscription affects the children involved, nineteen male soldiers (mean age 19 years, range 16 to 24 years) were interviewed with a questionnaire using standardized questions. The mean age of conscription was 14.5 years (range 10 to 17 years)

(D.G.H. de Silva, Jayawardena, Rajeendrajith, Gunarathna, & Mahendra-jith, 1997). The children reported performing various forms of manual la-bor, involving varied degrees of danger. Two children performed radio communication tasks, and fifteen performed guard duty. Fifteen of the chil-dren performed tasks such as digging trenches or doing kitchen work. Seven of the children engaged in front-line fighting, five manufactured bombs, and five set land mines. Fifteen of the children had been trained in firearm use, and fourteen had been trained to commit suicide if captured.

According to the nineteen children interviewed, life with the militants was not pleasant. All of the children underwent some form of indoctrination designed, in part, to create a hatred of the enemy. Twelve of the nineteen children ran away or attempted to run away at least once, and eleven of the nineteen reported arguing about or refusing to obey orders. Disobedience led to various forms of punishment, including kitchen duty, beatings, im-prisonment, blackmail, or death threats. A majority of the children felt sad and emotionally upset when they thought about their mothers or families.

Surprisingly, only one out of nineteen children reported being abducted and forced to join the army. The other eighteen reported that they had "volunteered." How is it that a majority of the children "volunteered" to join the armed group? The BBC's *Inside Story* (1991) (although not inten-tionally) illustrates many of the different methods adopted to motivate child "volunteers" to join the armed groups. Some of these methods include pub-lic address systems that continuously broadcast "reasons" and "justifica-tions" for volunteering, and literature encouraging volunteerism aimed at children and adolescents. Model automatic rifles were even attached to see-saws in one playground to attract "volunteers." The dead have been glorified as martyrs through monuments and posters of martyrs on display. School children and school bands parade at funerals of these dead "martyrs." Ex-cerpts of a poem, addressed to a girl, ridicule her ambition of becoming a doctor and ask her to compromise, to "study while fighting, fight while studying." A poem to an adolescent boy ridicules him: "you are idling and growing fat in your youth."

Our interviews with the nineteen soldiers suggest that these tactics (or a combination of them) are often successful. Nine of the nineteen said that they joined for the virtue of being a freedom fighter and martyr. Seven said they joined for fear of being abducted by the enemy, and five said they joined to revenge a family member who had been killed by an enemy. Only three of the nineteen indicated that they joined for economic reasons (i.e., to support their family).

Given the public's tendency to view these child soldiers as heroes, it may be difficult for many to recognize the abusive effects of conscription. Con-scripted children face a variety of experiences and influences that clearly appear abusive, particularly when considered from the standpoint of their emotional impact. For example, conscription corrupts a child by making him engage in violent, destructive, and antisocial behavior, such as killing and destruction of property, thus making him unfit for normal social experience. Conscription terrorizes a child with verbal assaults, bullying, blackmail, and death threats, all in the name of discipline. Conscription isolates a child from normal social experiences, and ignores his emotional and developmental needs by removing him from normal family life and schooling. Each of these circumstances adversely affects the child's right to unhindered growth and identity formation as a child.

Moreover, conscription may lead children to commit suicide, an act of self-destruction that a child cannot fully comprehend. Usually, all conscripts, irrespective of age, wear cyanide capsules, which they are trained to bite on during "suicide missions" or when captured (BBC, 1991). The prominent place given to martyrs and the oath taken by the child soldier in which he vows to sacrifice his life are likely contributing factors to this phenomenon.

Such conditions require us to expand our traditional view of child abuse. Indoctrinating and convincing a child to commit suicide for any cause should constitute both emotional abuse and intentional poisoning. When an adult persuades a child to commit suicide—an act the child cannot comprehend—for personal, social, economic, or political reasons that the child cannot understand, such persuasion constitutes a form of child abuse that may be called "suicide by proxy."

Moreover, conscription itself—the involvement of dependent, developmentally immature children and adolescents in an armed conflict that they do not truly comprehend, to which they are unable to give consent, and which adversely affects their right to unhindered growth and identity as children—should also be viewed as a form of child abuse. Defining conscription as a form of child abuse does not require a great leap of imagination, as many of the traditional elements of child abuse are already contained within it. The severe physical punishment called "discipline" is simply physical abuse. Getting a child to perform guard duty in a war zone, involving the child in military operations, making the child manufacture bombs and set sea mines, all increase the likelihood that the child will suffer serious injury or death and subject the child to intense psychological and emotional pressure. Moreover, child conscription is a thinly veiled method of exploiting child labor.

The public in affected areas must recognize the long-term implications that childhood conscription may have on their society. Political bias should not come into play when such a call for awareness is made. The common objective should be to prevent child conscription and protect children of all races, religions, and political groups from the physical and emotional trauma and potential death that conscription brings, and to initiate a program to rehabilitate those child conscripts who have been deeply damaged emotionally.

PREVALENCE

Even though the medical profession and the public did not widely recognize child abuse during 1994 and 1995, police data from this period show a significant number of reported physical and sexual abuse incidents, including 179 cases of abuse, incest, or intimidation, 43 cases of voluntarily hurting a child, and 172 cases of sexual violence against a child (Nizam, 1996). Surprisingly, the data list physical abuse, child prostitution, child pornography, and encouraging the seduction of a girl as "minor offenses." In instances of prostitution, the data list the child as an offender rather than as a sexually exploited victim. These records reflect the difficulties in management and investigation of child abuse that have led to discussion and agitation within the medical and legal community (D.G.H. de Silva, 1996a).

Although reliable official statistics on the type and incidence of child abuse in Sri Lanka are not available, the author, along with other pediatricians, has conducted a number of studies to investigate these issues. After seeing many children present complaints of incest, rape, and other forms of sexual abuse, we studied case histories of abused children in a detention home. In general, the case studies reveal that the abused children were from broken families with marital problems. Illegal adoption, domestic employment, or abuse by a stepfather or employer was common. Usually, the abuse was detected because the children ran away (D.G.H. de Silva, 1996a; de Silva, Jayawardena, Rajeendrajith, & Gunarathna, 1997).

Observations from this study and police data mentioned above prompted us to look at the incidence of sexual abuse of children in domestic situations as well. We began by administering an initial anonymous questionnaire to 899 university students. The same questionnaire was also administered to 818 university students who heard a lecture on child abuse prior to completing the survey. The lecture described all forms of child abuse, including physical abuse, sexual abuse, neglect, exploitation of child labor, and conscription. The lecture also explained the long-term consequences of abuse and included definitions of abuse such as "an act or omission by an adult care-giver, which could cause actual or potential damage to a child's health and development and lead to unnecessary suffering" or "the involvement of dependent, developmentally immature children and adolescents in sexual activities they do not truly comprehend, to which they are unable to give informed consent; or which violate social taboos of family roles" (Schechter & Robergo, 1976).

In the initial study, eighty-five (18 percent) males admitted having been sexually abused during childhood. Nineteen (5 percent) of the females reported having been abused. In the group that was given a prior lecture on child abuse, however, 21 percent of males and a higher percentage of females (11 percent) reported sex abuse.

We grouped the first sample of 899 student responses into three social classes, depending on the occupation of the students' parents. The incidence of sex abuse in the higher social class appeared high, but the numbers were relatively small. Twenty-five percent of the poorer males had been sexually abused during childhood as compared with 15 percent of middle-class boys. For females, the incidence of abuse was 7 percent in the lower social group and 3 percent in the middle social group. In the group that heard the lecture, a similar trend was observed, with a higher reported incidence in the lower social class than in the middle class.

A majority of the males who had been abused had been abused either by a relative or a neighbor. Other reported abusers included brothers, teachers, and priests. Older women had abused nineteen of the boys. A majority of females did not divulge the abuser, suggesting that the abuser may have been an immediate family member. Females in the group that heard the lecture about abuse were more likely to divulge the identity of the abuser than those who had not heard the lecture.

In addition, 28 (6 percent) of the males in the initial study admitted they had sexually abused (or were still abusing) other boys and/or girls. A significant finding was that 71 percent of these males reported having been sexually abused during childhood. In the group of students who heard the lecture on child abuse, an alarming 12 percent of the males admitted having sexually abused a child at least once, and 64 percent of them reported having been sexually abused as children. These findings support the view that "today's abused may become tomorrow's abusers."

Another study conducted at the sexually transmitted disease clinic at Teaching Hospital Karapitiya found that individuals who admitted promiscuous behavior reported a very high incidence of childhood sex abuse (D.G.H. de Silva, Rubesinghe, Jayasekera, Wijayasooriya, Hewamanne, & Ginige, 1997). Commercial sex workers reported the highest incidence, at 40 percent. When the total promiscuous male sample of fifty was considered, 21 percent admitted pedophilic activity, while 64 percent of these child abusers had been abused as children. In yet another study, we found that children in a detention home had been abused sexually, neglected nutritionally and medically, deprived of an education, and exploited for labor in the name of "vocational training" (D.G.H. de Silva, Rubesinghe, Jayasekera, Fernando, Hewamanne, & Wijesooriya, 1997).

In summary, our data show widespread sexual abuse in Sri Lanka during childhood, especially in boys and in the lower social group. The actual prevalence is probably higher, because our study sample was selected (i.e., limited to university students and university entrance class students). Thus, those who were more likely to have been abused may have been weeded out. Our study also found that subjects were more likely to divulge abuse when they had been educated about child abuse.

Furthermore, the incidence of sex abuse in our study was unusually high for boys. This higher rate was not due to sex tourism, as *none* of the perpetrators was reported to be a tourist. Although the media highlight sex tourism as a major form of child abuse in Sri Lanka, our study suggests that it plays a small role when compared to domestic abuse. This should not be surprising, as many people may know if a tourist abuses a child, whereas domestic abuse may not be seen so easily. However, because we studied a selected group of university students, we may not have heard from children exploited by tourists, who may have been more likely to drop out of school.

Why is abuse of boys more common than abuse of girls in Sri Lanka? Several social factors may explain this fact. A girl's virginity is considered important at the time of marriage in traditional Sri Lankan society, and thus girls are more protected than boys. In traditional society, it is customary to show a blood-stained bedsheet to the groom's mother to prove a girl's virginity at the homecoming ceremony. However, this practice is slowly disappearing from society, and is nowadays often considered an insult to the bride. For the same reason, premarital sex is unusual in traditional society. As a result, hormonally primed young adult males may only have access to other boys or prepubescent girls.

Moreover, there are many misconceptions about boys' abuse in Sri Lankan society, and the problem may not be taken seriously. One journalist reacted to the observations of the author in the following way:

That is not to justify the crime. But it is to say that a sudden persecution psychosis may not be the proper answer to a problem that has a cultural genesis in a society that is still wedded to Victorian values (i.e., virginity among adults too is at a premium, therefore, seeking other means of gratification has become almost a cultural alternative, practiced albeit illegitimately by some Buddhist monks in their "viharages" [temples]). (Abeynayake, 1998, p. 11)

This journalist not only tries to portray sexual abuse as a "cultural norm," but also tries to label accountability to the laws as "persecution psychosis." However, he too suggests that young men cause boys' abuse by "seeking other means of gratification" in a society that values the virginity of a female at the time of marriage. Similarly, Carl Muller, in his novel *Colombo* (1994), describes the feeling of a young man who cannot have sex with his girlfriend as "the great wanting, the denial of relief" (p. 138), a characterization which is followed by the young man masturbating.

TREATMENT

The difficulties one faces when treating and managing child abuse in Sri Lanka are exemplified by a few case histories of physically abused children who were seen by the author. For example, N. was a seven-month-old girl whose mother lived alone and whose father worked in Colombo. N. displayed multiple injuries, including an obvious laceration to her nasal septum, several scars on her face and body, linear abrasions characteristic of an injury caused by a stick or cane, a fractured skull, and multiple "bucket handle" fractures to her femur and tibia/fibula. She also presented severe nutritional neglect.

N. was given "protection" in the pediatric ward for several months (since there are no registered temporary care foster homes in Sri Lanka) until she was sent to her grandmother for temporary care. Regular visits by childcare officers and follow-up care in the clinic were recommended, but these did not occur due in large part to a shortage of childcare workers and other resources. Irregular visits indicated that N. was subsequently well cared for.

The case of N. K. provides another striking example of the effect of insufficient resources on child care in Sri Lanka. N. K. suffered multiple injuries at the hands of a male friend of his mother's. The man used a firebrand to inflict multiple burns to N. K.'s arm and forehand. In addition, N. K. had burns on his chin and chest, along with other scars. X-rays revealed that N. K. had multiple fractures to the limbs and ribs that were at different stages of healing. Unfortunately, the child and the mother spent ten months in the pediatric ward because probation and childcare services were not equipped at the time to take action.

Inadequate resources are not the sole reason for insufficient or delayed responses to children in need. M. was treated at the pediatric ward for multiple fractures, but further action was prevented by political interference from both candidates during an election, and by delayed investigation by the police and Probation and Child Care Services. Although the resources of the Probation and Child Care department have not changed dramatically in the last few years, wider recognition of child abuse and improvement in multidisciplinary coordination have changed the manner in which child abuse is managed.

LEGAL INNOVATIONS

Political Commitment

In 1994, the Chief Minister of the Western Province, Hon. Chandrika Bandaranaike Kumarantunga, took up the issue of sexual exploitation of children by foreigners and discussed the matter with NGOs. Chief Minister Bandaranaike was then elected President, and the commitment of the President and the cabinet to the cause of child abuse was reflected in the Penal Code (amendment) Act No. 22 of 1995. The highlight of the amendment was a provision that strengthened the law governing sexual offenses and offenses against children. The amendment concentrated on (a) defining offenses that were previously not defined or described adequately, (b) increasing sentences, and (c) introducing mandatory jail sentences for some

Table 15.1
Summary of 1995 Penal Code Amendments

Offense	Previous law	Amended law
Child pornography	Up to 3 months imprisonment or fine or both	Minimum 2 years, maximum 10 years, plus fine at discretion of court
Cruelty to children	Maximum 3 years or fine	Minimum 2 years, maximum 10 years with fine and compensation at discretion of court
Procuring girls or women	Not described previously	Minimum 2 years, maximum 10 years with fine at discretion of court
Trafficking	Previously defined as "slavery"	Minimum 5 years (2 years for adult trafficking), maximum 20 years
Statutory rape	Age of victim 12 years	Age of victim increased to 16 years; minimum sentence 7 years
Custodial rape Rape of pregnant women Rape of females <18 yrs. Gang rape	Not previously described adequately	Physical injury not essential to prove lack of consent Minimum 10 years, maximum 20 years
Grave sexual abuse	Not described previously	Minimum 7 years, maximum 20 years
Incest	Offense under marriages law	Minimum 7 years, maximum 20 years, with Compensation
Publication of matters relating to sex offenses, identifying the victims	Previously not an offense	Up to 2 years imprisonment or fine or both for guilty media personnel

offenses. Major changes relating to child abuse are summarized in Table 15.1.

In December 1996, the President appointed a task force on child protection, of which the author was the chairman. The task force recommended several legal amendments, including the establishment of a National Child Protection Authority (NCPA). In addition, the task force recommended a number of amendments to existing law that were subsequently enacted and are now in force. For example, in cases of rape prior to the amendments, a magistrate would perform a preliminary, non-summary inquiry before an indictment was filed in High Court. This preliminary hearing was often protracted and sometimes psychologically traumatized the child. The new amendment to the judicature act dispenses with the non-summary inquiry in the case of statutory rape (the rape of children below sixteen years of age), thereby reducing the duration of the court procedure that the child must undergo.

Another amendment expanded the magistrate's authority to detain alleged perpetrators of child abuse (Code of Criminal Procedure Amendment, Act No. 28 of 1998). Previously, the magistrate was only empowered to detain an alleged perpetrator of child abuse for investigative purposes without a warrant for one day. The new amendment expands the allowable period of investigative detention to three days. The amendment also gives priority to cases of child abuse and introduces a referral form for victims of child abuse.

Other amendments increased the scope of prohibited conduct. For example, Act No. 29 of 1998 amended the penal code to prohibit the use of children for purposes of begging, procuring sexual intercourse, and trafficking in restricted articles. The amended penal code also imposes a legal obligation on developers of films and photographs to inform the police of indecent or obscene material involving children.

The Presidential Task Force recommended other legal amendments that are now in the process of being enacted and implemented. One proposed amendment to the Evidence Ordinance, currently before Parliament, would admit video evidence of a child witness's preliminary interview. Other recommendations currently being drafted into bills include dispensing with the requirement that a child witness take an oath and enabling age indication on a doctor's certificate to serve as prima facie proof of age where age is relevant in a case and there is no better evidence available.

One of the most important recommendations of the Presidential Task Force on Child Protection was the establishment of a National Child Protection Authority (NCPA). The NCPA bill was presented in Parliament by the Minister of Justice in August 1998 and was passed unanimously in November 1998 (NCPA Act, 1998). The act was gazetted in January 1999, and the board of the NCPA was appointed in June 1999, with the author serving as the present chairman.

The NCPA's mandate includes a broad range of authority, objectives, and duties, such as advising government on national policy and measures regarding the protection of children and the prevention and treatment of child abuse; consulting and coordinating with relevant ministries, local authorities, and public and private sector organizations and recommending measures for the prevention of child abuse and the protection of victims; recommending legal, administrative, and other reforms for the effective implementation of national policy; monitoring the implementation of the law and the progress of investigations and criminal proceedings in child abuse cases; recommending measures regarding the protection, rehabilitation, and reintegration into society of children affected by armed conflict; taking appropriate steps for the safety and protection of children in conflict with the law (i.e., "juvenile offenders"); receiving reports of child abuse from the public; advising and assisting local bodies and NGOs to coordinate campaigns against child abuse; coordinating, promoting, and conducting research on child abuse; coordinating and assisting the tourist industry to prevent child abuse; preparing and maintaining a national database on child abuse; monitoring organizations that provide care for children; and serving as liaison to and exchanging information with foreign governments and international organizations.

To oversee such a broad mandate, the NCPA needs the participation of professionals with a broad range of experience and skills. To this end, the NCPA is comprised of pediatricians, forensic pathologists, psychiatrists, psychologists, a senior police officer, a senior lawyer from the Attorney General's department, and five other members associated with child protection efforts, including members from NGOs. Ex-officio members would include the Commissioners of Labor and Probation and Child Care Services, and the chairman of the monitoring committee of the CRC (Convention on the Rights of the Child). Another panel of ex-officio members would include senior officers from the ministries of Justice, Education, Defense, Health, Social Services, Provincial Councils, Women's Affairs, Labor, Tourism, and Media. The NCPA has the advantage of reporting directly to the President, and the presence of high-ranking officials facilitates the implementation and coordination of mechanisms of action suggested at the NCPA meetings.

In the author's experience, conflicts between different organizations and entities involved in child protection are major obstacles in the fight against child abuse. In developing countries where funding resources are limited, NGOs compete with one another, and there is a tendency for each organization to emphasize its own importance, while downplaying and criticizing others' activities. Professionals, academics, and officials have similar conflicts among themselves, and negative interactions often spread between the different actors. The NGO activists often accuse and criticize officials. The officials often view the activists as "antagonistic and terrorist," which in turn leads the officials to take a defensive approach and to view their area of activity as their own personal territory. This negative interaction between groups who share a common goal of protecting children is a crucial problem in the campaign against child abuse and should be addressed head-on, particularly in developing countries. The inclusion of all three categories (i.e., professionals, officials, and NGO representatives) in the NCPA was designed to reduce this antagonism.

The author appreciates that child abuse reforms may best be initiated at the grass-roots level with a bottom-up approach rather than a top-down approach. However, in a developing country in which day-to-day survival poses a variety of problems, one cannot expect a spontaneous social evolution at the grass roots to make child protection a priority. A top-down approach, such as the National Child Protection Act 1998, can help to initiate, coordinate, and direct grass-roots level activity. For this reason, many of the NCPA's activities are directed toward grass-roots activities.

CONCLUSION: THE PRESENT STATUS IN SRI LANKA

Recent studies reveal that there is a sharp rise in reports and prosecutions of child abuse in the southern province, and there are signs that the new laws are taking effect and reaching perpetrators both at home and abroad.

For example, a Norwegian pedophile was sentenced to fourteen years of rigorous imprisonment under the new penal code amendment of 1995, which established a minimum sentence of seven years. The importance of cooperation between countries in the war against commercial sexual exploitation of children is underscored by the successful prosecution of two pedophiles in Switzerland and one from the Netherlands for crimes committed in Sri Lanka. Charges have also been requested for the trial of a Belgian who escaped while on bail. These prosecutions would not have been possible without the cooperation of the Sri Lanka government and NGOs.

Despite these successes, the legal system has still not fully implemented the recent changes in the law. Further, it sometimes appears that officials do not implement the new laws appropriately or that judgments do not conform to the new mandatory sentences (D.G.H. de Silva, Chandrasiri, Sandya Kumari, Premaratne Evanthi, & Prasantha Kumara, 1998). Because the NCPA has a mandate to monitor investigation and law enforcement in cases of child abuse, several NGOs now send the NCPA their complaints regarding these inappropriate actions and judgments. The NCPA now asks the Attorney General to reopen trials in cases where the judgments are "inappropriate" under the new law.

Although child abuse was historically present in Sri Lanka, it went through a long phase of denial, until it was acknowledged initially in the mid-1980s in the form of physical abuse and subsequently in the form of sexual abuse in the early 1990s. Childhood sexual abuse is prevalent in Sri Lanka, especially among boys. Recently, child labor, particularly in domestic households and in conscription, has received wide attention as a form of child abuse. Although Sri Lanka was a signatory to the CRC in 1991, actual political commitment was recognized only after the appointment of a Presidential Task Force, a series of amendments to the laws, the allocation of resources to child protection, and the establishment of the National Child Protection Authority, which has a wide mandate in all aspects of child abuse prevention and action.

REFERENCES

Abeynayake, R. (1998, April 12). *Sunday Times* (Sri Lanka), p. 11.

Alles, A. C. (1962). The Kadugannawa postal bomb murder case. In *Infamous Criminal Cases of Sri Lanka* (pp. 89–116). Colombo: Mervyn Mendis, the Colombo Apothecaries Co.

Arulanantham, T. (1992, July). In a Symposium on Child Prostitution [paper], at the Conference on Sexually Transmitted Diseases and AIDS, organized by the Department of Child Care Services, and PEACE, Mt. Lavinia, Sri Lanka.

Bond, T. (1980). *Boy prostitution in Sri Lanka*. Lausanne: Terres des Zommes.

Chandrasiri, N., Lamabadusuriya, S., & de Silva, D.G.H. (1988). Non-accidental injuries to children in Sri Lanka. *Medicine, Science, & the Law, 28*, 123–126.

Code of Criminal Procedure. Amendment, Act 28 of 1998. Colombo: Government Publications Bureau of Sri Lanka.

de Silva, D.G.H. (1995, September). *Management of child abuse in Sri Lanka*. [paper]. Seminar organized by UNICEF & Faculty of Medicine, Colombo, Identification of Child Abuse and Problems in the Clinical Management, Colombo, Sri Lanka.

de Silva, D.G.H. (1996a). *Child abuse: The gravity of the problem and dilemmas in management in Sri Lanka*. Colombo, Sri Lanka: UNICEF.

de Silva, D.G.H. (1996b, March). *Child abuse: How big is the problem?* Plenary lecture, presented at the meeting of the Sri Lanka Medical Association (SLMA) Annual Sessions, Colombo, Sri Lanka.

de Silva, D.G.H. (1997). Child abuse in Sri Lanka. C. C. de Silva Memorial Oration, 1997. *Ceylon Journal of Child Health, 26*, 20–28.

de Silva, D.G.H., Chandrasiri, N., Sandya Kumari, L., Premaratne Evanthi, W., & Prasantha Kumara, U.G.P. (1998, August). *How accountable is the legal system?* [paper]. Child Abuse: Annual Sessions of the Galle Medical Association, Galle, Sri Lanka.

de Silva, D.G.H., Jayawardena P., Rajeendrajith, S., Gunarathna, A. M. S. W., & Mahendrajith, W. S. P. L. (1997). Conscription in armed conflict: Is it martyrdom or child abuse? *Journal of Paediatrics and Child Health, 33*, 564.

de Silva, D.G.H., Jayawardena, P., Rajeendrajith, S., & Gunarathna, M. (1997). Sexual abuse of illegally adopted children. *Ceylon Medical Journal, 42*, 44.

de Silva, D.G.H., Jayawardena P., Rajeendrajith, S., Gunarathna, M., Hewamanna, T., Rubesinghe, N., & Jayasekara, A. (1997). Sexual abuse in childhood in southern Sri Lanka. *Journal of Paediatrics and Child Health, 33*, 564.

de Silva, D.G.H., Rubesinghe, N. K., Jayasekera, A., Fernando, R., Hewamanna, T., & Wijesooriya, W.P.K. (1997, July). *Sex abuse in a home meant for protection of children*. Paper presented at the First Annual Congress of the Sri Lanka College of Paediatricians, Colombo, Sri Lanka.

de Silva, D.G.H., Rubesinghe, N. K., Jayasekera, A., Wijayasooriya, W., Hewamanna, T., & Ginige, V. (1997, July). *Incidence of childhood sex abuse and paedophiles in a promiscuous group*. Paper presented at the First Annual Congress of the Sri Lanka College of Paediatricians, Colombo, Sri Lanka.

de Silva, S. G. (1993). Child abuse [editorial], *Ceylon Journal of Child Health, 22*, 1–2.

Fernando, A. D., & de Silva, D.G.H. (1996). Child abuse: Time for action. *Ceylon Medical Journal, 41*, 121.

Fernando, R., Soysa, P. E., & Nanayakkara, J. C. (1987). Non-accidental injury to children—report of a fatal case in Sri Lanka. *Ceylon Medical Journal, 31*, 193–196.

Gmünder, B. (Ed.). (1995–1996). *The International Gay Guide* (24th ed.) Verlag: Spartacus Magazine.

Hamann, P. (Executive Producer). (1991). *Inside Story*. British Broadcasting Company.

Mahendrarajah, V., Rajagopalan, L., & Wickremasinghe, N. (1993). Child abuse as seen in the North Colombo Teaching Hospital. *Ceylon Journal of Child Health, 22*, 25–26.

Mirando, E. H. (1965–1966). The neglected child. *Ceylon Journal of Child Health*, 3–12.

Muller, C. (1993). *Jam fruit tree*. New Delhi, India: Penguin Books.

Muller, C. (1994). *Colombo*. New Delhi, India: Penguin Books.

Muller, C. (1995). *Once upon a tender time*. New Delhi, India: Penguin Books.

National Child Protection Authority (NCPA) of Sri Lanka, Act No. 50, November 14, 1998.

Nizam, M.S.M. (1996). Personal communication, Senior Deputy Inspector of Police (Crimes), Police Headquarters, Colombo, Sri Lanka.

Penal Code Amendment, Act No. 22 of 1995.

Ratnapala, N. (1999). *Sex workers of Sri Lanka*. Ratmalana, Sri Lanka: Sarvodaya Vishvalekha.

Regulations for the Instruction and Guidance of Teachers in Government Schools. Education Ordinance of 1939—Ceylon. Regulation 23.

Schechter, M., & Robergo, L. (1976). Child sexual abuse. In R. Helfer & C. Kempe (Eds.), *Child abuse and neglect: The family and community*. Cambridge, MA: Ballinger.

Seneviratne, M. (former Tourist Board official) (1997). Personal communication.

United Nations Convention on the Rights of the Child. (1989). Article 28 (2).

16

UNITED STATES

Michelle McCauley, Beth M. Schwartz-Kenney, Michelle A. Epstein, and Elizabeth J. Tucker

PROFILE OF THE UNITED STATES

The United States of America, located in North America and bordering both the North Atlantic and the North Pacific, has an area of 9.2 million square kilometers. The capital is Washington, D.C., and its 272.6 million people are of varied ethnic backgrounds, including European, African, Asian, and Native American. The languages spoken are English and Spanish (sizable minority) and the practiced religious faiths include Protestant (56 percent), Roman Catholic (28 percent), and Jewish (2 percent). The infant mortality rate is 6.33 per 1,000, and the life expectancy is 72.95 years for males and 79.67 years for females. Education, though not a constitutional right, is provided by most states without cost. The ages at which education is compulsory vary by state, ranging from five to eighteen years of age. The literacy rate is 97 percent. The government is a federal republic with a strong democratic tendency. Suffrage is universal at the age of eighteen. In 1998, the gross national product per capita was $29,340 (U.S.).

A CASE STUDY

A few days following Thanksgiving, "Ashley's" stepmother led police to the shallow grave where Ashley was buried. Later, her father admitted that he had hit Ashley repeatedly with a wooden discipline paddle and threw her against a wall, killing her. Ashley had been living with her aunt and uncle while her mother tried to recover from her abusive relationship with Ashley's father. Ashley was eventually placed in her father's care against her mother's wishes. Ashley's mother made several attempts to regain custody of the child, but her father refused. Retrospective reports revealed that Ashley had been physically abused on many prior occasions. Specifically, Ashley had reportedly come to school on several occasions with visible physical injuries, including black eyes on three occasions and a fractured nose. Ashley's injuries were allegedly reported to the police, but no official action was taken. Further, records indicated that Ashley's father had been investigated by social service agencies on three separate occasions and had a documented criminal record for violent behavior. Ashley's father acknowledged having difficulties controlling his anger, but claimed that he had previously asked for help from social service workers but had not received any.

INTRODUCTION

In the United States, reports of child maltreatment have increased dramatically over the last fifteen years, with the number of investigated cases in 1997 approaching 3 million (U.S. Department of Health and Human Services [USDHHS], 1997). Approximately 56 percent of such cases involve neglect, 25 percent physical abuse, 13 percent sexual abuse, 6 percent emotional maltreatment, and 13 percent other forms of maltreatment.[1] Unfortunately, these disturbing figures may actually constitute less than half of all cases of child maltreatment, as many cases go unreported (USDHHS, 1997). Given the staggering number of child maltreatment reports, the U.S. Advisory Board on Child Abuse and Neglect (1990) rightfully declared child maltreatment a "national emergency" (Krugman, 1996).

HISTORY

Historically, child protection in the United States focused on aiding economically disadvantaged children. This assistance, however, primarily involved removal of the child from the home and was performed mainly by private organizations. In colonial America during the late eighteenth century, children from indigent families were often placed in institutions or foster homes (Schene, 1996). By the mid-nineteenth century, such children were often sent to work in factories, as apprentices, or on farms (Giovannoni, 1989; Schene, 1996). The motivating force behind removal of children from economically disadvantaged homes was to ensure that the child developed into a moral and valuable member of society rather than to alleviate the child's hardship (Giovannoni, 1989).

During this early period (i.e., the late eighteenth and early nineteenth centuries), there was little focus on physical or sexual abuse of children. Much of what U.S. society now considers to be physical abuse (e.g., beating a child for wrongdoing) was condoned during this period. In fact, there was a complete absence of legislation designed to protect children from physical maltreatment. One of the earliest cases of physical abuse to receive widespread attention was that of Mary Ellen, an eight-year-old girl who was seriously abused by her adoptive parents in 1874. Although the little girl had been chained and beaten and was clearly malnourished, existing laws did not permit her to be removed from her home. The media attention generated for little Mary Ellen led to the establishment of the Society for the Prevention of Cruelty to Children in 1875 (Zigler & Hall, 1989). Within the next twenty-five years, over 160 organizations were established to protect children (Giovannoni, 1989). Although these organizations were established specifically for aiding children, many of them still failed to focus on the needs of abused and neglected children. For example, the American Humane Association (AHA), which was established in the late 1870s, initially focused on maternal health and high infant mortality rates. In fact, the AHA did not directly address the problem of child maltreatment until the 1950s (Kalichman, 1993; Schene, 1996).

Sexual abuse was also rarely identified during this period, even though it clearly occurred. During the nineteenth century, numerous articles published in American medical journals discussed children with venereal diseases—usually syphilis and gonorrhea. Although doctors clearly acknowledged that adults contracted such diseases through intimate sexual contact, they believed that children contracted them either through nonsexual contact, such as breast-feeding or hugging, or through the use of shared eating utensils and bedding (Taylor, 1985). In fact, as late as 1889, Dr. Lucius Buckley stated that there were in fact three types of syphilis: (1) congenital syphilis, which one was born with; (2) syphilis contracted through "legitimate" sexual contact within marriage; and (3) syphilis transmitted without sexual contact (Taylor, 1985). Dr. Buckley's multiple syphilis theory allowed doctors to diagnose and treat children with venereal diseases without acknowledging a violation of society's incest taboos. Unfortunately, this societal denial of the sexual origin of child syphilis cases allowed sexual abuse to go under-identified and under-punished.

In summary, during the first hundred years of this country's existence, societal response to child abuse and neglect involved either ignoring it or removing the child from the family. There were few attempts to ameliorate abuse by providing the support needed to educate families, rehabilitate parents, and keep the family intact (Giovannoni, 1989, Schene, 1996). As noted, there were few regulations prohibiting forced labor or physical abuse during this period of U.S. history and essentially no enforcement. In addition, the mere existence of sexual abuse seemed essentially ignored.

In 1920, the development of the Child Welfare League of America (CWLA) helped change preexisting approaches to child maltreatment. The CWLA emphasized maintenance of the natural family whenever possible, and advocated temporary, rather than permanent, institutionalization of children. Eventually, in the 1930s, the American Humane Association created a set of standards for all state-based agencies that stressed the need for prevention of child abuse and neglect (Antler & Antler, 1979). During this time, medical understanding of venereal diseases advanced considerably, making it difficult for professionals to deny that such diseases in children were contracted through sexual contact (Taylor, 1985).

Although public awareness and acknowledgment of sexual and physical abuse were increasing, early legislation regarding child abuse and neglect nonetheless focused almost exclusively on the neglect of children. The first such legislation was passed as part of the 1935 Social Security Act and marked the first time the federal government provided funding for child welfare services (USDHHS, 1988). Under the act, suspected child abuse could be reported to child protection agencies. Mandatory reporting requirements and widespread social awareness of the problem, however, still did not emerge until the 1960s.

This increased awareness was primarily due to Kempe, Silverman, Steele, Droegemueller, and Silver's (1962) identification of the battered-child syndrome, which led to objective medical definitions for physical abuse and stressed the importance of reporting abnormal physical examinations that might be suggestive of abuse (see also Bain, 1963; Fontana, Donovan, & Wong, 1963). Discussions generated by Kempe and his colleagues' research resulted in mandatory reporting legislation. By 1966, all states had enacted laws requiring physicians to report suspected abuse (Kalichman, 1993). These reporting laws were intended to (a) accelerate identification of abused children by child protection professionals, (b) appoint specific professionals to respond to abuse reports, (c) prevent further abuse by implementing protective services, and (d) provide support to help sustain the unity of the family. Soon thereafter, the types of abuse that required mandatory reporting expanded to include emotional and nutritional maltreatment, as well as suspected sexual abuse. In addition, human service professionals (such as therapists, social workers, and teachers) were also mandated by law to report suspected abuse (Giovannoni, 1989). Despite these advances, modern research on childhood sexual abuse still did not begin until the late 1970s, lagging well behind childhood physical abuse. Not until almost two decades after Kempe and his colleagues' discovery of the battered child syndrome, when child advocates and feminists finally made childhood sexual abuse a political issue, did Americans truly acknowledge the existence of such abhorrent sexual crimes against children (Finkelhor, 1979; 1984; Russell, 1986).

Fortunately, with the creation of the Child Abuse Prevention and Treatment Act of 1974 (CAPTA), a federal definition of child abuse and neglect was established and standards for mandatory reporting were created. CAPTA defined child abuse and neglect as

[t]he physical or mental injury, sexual abuse, negligent treatment, or maltreatment of a child under the age of 18 by a person who is responsible for the child's welfare

under the circumstances which indicate the child's health or welfare is harmed or threatened thereby as determined in accordance with regulations prescribed. (Child Abuse Prevention and Treatment Act of 1974, 42 U.S.C. §5106g [4] [1974])

Although this definition was overly broad, it provided a comprehensive view of child abuse that increased governmental and public awareness and response.

States rapidly adopted CAPTA's definition, in part because doing so was a requirement for receiving federal funding for development of services for abused and neglected children. CAPTA also established the National Center for Child Abuse and Neglect (NCCAN). NCCAN is a governmental agency, whose mission is to conduct research and provide public education to prevent child abuse and neglect (Giovannoni, 1989).

Unfortunately, when NCCAN was first established, adequate funding was not available to provide sufficient services to those children and families who were in need of them. Initial funds were used primarily at the state level to provide training for social service workers rather than to provide support to victims and their families. In the early 1980s, the Social Security Act was intended to allocate funds at the state level necessary for provision of direct services for children and families. Additional legislation in the 1980s, such as the Adoption Assistance and Child Welfare Act of 1980 provided resources to prevent child abuse and identify alternative interventions other than removal of children from their natural families. In 1993, additional changes to the Social Security Act were made to support services and education for high-risk families before abuse and neglect occurred (Schene, 1996).

DEFINITION

However, in 1996, Congress changed the federal definition of "child abuse and neglect" to its current reading: "[T]he term 'child abuse and neglect' means, at a minimum, any recent act or failure to act on the part of a parent or caretaker, which results in death, serious physical or emotional harm, sexual abuse or exploitation, or an act or failure to act which presents an imminent risk of serious harm" (42 U.S.C. §5106g[2] [1999]). According to the Senate, the new definition is intended to protect the states' child protection agencies from a perceived burden of "unrealistic expectations and inadequate resources":

This definition allows States to limit abuse and neglect definitions to serious harm to a child. At the same time, the definition, by specifying "at a minimum," allows States, if they wish, to define child abuse and neglect more broadly. The intent of this legislation is not to force States to change their current definitions; instead, the new definition accommodates those States which choose to limit the scope of Child

Protection interventions to cases involving serious harm. (104 S.Rpt 117 [July 20, 1995])

It remains to be seen whether the new definition will lead to widespread reductions in the funding and focus of child protection agencies.

Fortunately, societal response and services designed to identify and ameliorate child abuse and neglect have not remained static. Initial efforts concentrated on identifying and removing children from abusive situations. Subsequent efforts focused not only on identifying potentially abused or neglected children, but also on providing services to empower families in need. More recent efforts have recognized the need for preventative services and for intervention in problematical situations before abuse occurs. Unfortunately, although resources allocated to ensure the welfare of children have increased dramatically during the twentieth century, the number of reported cases has increased as well.

PREVALENCE

Unlike many other countries, the United States has successfully compiled fairly reliable statistics on the prevalence of child abuse and neglect. This is primarily as a result of several national research studies and federally funded comprehensive incidence studies (e.g., National Incidence Study of Child Abuse and Neglect and Reports from the States to the National Center on Child Abuse and Neglect). Unfortunately, these reports reveal alarming rates of abuse and neglect and suggest that the incidence of child maltreatment continues to rise in the United States. In fact, based on the most recent statistics to date, in 1993, a child was one and one-half times more likely to experience harm by abuse or neglect than in 1989 (Sedlak & Broadhurst, 1996). Based on *The Third National Incidence Study of Child Abuse and Neglect* (Sedlack & Broadhurst, 1996), which was conducted jointly by several federal agencies, the prevalence of all types of maltreatment (i.e., physical abuse, sexual abuse, emotional abuse, and neglect) was significantly higher than in 1989. Disturbingly, child protective services were noted to investigate only 28 percent of cases in which children were harmed due to abuse or neglect.

Several factors appear to increase a child's level of risk of being harmed, including a child's gender, family income, and parental marital status. Findings reveal gender differences in experiences of sexual victimization. Girls are more likely to experience such abuse than boys. Boys, however, are slightly more likely to be the victims of particularly serious injuries (Sedlack & Broadhurst, 1996). Experiences of abuse also tend to be related to parental class and family income or socioeconomic status (SES), with violence occurring more often in homes with lower SES (e.g., Pelton, 1981; Sedlack & Broadhurst, 1996; Straus, 1994; Straus, Gelles, & Steinmetz, 1980) and in single-parent homes. Despite such relationships, however, it is important to note that abuse occurs across all levels of parental class, income, and education, and that discrepancies in victimization rates may be due to differences in reporting across different SES groups. Furthermore, there is reason to believe that all of these prevalence estimates may be low. National research surveys that ask adults to report retrospectively whether they were abused as children have revealed much higher levels of abuse than those reported above. In particular, childhood sexual victimization is reported by approximately one in four women (e.g., Elliot & Briere, 1995; Epstein & Bottoms, 1998; Finkelhor, Hotaling, Lewis, & Smith, 1990) and by approximately one in ten men (e.g., Elliot & Briere, 1995; Epstein & Bottoms, 1998; Haugaard & Emery, 1989).

INVESTIGATION

Because state and federal laws require human service professionals to report known or suspected cases of child abuse and neglect, over half of child maltreatment cases are reported by individuals working in day-care centers, hospitals, schools, or mental health/social service agencies (USDHHS, 1997). Virtually every state in the United States has a state-funded child protective agency that is responsible for investigating reports of child abuse or neglect. Once a child protective agency receives a report of abuse or neglect, state law provides specific procedures that the agency must follow. Usually, when an agency receives a report, a child protection investigator visits the alleged victim's home and interviews the child, the child's parents, and the child's siblings regarding the specific allegations. Other persons who have considerable contact with the child or family (e.g., teachers) might also be interviewed during the initial investigation. Information obtained during these interviews helps agency workers to assess the child's present living situation and determine the child's current level of risk. If the initial investigation indicates the need for additional information or assessment, more in-depth evaluations may be conducted (Pecora, 1991).

Child protection investigations may yield three different outcomes (Kalichman, 1993). First, the report may be *substantiated*, indicating that the child required protection and that the family was in need of assistance. In such cases, either the identified perpetrator or the child victim is removed from the home. Additionally, services are provided to the family to address sequelae of the abuse. Second, the report may be *unsubstantiated*, indicating that the evidence did not support child maltreatment charges. In such cases, the agency may nonetheless refer the family for various types of assistance, perhaps focused on education and prevention. Finally, some reports may be deemed *inconclusive*, meaning that the agency is unable to confirm or deny reported maltreatment. In these cases, questions often remain unanswered because there is inadequate evidence available to corroborate the report of abuse, individuals needed for questioning are unavailable, or the child does not disclose abuse when questioned by child protection workers. A report from the U.S. Department of Health and Human Services (1988) indicates that about 50 percent of all reported cases are substantiated. This percentage is even higher when only mandated reports are considered. This increased substantiation among reports made by health service professionals is probably due to the degree of specific evidence provided in such cases, as these professionals generally have more resources and expertise available to identify abuse than individuals in the lay community (Kalichman, 1993). This highlights the importance of adequate education regarding signs of abuse for individuals who have considerable contact with children (e.g., teachers or pediatricians).

PROTECTION OF VICTIMS

Merely because a reported case of child abuse or neglect is substantiated by child protection services does not mean that the case will be legally prosecuted. In fact, most cases of abuse and neglect are not prosecuted. This often occurs because there is insufficient legal evidence to prove that abuse occurred "beyond a reasonable doubt," the legal burden that must be met in criminal cases in the United States. Consequently, even when a child makes a credible report of abuse, and child protection services substantiate the case, the perpetrator may go unpunished. Luckily, in such cases, child protection can still intervene to ensure the child's protection. In cases of intrafamilial abuse, children are usually removed from the home and placed in temporary foster care. During this time, parents are often mandated to receive remedial counseling and educational services to ensure against further abuse. If parents successfully comply with the demands placed upon them by the courts and/or child protection services, children are often returned to their custody. If parents fail to cooperate, however, parental rights are often terminated. Further, in cases where the abuser is not a family member, particularly in cases of sexual abuse, victims and families usually remain intact and are often referred for mental health services to address sequelae of the abuse.

LEGAL INNOVATIONS

A child's testimony is always a critical element in child abuse cases, in that the child is often the sole witness to the events in question. In order for any witness to take the stand, he or she must be deemed competent to testify. This can pose unique problems when the witness is a child. Approximately one-third of all states in the United States have adopted Rule 601 of the Federal Rules of Evidence, which presumes that all persons are competent to testify regardless of age (Bulkley, Feller, Stern, & Roe, 1996). In such states, no special inquiry is made into a child's competence, unless the child's competency is specifically challenged. In those states that have not adopted Rule 601's presumption, however, competence of young children must be determined during a pretrial *voir dire* hearing. Although the age range of children who require such hearings varies from state to state, it generally falls somewhere between ten and fourteen years of age. During the competency hearing, the child is asked a number of questions, including whether he or she is aware of the difference between telling the truth and telling a lie. The belief is that children who can demonstrate such an understanding will present credible and veracious testimony.

Researchers have demonstrated that a number of factors affect children's recall and testimony, including the child's level of cognitive development, stress, and fear (Ceci & Bruck, 1995; Poole & Lamb, 1998). In an effort to ameliorate the negative effects of such factors, many reforms have been proposed and implemented in the United States over the last two decades to accommodate child witnesses. These reforms are designed to obtain accurate information from potentially abused children in the least stressful manner. Bulkley et al. (1996) identified several desirable legal innovations in child abuse cases, including (a) the use of interdisciplinary investigation teams; (b) coordination between juvenile and criminal courts; (c) making a special advocate available for the child; (d) a reduction in the number of interviews a child has through the use of videotaped interviewing and other methods; and (e) the use of alternative methods, such as closed-circuit television and one-way mirrors, during a child's testimony to save the child from testifying in open court at trial. Not every state has instituted these legal innovations, and some of these innovations have been controversial. For example, in 1986, the constitutionality of the use of closed-circuit televisions and one-way mirrors was challenged in *Maryland v. Craig* (1990). Fortunately, many of these interventions have been deemed constitutional in certain situations, and thus permitted in U.S. courts.

Some interviewing practices, such as the use of developmentally insensitive language, coercive or repeated interviewing, and the necessity of several court appearances, also appear to compromise the accuracy of children's reports (Bruck, Ceci, Francoeur, & Barr, 1995; Poole & White, 1993; Saywitz & Goodman, 1996). Further, being forced to continually recount abusive experiences may be particularly traumatizing for some child victims. Thus, additional reforms have been designed to improve the accuracy of children's recall and eliminate the need for multiple interviews by different professionals involved in the investigation and prosecution of child abuse cases (e.g., law enforcement, attorneys). Such innovations include the use of innovative questioning techniques such as the cognitive interview (McCauley & Fisher, 1995), or narrative elaboration (Saywitz & Snyder, 1993). These techniques incorporate interviewing tactics intended to facilitate a child's recall without being leading or coercive.

In many states, community-based programs called Children's Advocacy Centers have been developed and provide child-focused programs that combine knowledge from many disciplines (e.g., law, mental health, child protection) in order to make decisions about investigation, treatment, and prosecution of child abuse cases (National Children's Advocacy Center, 1999). The primary purpose of these programs is to prevent further victimization of children. Additional goals include minimizing the level of re-traumatization the child experiences as a consequence of having to disclose the abuse, providing families and children with remedial services, and preserving the legal integrity of the child's disclosure. Specially trained interviewers conduct interviews that integrate techniques that are known to increase a child's recall without being coercive or misleading. Further, professionals from varied disciplines work together within the advocacy center to facilitate more efficient medical and mental health referrals for child victims and successful prosecution of identified perpetrators.

Additionally, some communities have adopted advocacy programs in which child witnesses receive information about the trial process to help facilitate recall and reduce their stress (i.e., they attend "court school"). These schools explain to children the roles of various court personnel, the process of testifying, and their role in the judicial process (Doueck, Weston, Filbert, Beekhuis, & Redlich, 1997; Saywitz, Nathanson, Snyder, & Lamphear, 1993; Saywitz & Snyder, 1993). Yet another reform designed to improve the accuracy of children's testimony is the exclusion of spectators from the courtroom and the presence of a parent or loved one to provide social support for the child while he or she testifies (Goodman et al., 1992). Additional research is needed to explore the degree to which these various innovations improve the accuracy of children's testimony and decrease additional trauma to the child. Only then will we know if, and under which circumstances, the innovations are beneficial in balancing the rights of victims and defendants.

Legal Ramifications for Convicted Perpetrators of Child Abuse

Cases of child abuse may be tried in criminal court, civil court, or both. When a person is convicted of child abuse, sentencing differs from state to state and is generally based on the type of abuse committed and the age of the victim. For example, the Vermont criminal code provides that a person convicted of sexual assault of a minor younger than sixteen years of age "shall be imprisoned for not more than 20 years, or fined not more than $10,000, or both" (13 V.S.A. § 3253 [a][3]). The Arizona criminal code draws even finer age distinctions: Sexual assault of a minor who is fifteen years of age or older is punishable by a presumptive sentence of seven years imprisonment; sexual assault of a minor between the ages of twelve and

fifteen is punishable by a presumptive sentence of twenty years imprisonment; and sexual assault of a minor younger than twelve years of age is
punishable by life imprisonment without hope of parole until at least thirty-
five years of the sentence have been served (Ariz. Rev. Stat. §§ 13–1406[B],
13–604.01[C], & 13–604.01[A]). Other states have mandatory minimum
sentencing for sexual abuse, requiring that the convicted perpetrator serve
a certain number of years without the possibility of parole (Bulkley et al.,
1996). Because few cases of abuse are reported and fewer still are prosecuted, however, many abusers never receive legal penalties at all. Those who
do often plea bargain, leading to more lenient punishments.

PREVENTION

Experts such as Edward Zigler at Yale University's Child Study Center
believe that in order to control child abuse and neglect, resources must focus
on preventing abuse by providing education and parental support to alleviate
family stressors, which he believes are at the root of the problem of abuse
and neglect. Child abuse prevention programs are often sponsored by a
variety of national agencies and corporations. For example, the National
Center to Prevent Child Abuse (NCPCA), the Ronald McDonald House
Charities, and the Freddie Mac Corporation sponsor programs such as the
Healthy Families America program. Through local hospitals and agencies
such as departments of health, this program encourages professionals and
neighbors to provide support for families of newborns, in hopes of creating
a supportive family environment (Rabasca, 1999).

Many experts believe that the most effective prevention programs are
community-based, such that community members are active in ensuring that
social support is available to parents and that children are safe. Community-
based programs are believed to be less threatening to a parent's self-esteem
and involve less stigma than government-sponsored programs. Examples of
community-based programs include the Moms and Cops program in Aiken,
South Carolina, which, for example, increases police involvement in child
protection, and the Well-Baby Plus program in Beaufort, South Carolina,
which links new parents to available resources. The American Psychological
Association is currently working with the National Child Abuse Coalition
to establish legislation that would provide federal funding in support of
community-based prevention programs (Rabasca, 1999).

In addition to family-focused prevention, a number of school-based child
sexual abuse prevention programs were developed during the late 1970s and
early 1980s (Kohl, 1993). These programs aim to reduce children's vulnerability to abuse and exploitation by teaching them about personal safety,
appropriate and inappropriate touching, and saying no. In addition, the programs teach children the skills needed to resist abuse and ways to obtain
support from others. The hope is that such training will help children feel

self-confident and efficacious, leading them to feel empowered to resist being abused. These programs are based on the premise that through training and discussion, children can learn to protect themselves from becoming victims of abuse or respond appropriately should abuse occur (e.g., tell an adult).

More recently, some prevention programs have included topics such as empathy training, problem solving, and anger management in hopes of preventing children not only from being victimized, but also from potentially abusing others. The training approach is dependent on the age group involved, such that programs for younger children use puppets and dolls, while training for older children uses lectures and role-playing (Kohl, 1993).

How effective are these training programs? Unfortunately, the benefits of prevention programs remain unclear, in part due to a lack of knowledge regarding the best way to implement them. Finkelhor and Strapko (1992) found that regardless of age, children learned about prevention from each of the various training approaches. Some types of training approaches, however, such as role-playing, were found to be more effective than others, suggesting that the method of prevention training used is important to consider.

Unfortunately, less than 10 percent of the $14 million in funding provided to child abuse and neglect agencies is applied to prevention. Why is prevention underfunded? Treatment programs seem to be favored over prevention programs, possibly because research has focused more on outcomes of treatment programs than prevention programs. As a result, there is empirical evidence regarding the efficacy of treatment, leading agencies to focus their limited funding in areas that may provide more predictable outcomes. Subsequently, prevention programs reach only a small minority of the many families in need of the support and education that they provide. Further, such programs still tend to be rare. Thus, until prevention of child abuse is better understood, treatment programs may continue to be the favored approach for dealing with child abuse.

CONCLUSION

Despite child protection agencies' stated goal of protecting children, and despite the millions of dollars of federal funding earmarked for prevention of child abuse and neglect, the number of reported cases has substantially increased over the past few decades and continues to do so (Krugman, 1996). As mentioned previously, this increase in reported cases prompted the U.S. Advisory Board on Child Abuse and Neglect to declare child abuse a national emergency in 1990. Although state agencies exist to address the problem, agency personnel often lack adequate training and support, and are burdened by voluminous caseloads. Although great strides have been made in the United States in addressing the problem of child abuse and neglect, it is obvious that even greater strides are needed to overcome this extremely prevalent and debilitating social problem.

NOTE

1. These numbers do not add up to 100 percent, because a child may be a victim of multiple types of abuses.

REFERENCES

Antler, J., & Antler, S. (1979). From child rescue to child protection. *Children and Youth Services Review, 1*, 177–204.

Ariz. Rev. Stat. §§ 13–1406(B), 13–604.01(C), & 13–604.01(A) (1999).

Bain, K. (1963). The physically abused child. *Pediatrics, 31*, 895–898.

Bruck, M., Ceci, S. J., Francoeur, E., & Barr, R. J. (1995). "I hardly cried when I got my shot!": Influencing children's reports about a visit to their pediatrician. *Child Development, 66*, 193–208.

Bulkley, J. A., Feller, J. N., Stern, P., & Roe, R. (1996). Child abuse and neglect laws and legal proceedings. In J. Briere, L. Berliner, J. A. Bulkley, C. Jenny, & T. Reid (Eds.), *The APSAC handbook on child maltreatment* (pp. 271–296). Thousand Oaks, CA: Sage.

Ceci, S. J., & Bruck, M. (1995). *Jeopardy in the courtroom: A scientific analysis of children's testimony.* Washington, DC: American Psychological Association.

Child Abuse Prevention and Treatment Act, 42 U.S.C. §5106g(2) (1999).

Child Abuse Prevention and Treatment Act, 42 U.S.C. §5106g(4) (1974).

Child Abuse Prevention and Treatment Act Amendments of 1995, 104 S.Rpt 117 (July 20, 1995).

Child Abuse Prevention and Treatment Act of 1974, 42 U.S.C. § 5101 et seq.

Doueck, H. J., Weston, E. A., Filbert, L., Beekhuis, R., & Redlich, H. F. (1997). A child witness advocacy program: Caretakers' and professionals' views. *Journal of Sexual Abuse, 6*, 113–132.

Elliot, D. M., & Briere, J. (1995). Posttraumatic stress associated with delayed recall of sexual abuse: A general population study. *Journal of Traumatic Stress, 8*, 629–647.

Epstein, M. A., & Bottoms, B. L. (1998). Memories of childhood sexual abuse: A survey of young adults. *Child Abuse and Neglect, 22*, 1217–1238.

Finkelhor, D. (1979). *Sexually victimized children.* New York: The Free Press.

Finkelhor, D. (1984). *Child sexual abuse: New theory and research.* New York: The Free Press.

Finkelhor, D., Hotaling, G., Lewis, I. A., & Smith, C. (1990). Sexual abuse in a national survey of adult men and women: Prevalence, characteristics, and risk factors. *Child Abuse and Neglect, 14*, 19–28.

Finkelhor, D., & Strapko, N. (1992). Sexual abuse prevention education: A review of evaluation studies. In D. Willis & W. Holden (Eds.), *Prevention of child maltreatment: Developmental and ecological perspectives* (pp. 150–167). New York: John Wiley & Sons.

Fontana, V. J., Donovan, D., & Wong, R. J. (1963). The "maltreatment syndrome" in children. *New England Journal of Medicine, 269*, 1389–1394.

Giovannoni, J. (1989). Definitional issues in child maltreatment. In D. Cicchetti & V. Carlson (Eds.), *Child maltreatment* (pp. 3–37). Cambridge, England: Cambridge University Press.

Goodman, G. S., Pyle-Taub, E. P., Hones, D.P.H., England, P., Port, L. K., Rudy, L., & Prado, L. (1992). The effects of criminal court testimony on child sexual assault victims. *Monographs of the Society for Research in Child Development, 57 (Serial No. 229),* 1–163.

Haugaard, J. J., & Emery, R. E. (1989). Methodological issues in child sexual abuse. *Child Abuse and Neglect, 13,* 89–100.

Kalichman, S. C. (1993). *Mandated reporting of suspected child abuse: Ethics, law, and policy.* Washington, DC: American Psychological Association.

Kempe, C., Silverman, F., Steele, B., Droegemueller, W., & Silver, H. (1962). The battered-child syndrome. *Journal of the American Medical Association, 181,* 17–24.

Kohl, J. (1993). School-based child sexual abuse prevention program. *Journal of Family Violence, 8,* 137–150.

Krugman, R. D. (1996). Epilogue. In J. Briere, L. Berliner, J. A. Bulkley, C. Jenny, & T. Reid (Eds.), *The APSAC handbook on child maltreatment* (pp. 420–422). Thousand Oaks, CA: Sage.

Lawton, H. (1988). *The psychohistorian's handbook.* New York: Psychohistory Press.

Maryland v. Craig, 110 S. Ct. 3157 (1990).

McCauley, M. R., & Fisher, R. P. (1995). Facilitating children's eyewitness recall with the revised Cognitive Interview. *Journal of Applied Psychology, 80,* 510–516.

National Center on Child Abuse and Neglect. (1989). *State statutes related to child abuse and neglect: 1988.* Washington, DC: Clearinghouse on Child Abuse and Neglect Information.

National Children's Advocacy Center. (1999). *What is a children's advocacy center?* [Brochure]. Huntsville, AL: National Children's Advocacy Center.

Pecora, P. J. (1991). Investigating allegations of child maltreatment: The strengths and limitation of current risk assessment systems. *Child and Youth Services, 15,* 73–92.

Pelton, L. H. (Ed.). (1981). *The social context of child abuse and neglect.* New York: Human Sciences Press.

Poole, D. A., & Lamb, M. E. (1998). *Investigative interviews of children.* Washington, DC: American Psychological Association.

Poole, D. A., & White, L. (1993). Effects of question repetition on the eyewitness testimony of children and adults. *Developmental Psychology, 27,* 975–986.

Rabasca, L. (1999, April). Child-abuse prevention efforts still too few. *APA Monitor* (p. 30). Washington, DC: American Psychological Association.

Russell, D.E.H. (1986). *The secret trauma: Incest in the lives of girls and women.* New York: Basic Books.

Saywitz, K., Nathanson, R., Snyder, L., & Lamphear, V. (1993). *Preparing children for the investigative and judicial process: Improving communication, memory, and emotional resiliency.* Final report to the National Center on Child Abuse & Neglect (Grant No. 90-CA-1179). Torrance: University of California, Los Angeles, Harbor-UCLA Medical Center, Department of Psychiatry.

Saywitz, K. J., & Goodman, G. S. (1996). Interviewing children in and out of court:

Current research and practice implications. In J. Briere, L. Berliner, J. A. Bulkley, C. Jenny, & T. Reid (Eds.), *The APSAC handbook on child maltreatment* (pp. 297–318). Thousand Oaks, CA: Sage.

Saywitz, K. J., & Snyder, L. (1993). Improving children's testimony with preparation. In G. S. Goodman & B. L. Bottoms (Eds.), *Child victims, child witnesses: Understanding and improving testimony* (pp. 117–146). New York: Guilford.

Schene, P. (1996). Child abuse and neglect policy: History, models, and future directions. In J. Briere, L. Berliner, J. A. Bulkley, C. Jenny, & T. Reid (Eds.), *The APSAC handbook on child maltreatment* (pp. 385–397). Thousand Oaks, CA: Sage.

Sedlack, A. J., & Broadhurst, D. D. (1996). *The third national incidence study of child abuse and neglect.* U.S. Department of Health and Human Services. Washington, DC: Government Printing Office.

Straus, M. A. (1994). *Beating the devil out of them: Corporal punishment in American families.* New York: Lexington Books.

Straus, M. A., Gelles, R., & Steinmetz, S. (1980). *Behind closed doors: Violence in the American Family,* Garden City, NY: Doubleday.

Taylor, K. J. (1985). Venereal disease in nineteenth-century children. *Journal of Psychohistory, 12,* 431–463.

13 V.S.A. § 3253(a)(3) (1999).

U.S. Advisory Board on Child Abuse and Neglect. (1990). *Child abuse and neglect: Critical first steps in response to a national emergency.* Washington, DC: Government Printing Office.

U.S. Department of Health and Human Services. (1988). *Study findings: Study of national incidence and prevalence of child abuse and neglect: 1988.* Bethesda, MD: Government Printing Office.

U.S. Department of Health and Human Services. (1997). Reports from the states to the national child abuse and neglect data system. Washington, DC: Government Printing Office.

Zigler, E., & Hall, N. W. (1989). Child abuse in America. In D. Cicchetti & V. Carlson (Eds.), *Child maltreatment* (pp. 38–75). Cambridge, England: Cambridge University Press.

INDEX

Page references to tables are indicated by *t* (e.g., 92–94*t*).

ABOUT THE EDITORS AND CONTRIBUTORS

BETH M. SCHWARTZ-KENNEY is Associate Professor of Psychology at Randolph-Macon Woman's College. She received her B.A. from Colby College and her M.A. and Ph.D. from the State University of New York at Buffalo. She has coauthored a number of book chapters and journal articles addressing the reliability of children's memory and techniques for improving children's testimony. She is currently researching the use of drawing when questioning children about witnessed events, and young children's understanding and use of deception.

MICHELLE MCCAULEY is Assistant Professor of Psychology at Middlebury College. She received her B.A. from the University of Iowa and her M.A. and Ph.D. from Florida International University. She has coauthored a number of journal articles and book chapters addressing the use of the Cognitive Interview with children. Her current research focuses on adults' perceptions of child victims.

MICHELLE A. EPSTEIN is the Postdoctoral Fellow in Childhood Trauma at La Rabida Children's Hospital and Research Center in Chicago, Illinois. She obtained her Ph.D. in clinical psychology from the University of Illinois at Chicago and completed her clinical internship at the Children's Hospital/ Harvard Medical School in Boston. She provides clinical treatment to victims of childhood sexual abuse and trauma, and conducts forensic interviews of child victims. She has coauthored journal articles on memories of childhood trauma and jurors' perceptions of child victims, and was the recipient of a National Institute of Mental Health Dissertation Research Grant in Developmental Psychopathology. She is currently researching individual differences in coping in childhood trauma victims and the decision-making process of juries in child sexual assault cases.

NICHOLAS BALA is a Professor of Law at Queen's University in Kingston, Canada, specializing in Family and Children's Law, and has been a Visiting Professor at McGill, the University of Calgary and Duke Law School. He has published extensively on legal issues related to divorce, child abuse and juvenile justice, and served as a legal consultant to government and non-governmental agencies. He is currently working on an interdisciplinary project on child witnesses and on an international comparative project on juvenile justice.

FREDERICK B. BERRIEN, M.D., is Associate Professor of Clinical Pediatrics at the University of Connecticut School of Medicine and the Director of the Aetna Foundation Children's Advocacy Center in Hartford, Connecticut. He also serves as the Director of the Siberian American Children's Health Program and has had extensive experience with children's health issues in Russia.

TAMAR COHEN is the founder and Director of Meital—Israel Center for the Treatment of Child Sexual Abuse. She has published a book on incest (in Hebrew) and has authored many professional articles on child maltreatment. She is an internationally known lecturer and trainer, whose main research interest is in the effects of child sexual abuse on future mothering. She received her B.S.W. from the Hebrew University, her M.S.W. from Yeshiva University, and her Ed.D. from Boston University.

JOAQUÍN DE PAÚL, a psychologist, is Associate Professor at the Department of Psychology at the University of Basque Country (San Sebastian, Spain). He is a researcher focused in basic and applied studies of physical child abuse and neglect. He has been working in the field of child maltreatment and child protection since 1986 and has developed and evaluated several programs for abusing families and other service studies all around Spain. He is author of several papers and books about child maltreatment.

D. G. HARENDRA DE SILVA is Professor and Head of Pediatrics at the University of Kelaniya, Sri Lanka. He received his MBBS and DCH from the University of Ceylon, Colombo, and the MRCP from the Royal College of Physicians of the UK. He also obtained a M.Sc. in pediatric gastroenterology from the University of Birmingham, UK. He was appointed a Fellow of the Royal Colleges of London and Edinburgh. He was awarded an honorary fellowship by the College of General Practitioners of Sri Lanka. Originally, his main research interests were gastroenterology and nutrition. However, following the description of the first cases of child abuse in Sri Lanka, his research has focused on child abuse and neglect. He has over eighty research publications. He was appointed Chairman of the Presidential Task Force on Child Protection and is the Founder Chairman of the National Child Protection Authority of Sri Lanka.

ANTONIO ESTRADA is Professor of Family Therapy at the University of Montemorelos, Mexico, and Guest Professor of Pastoral Counseling at Cento Univesitario Adventista do Brazil (IAE). He received his B.A. from the University of Montemorelos, his M.A. from Las Americas University and Andrews University, and his Ph.D. from Fuller Theological Seminary. He has authored two books as well as a number of journal articles addressing family issues and physical child abuse and three videos on parental discipline. He is currently researching the relationship between abuse and religion.

HARRY FERGUSON is Professor of Social Policy and Social Work at University College, Dublin, Ireland. He previously worked as a senior lecturer in the Department of Applied Social Studies, University College, Cork. He has researched and published widely in the areas of child protection, domestic violence, gender relations, and the critical study of men and masculinities. He is the author or coauthor of seven books, including *Protecting Irish Children: Investigation, Protection and Welfare* (1996, with T. McNamara) and *Changing Fathers? Fatherhood and Family Life in Modern Ireland* (1998, with K. McKeown and D. Rooney). He has just completed *Keeping Children Safe?*, a book based on a three-year research project into child abuse and child protection practices in Ireland.

DAVID FINKELHOR is Co-Director of the Family Research Laboratory and Professor of Sociology at the University of New Hampshire. He has been studying the problems of child victimization, child maltreatment, and family violence since 1977. He is well known for his conceptual and empirical work on the problem of child sexual abuse, reflected in publications such as *Sourcebook on Child Sexual Abuse* (1986) and *Nursery Crimes* (1988). He has also written about child homicide, missing and abducted children, and children exposed to domestic and peer violence and other forms of family violence. In his recent work, he has tried to unify and integrate knowledge about all the diverse forms of child victimization in a field he has termed developmental victimology. He is editor and author of ten books and over seventy-five journal articles and book chapters. He has received grants from the National Institute of Mental Health, the National Center on Child Abuse and Neglect, the U.S. Department of Justice, and a variety of other sources. In 1994 he was given the Distinguished Child Abuse Professional Award by the American Professional Society on the Abuse of Children.

OLAYO GONZÁLEZ is a lawyer and Attorney in Chief in a Spanish county. He is an expert in legal aspects of Spanish and European child protection systems. He is author of several papers about legal implications of the Spanish child protection system and, more specifically, about the relation between the judicial system and clinical intervention of perpetrators.

JAMES HATTY is Honorary Research Associate in the College of Humanities and Social Sciences at the University of Sydney. He received his B.A. and M.Phil. from the University of Sydney. He has authored and coauthored books and book chapters on the societal impact of epidemics, and on the body in society. He is currently researching and writing on the history of childhood, child abuse, and the problems faced by boys in the postmodern period.

SUZANNE E. HATTY is Associate Professor of Social Medicine at Ohio University. Previously she was Associate Professor of Humanities and Human Sciences at Australian Universities. She received her B.A. from Macquarie University (Sydney) and her Ph.D. from the University of Sydney. She has authored and coauthored a number of books, monographs, book chapters, and journal articles addressing issues such as domestic violence, child abuse, masculinity, prostitution, and victimization of marginalized groups. She is currently researching and writing on the body in society, and on problems for boys in the postmodern period.

CHARLES FELZEN JOHNSON, M.D., is director of the Child Abuse Program at Children's Hospital, Columbus, Ohio, and Professor of Pediatrics at the Ohio State University College of Medicine. He is the author of over fifty articles appearing in scientific journals and eleven book chapters. He edits *SCAN*, the newsletter of the Section on Child Abuse of the American Academy of Pediatrics, and serves on the Academy's Committee on Child Abuse.

MOHD SHAM KASIM is Professor of Pediatrics at the Faculty of Medicine, Universiti Putra Malaysia. He obtained his medical degree from Sydney University, New South Wales, Australia, in 1971, a diploma in child health in Glasgow, Scotland, in 1974, and membership in the Royal College of Physicians and Surgeons of Glasgow, Scotland, United Kingdom, in 1975. The Royal College of Physicians of Edinburgh awarded him a Fellowship in 1987. He has authored a book chapter on child abuse and forty articles in referred journals, more than half of which are on child abuse and neglect. He was instrumental in setting up the Suspected Child Abuse and Neglect Team in Malaysia and was part of the committee that drafted Malaysia's Child Protection Act. He is actively involved in highlighting issues of child abuse and its prevention in Malaysia.

VICTORIA W. M. KATTAMBO is a lawyer by profession. Currently she is the Senior Principal State Counsel in Kenya. She has done research and published widely on law as it relates to children. She was formerly the secretary to the Task Force on Child Law Review in Kenya.

KARI KILLÉN is First Researcher at NOVA, Norwegian Social Institute.

AKIHISA KOUNO is Executive Director and Chief Anesthesiologist of Kouno Clinic, Sakai–Osaka. He is also Medical Examiner of Osaka Prefecture. He received his M.D. from Fujita–Gakuen University School of Medicine and his Ph.D. from Osaka University Medical School. He has authored a number of book chapters and journal articles addressing differential diagnosis among sudden infant death cases including child abuse, neglect, SIDS, suffocation, and infectious diseases. He is currently researching pathophysiological and sociomedical characteristics of sudden infant death cases.

HARRIET MACMILLAN, M.D., M.Sc. FRCPCb, works with the Child Advocacy and Assessment Program at Hamilton Health Sciences Corporation. In addition, she is an Associate Professor on the Faculty of Health Sciences at McMaster University in Hamilton, Ontario.

MARCELLINA MIAN is Associate Professor of Pediatrics in the Faculty of Medicine, University of Toronto, and a member of the Suspected Child Abuse and Neglect Program at the Hospital for Sick Children in Toronto. She received her MDCM from McGill University and completed her residency in pediatrics at the Boston Floating Hospital in Boston, Massachusetts. She has been active in a clinical practice and in teaching multiprofessional audiences about various aspects of child abuse. In addition, she has conducted research and published articles on the effects of child sexual abuse and presented at international conferences on a number of topics. She is a member of the executive council of the International Society on Child Abuse and Neglect (ISPCAN) and is actively involved with other world organizations in developing an integrated approach for the response to child maltreatment for global use.

ANA MUNTEAN is a Lecturer in the Social Work Department at the University of West Timisoara. She received her B.A. and her Ph.D. from Babes-Bolyai University of Cluj, Romania. She has coauthored a number of book chapters and journal articles addressing child abuse and neglect in Romania. As a chairperson of SCOP (Society for Children and Parents), she organized the first National Conference on Child Abuse and Neglect Prevention in Romania in 1996, with international participation. She is the coordinator of the training program for postgraduates in the field of child abuse and neglect prevention. This program was set up at the University of West Timisoara in

1999 with European Community support within the Tempus–Phare Program.

PHILISTA P. M. ONYANGO, a sociologist by profession, has been teaching and doing research at the University of Nairobi for many years. Currently she is the Chief Executive of ANPPCAN Regional. She has coauthored several publications and written papers for publications.

JEREMY ROCHE is a Lecturer in the School of Health and Social Welfare at the Open University (the UK's distance learning university). He writes and researches in the field of children's rights and the law and is co-editor of *Youth in Society* (1997) and *Changing Experiences of Youth* (1997).

WENDY STAINTON ROGERS is a Senior Lecturer in the School of Health and Social Welfare at the Open University (the UK's distance learning university). A psychologist by background, much of her theoretical work and research have been carried out in the field of critical and health psychology. She has also worked extensively in the field of child welfare, publishing, researching, and teaching around the topics of child protection, child welfare law, and children's quality of life. She has acted as an advisor to government agencies in the UK and Spain, especially in relation to training professionals working in child protection.

MARIA ROTH is Senior Lecturer in the Social Work Department at Babes-Bolyai University in Cluj, Romania. She is one of the professionals who laid the basis of social work training in the country after the political change in 1989. She received her Ph.D. in psychology from the same university, based on research in the field of cognitive educability of preschool children. Her research is motivated by her thirteen years of experience with children living in disadvantaged situations. She is the author and coauthor of many books and chapters that discuss cases, data, theoretical views, investigation procedures, and intervention possibilities in the area of child abuse and neglect.

TAMARA YAKOVLEVNA SAFONOVA is a pediatrician in Moscow who has specialized in the social problems of children. She has been awarded the advanced degree of Medical Science. She is the Director of the OZON Center, where she advocates for social and legal protections of child victims of abuse.

UMA A. SEGAL is Associate Professor of Social Work at the University of Missouri–St. Louis. She received her B.A. from Barnard College, her M.S.S.W. from the University of Texas at Arlington, and her Ph.D. from Washington University in St. Louis. She has authored several articles on child abuse in India and on cross-national/cross-cultural issues and implications for methods of research and intervention with diverse populations. Her current research focuses on a comparison of perceptions of abuse among professionals in the United States, Japan, and India.

EVGENY IOSIFIVICH TSIMBAL, a pediatrician, is a Senior Scientist at the Institute for Law and Order Problem Enforcement located in the office of the General Prosecutor of the Russian Federation. He is a senior staff member of the OZON Center in Moscow.

ELIZABETH J. TUCKER is pursuing her master's degree in counseling at Lynchburg College. She received her B.A. from Randolph-Macon Woman's College, graduating with a dual degree in psychology and philosophy. She has worked in the counseling setting with emotionally disturbed children in treatment, residential, and school environments. Currently, she is serving as a nursery school teacher at the Randolph-Macon Nursery School in Lynchburg, Virginia.